Deliberative Democracy
and the Plural Polity

Deliberative Democracy and the Plural Polity

Michael Rabinder James

University Press of Kansas

© 2004 by the University Press of Kansas
All rights reserved

Published by the University Press of Kansas (Lawrence, Kansas 66049), which was organized by the Kansas Board of Regents and is operated and funded by Emporia State University, Fort Hays State University, Kansas State University, Pittsburg State University, the University of Kansas, and Wichita State University

Library of Congress Cataloging-in-Publication Data

James, Michael Rabinder.
    Deliberative democracy and the plural polity / Michael Rabinder James.
      p. cm.
    Includes bibliographical references and index.
    ISBN 0-7006-1318-8 (cloth : alk. paper) — ISBN 0-7006-1319-6 (pbk. : alk. paper)
  1. Decision making.   2. Political participation.   3. Pluralism (Social sciences).
4. Representative government and representation.   I. Title.
    JF1525.D4J36   2004
    321.8—dc22
                                           2004001997

British Library Cataloguing-in-Publication Data is available.

Printed in the United States of America

10 9 8 7 6 5 4 3 2 1

The paper used in this publication meets the minimum requirements of the American National Standard for Permanence of Paper for Printed Library Materials Z39.48-1984.

To my parents,
Dr. Esther Kamala James and Dr. Adolf Frederick James

Contents

Preface

In 1989, along with millions of others in India, I witnessed the historic electoral defeat of the Congress Party. Although Congress won the largest share of the seats in the lower house of Parliament, they remained far short of a majority and were subsequently replaced as the governing party by the Janata Dal. This event evoked mixed feelings in me. On the one hand, I was (naively) heartened by the ascension of the reformist Janata Dal leader, V. P. Singh, who had successfully campaigned against the rampant corruption within the Congress government. On the other hand, I felt queasy about the fact that the Janata Dal's minority government was forced to rely on the Hindu-nationalist BJP party for parliamentary support. My fears proved to be justified, when barely a year later the BJP sparked widespread Hindu–Muslim violence by attempting to destroy a Muslim mosque in the town of Ayodhya. While the BJP claimed that Muslim conquerors had unjustly built the mosque over a Hindu temple honoring the birthplace of Ram, their real motivation stemmed from political calculations. In August of 1990, the Janata Dal government announced its intention to implement the Mandal Commission Report, which recommended expanding quotas in education and government employment for members of lower castes. This policy, the BJP feared, would divide India's overwhelming Hindu majority along caste lines, thereby hindering its ability to garner votes through appeals to religious nationalism. This fear was probably well founded. For while V. P. Singh justified the Mandal Commission Report on the grounds of justice to oppressed castes, he too, was probably motivated by his own political calculations regarding the need to secure a loyal base of support in order to ward off intraparty challengers.*

*For a basic discussion of the 1989 elections, the Mandal Commission, and Ayodhya, see Craig Baxter, Yogendra K. Malik, Charles H. Kennedy, and Robert C. Oberst, *Government and Politics in South Asia,* 4th ed. (Boulder, CO: Westview Press, 1998), 104–105, and Robert L. Hardgrave and Stanley A. Kochanek, India: *Government and Politics in a Developing Nation,* 5th ed. (New York: Harcourt Brace Jovanovich, 1993), 310–311.

This story illustrates some of the problems that can emerge within the politics of a plural democratic polity. It reveals how parliamentary calculations can encourage parties to form cynical alliances, how electoral incentives can lead politicians to divide populations against one another, how such parliamentary and electoral strategies can lead to violent group conflict, and how claims of justice can be opportunistically employed to garner political power. Of course, this is a rather jaded take on politics in a plural polity, and it is not meant to obscure the real and justified struggles against oppression mounted by disadvantaged groups in India or elsewhere. Moreover, it is not meant to deny that the diverse collective identities inhabited by individuals are important only with respect to social, economic, or political costs and benefits. Indeed, my own reasons for being in India at that time reflect the more personal and cultural dimensions to collective identity.

I had come to India to seek my roots, so to speak. Like many young people of Indian descent, I grew up with a rather negative image of my parents' homeland. Succumbing to the stereotypes propagated by North American media and society, I associated being Indian with being physically weak, nerdy, and socially inept. To use Iris Marion Young's term, I suffered from cultural imperialism. But apart from this, I also had difficulty appropriating a positive perception of my ethnic identity, as I did not conform well with the Indian community of my small town. My family is South Indian and Christian, unlike the predominantly North Indian and Hindu families in my hometown. These religious, linguistic, and cultural differences led me to grow up with the uneasy feeling of not quite fitting in with either the majority White* population or even the Indian minority. Coming to India, specifically the South Indian, Christian community of my family, was my attempt to search for a positive sense of personal and collective identity that had eluded me for much of my life.

Although my personal experiences in India did much to rehabilitate my sense of identity, my encounter with Indian politics fostered a variety of conflicting responses. On the one hand, it strengthened my commitment to pursuing questions of justice related to racial, ethnic, and cultural groups. But on the other hand, it impressed upon me a need to recognize the dangers and uncertainties of real-world ethnic politics. Collective identities can be personally significant, but they can also be manipulated for political or economic gain. Political parties and social movements can pursue real claims of justice, but they can also exacerbate tensions that can lead to violence. And democratic political institutions can enable oppressed groups to protect themselves from social exploitation, but they can also encourage

---

*Throughout this text, I capitalize the terms "White" and "Black" when used to identify racial identities. In chapter 1, I argue that all racial or quasi-racial identities are socially constructed. "White" and "Black" are as equally socially constructed as "Asian" or "Hispanic" or "Native American," terms which are commonly capitalized. Because I use "White," "Black," "Asian," "Hispanic," and "Native," as racialized, not ethnic, identities, I feel that it would be inappropriate to capitalize some (Asian, Native, and Hispanic) while not capitalizing others (White and Black).

dangerous forms of group conflict. Over time, I came to recognize that the struggle for justice must remain cognizant of the dangers of politics.

Clearly, the relationship between justice and political conflict remains a source of ambivalence not just in India but in most plural polities, be they in the developing world, in the transitional polities of the former Eastern bloc, or even in wealthy Western democracies. In this book, I examine questions of justice and stability among diverse racial, ethnic, and cultural groups within the United States. More precisely, I develop and apply criteria for assessing democratic institutions within a plural polity, in order to determine whether they achieve democratic fairness, whether they respond to the multifaceted character of collective identities, and whether they exacerbate or mitigate conflict among groups. The normative core of my study is a model of democratic deliberation aimed at elucidating how members of diverse collective identities can communicate and make collective decisions in a fair manner. Complementing this model is an account of how collective identities are formed and transformed and an analysis of the strategic incentives toward group conflict. I then use my discussions of fair deliberation, collective identity formation, and group conflict to assess a variety of democratic institutions and phenomena, specifically electoral systems, social movements, associations, and the mass media. In doing so, I provide a portrait of deliberative democracy in the plural polity that can help political theorists, social scientists, and interested citizens better understand how democratic processes can more feasibly realize justice and stability among a plurality of groups.

A number of presses have helped me to bring this project to fruition. Chapter 3 is a much-revised version of my article "Communicative Action, Strategic Action, and Intergroup Dialogue," *The European Journal of Political Theory* 2 (2003), and I am grateful to Sage for permitting me to use this material. I also wish to thank the Northeastern Political Science Association for allowing me to use portions of my article, "Critical Intercultural Dialogue," *Polity* 31 (Summer, 1999), in chapter 2. Finally, I wish to extend my deepest gratitude to Fred Woodward of the University Press of Kansas, for encouraging this project at an early stage and for shepherding the manuscript through the review process. Fred had the foresight to select two astute anonymous reviewers, later revealed to be Richard Dagger and David Ingram, whose thoughtful suggestions and constructive criticisms improved the final manuscript immensely.

In developing this book, I have relied upon a variety of philosophical and social scientific sources, ranging across the fields of political theory, comparative politics, American politics, sociology, anthropology, and media studies. In weaving my way through this maze of disciplines, I have benefited from the advice, criticism, and encouragement of many colleagues. I especially wish to thank Johnny Goldfinger, Emily Hauptmann, James Johnson, Mark Warren, Stephen White, and Melissa Williams for reading and commenting on earlier versions of various chapters. Beyond this, Stephen gave me wise counsel while I was developing the framework for this project, helping me to transform it from a mélange of vaguely related

thoughts into a coherent argument. Mark encouraged me when I was an enthusi-
astic but confused undergraduate at Georgetown University, advised me when I
was first considering graduate study, hired me as a visiting professor at Georgetown after I had finished my Ph.D., and supported me as I made the transition from
student to scholar. At Duke University, where I received my graduate training, Tom
Spragens, Rom Coles, and Michael Gillespie guided my development as a political
theorist and supported my efforts to find employment as one. Tom deserves special thanks for shepherding me through the dissertation process and helping me to
become an independent thinker and writer.

Most of this book was written at Bucknell University, a small undergraduate
institution with a lively, energetic, and gifted faculty. Despite teaching six courses
per year, my colleagues manage to support an intellectual environment that allows
inspiring and devoted teachers to produce rigorous scholarship. Among my fellow
teacher-scholars, I especially wish to thank Pawan Dhingra, Tony Massoud, John
Peeler, and Amy McCready. Pawan shared with me his deep and broad understanding of how sociologists address problems of collective identity construction,
an issue often overlooked by political theorists and political scientists. Tony and
John each read preliminary portions of the manuscript and lent me their insights
as scholars of comparative politics. Amy, my fellow political theorist at Bucknell,
has been an ideal colleague and a dear friend. She carefully read the entire manuscript, fixed innumerable infelicities in my language, and helped me to surmount
countless leaps of logic. More important, she has provided measureless intellectual and moral support. I can think of no better person to have as my senior colleague in political theory. I also wish to thank Linda Danowsky, our wonderful
departmental secretary, for her invaluable clerical assistance.

I could not have completed this book without the support of friends and family. Over the years, David Bird, Cathie Caimano, Johnny Goldfinger, Claudia
Kinkela, Damon Palmer, and Jacquie Pfeffer have given me the intellectual and
emotional support to continue down the lonely path of the political theorist, even
when the costs seemed to occlude the distant benefits. My sisters, Anita, Kalpana,
and Sheila James, have influenced me in diverse ways: as fellow children of immigrants, they have helped me to struggle with and appreciate the meaning of identity,
and as social activists, they have prodded me to struggle for justice. Nicole Tron-
zano-Speletic has supported me during the darkest points in the writing process,
when it truly seemed like this project would never reach fruition. Her insights as
a political philosopher forced me to rethink my positions and avoid easy dogmas,
her creativity as a modern dancer inspired me to see beauty beyond the sometimes
staid world of academia, and her love and joy keep me buoyant amidst the waves
and shoals of life. My greatest debt is to my parents, Adolf and Kamala James.
Their will and determination to succeed in a new environment have afforded me
the opportunity to reflect upon intellectual matters, and their lives have provided
me with models for success amidst unfavorable odds. For all that they have done,
I dedicate this book to them.

Introduction

Controversies related to racial, ethnic, and cultural pluralism have assumed a central place in the theory and practice of democracy. Most spectacular have been the violent, ethnic civil wars that have erupted in polities undergoing transitions to democracy, like the former Yugoslavia and Rwanda. In addition, established but poor democracies have experienced intergroup violence, as exemplified by Hindu–Muslim conflict in India and Tamil–Sinhalese conflict in Sri Lanka. Even established, wealthy democracies, like Canada, the United States, and Great Britain, have not been immune to problems of pluralism. In these countries, political conflict among intergenerational groups has usually remained peaceful, and disputes have centered on the fairness of measures to remedy inequality among groups or to preserve threatened cultures. Most typical are Canadian debates over the status of minority nations, like Quebec or aboriginal nations; American disputes over racial gerrymandering and affirmative action; and British concerns with the political and cultural incorporation of immigrant minorities. However, established but poor democracies have also engaged in peaceful arguments concerning the fairness of measures to remedy inequality among groups and to preserve threatened cultures, as exemplified by Indian debates over preferential policies for backward castes and the separate Muslim civil code. Even the established, wealthy democracies have recently confronted problems of intergroup violence, such as the Oka standoff between Mohawks and police in Quebec, the Los Angeles riots, the paramilitary civil war in Northern Ireland, and the race riots in northern England.

Clearly, political relations among diverse racial, ethnic, or cultural groups raise questions of justice and stability. Questions of justice are most clearly associated with group-based inequalities in resources or political power. Where discrimination hinders disadvantaged groups from securing jobs, education, or political power, justice may require altering a polity's political structure, perhaps by creating group-specific rights, policies, or institutions. Questions of stability typically

1

concern the causes of group conflict, such as economic incentives to compete over scarce resources, political incentives to compete for political power, or psychological and cultural factors that engender prejudice. Of course, these two types of questions can be interrelated. Perceptions of injustice may foster conflict when one group feels that another group enjoys unfair advantages in securing jobs or educational opportunities. Similarly, institutions designed to realize a just distribution of political power among groups may inadvertently provide fuel for group conflict. But while questions of stability and justice arise within plural polities, they are not often integrated into scholarly analyses of the politics of pluralism.

Questions of stability primarily concern social scientists, who examine the economic, social, psychological, and institutional causes of group conflict. Tracing the genesis of conflict often requires examining the origins of the conflicting groups themselves, partially because these collective identities may have gained salience only recently. Despite the popular belief in ancient hatreds, many instances of racial, ethnic, or cultural violence involve collective identities that have emerged only in the last century. An analysis of the causes of group conflict is often followed by policy or institutional recommendations to mitigate, if not eliminate, conflict. Yet these recommendations, and the problems to which they respond, imply important normative commitments, to which social scientists pay relatively little attention. The most common, if unstated, normative goal is the Hobbesian concern with peace and stability: violent conflict must be minimized at all costs. Anyone who has followed the ethnic civil wars in the Balkans or Africa cannot help but cede the importance of peace and stability. However, we cannot and should not overlook the normative status of this goal, as in some circumstances the desire for peace may contradict the desire for fairness. A stable tyranny is hardly a self-justifying goal.

Normative questions have even greater pertinence when social scientists examine the prospects for achieving democracy in plural polities. In the past, some social scientists argued that democracy is undesirable in a polity populated by diverse, intergenerational groups.[1] These scholars claimed that democratic institutions provide too many incentives for ethnic political elites to enhance their power by manipulating animosities among groups. When this claim proved to be overstated,[2] social scientists then debated which democratic institutions would be best suited to enhance stability in plural polities. One locus of debate concerned the electoral and legislative institutions of the state, with scholars disagreeing over whether legislative seats and administrative jobs should be proportionally distributed among members of different groups.[3] Although this debate clearly raised questions of distributive justice and fair representation, social scientists only parenthetically addressed these normative issues. Another locus of debate was the role of civil society and the mass media in plural polities, specifically the role of group-specific media sources.[4] Here again, debate addressed only the causal question of whether these media sources contribute to group conflict, and not the normative question of whether they help to realize political fairness among diverse groups.

Questions of justice occupy normative political philosophers. Scholars examine some of the same institutions and policies studied by empirical social scientists, but through a very different set of lenses. Some develop sophisticated arguments to clarify what would be the fair representation of groups within political institutions.[5] Others construct models of distributive justice that defend group-specific rights and policies as ways to distribute resources and opportunities more fairly among diverse groups.[6] Finally, certain theorists argue that group-specific civil society associations and media sources can help members of disadvantaged groups protect their cultural practices, counter demeaning stereotypes, and debate advantaged groups on fairer terms.[7] In each case, normative political philosophers reconstruct the moral intuitions that most members of democratic polities claim to share. They then test whether existing or alternative political arrangements would realize these tenets in a plural polity.

But whereas social scientists insufficiently examine the normative presuppositions behind measures to enhance stability, normative political philosophers insufficiently incorporate social-scientific insights into their recommendations for realizing justice among groups. For instance, some normative political philosophers tend to assume that the groups in a plural polity are fixed and stable. These philosophers seek rights, policies, and institutions that can better attain justice among groups, but they insufficiently examine how these groups came into existence and how they might change in the future. Collective identities can incorporate other groups or disintegrate into smaller groups; groups can include subgroups that experience conditions quite different from those of the larger, more encompassing groups; and economic and political incentives can encourage individuals to identify with certain collective identities rather than with others. If a group-specific policy leads an individual to identify with a specific group simply to get an attractive job, the distributive justice of this policy should come into question. These problems of identity construction are frequently addressed by social scientists, but they occupy relatively little attention among normative political philosophers.[8]

In addition, normative theorists inadequately address the dynamics of group conflict within plural polities. Although many normative theorists do recognize instability as a problem for plural polities and even modify their proposals in response to this problem, they do not carefully examine which motivations or incentives will lead members of different groups to pursue justice and fairness rather than conflict and violence.[9] To a significant extent, this lacuna derives from their primary interest in the politics of established, wealthy democracies, regimes that have not recently experienced large-scale ethnic wars. But because even these democracies are not immune to smaller forms of group conflict, ignoring this issue is misguided. Even if group violence does not emerge, motivations and incentives toward group conflict can undermine the willingness to adopt the measures that normative political theorists believe will enhance justice.

Inattention to motivations and incentives also affects the viability of the institutional reforms normative political philosophers seek. Although they use models of justice to advocate certain group-specific representational, electoral, and civil society institutions, they pay insufficient attention to the incentive structures within these institutions. For example, an electoral system that enhances the representation of minority groups may also provide incentives for candidates to aggravate racial, ethnic, or cultural tensions. Similar incentives may apply to group-specific associations and media sources, which ideally should realize fairer terms of deliberation among diverse groups but which may actually exacerbate prejudices among them. Normative theorists would do best to advocate those institutions that can simultaneously enhance minority representation, realize fair deliberation, and mitigate group conflict.

Although social scientists and normative philosophers are aware of each other's concerns, few seek to integrate questions of justice and stability within a single approach to pluralism. Unfortunately, the politics of a plural polity can raise questions of justice and stability simultaneously. The constructed character of collective identities can complicate most theories of justice between groups, conceptions of fairness will invariably permeate institutions designed to enhance stability, and complex motivations may either support or undermine political measures to achieve justice or stability. In light of these issues, I integrate questions of justice and stability through a deliberative, institutional approach to democracy in a plural polity.

For over a decade, the idea of deliberative democracy has attracted the attention of political theorists. This idea presents democracy, the rule of the people, not simply as a process in which citizens vote according to their preexisting political preferences. Instead, deliberative democrats envision citizens engaged in spirited discussions that inform and transform their political preferences before they step into the voting booth. Such discussions should, at minimum, allow citizens to obtain better information about which policies will best satisfy their individual or common interests. But more important, democratic discussion should go beyond gathering information to include dialogues aimed at understanding other participants' situations, beliefs, and interests, along with vigorous debates meant to assess the desirability of proposed measures. More precisely, such discussions should encourage citizens and their representatives to justify the measures they favor while criticizing those they reject. This process should, ideally, proceed under conditions that all participants can accept as fair, thus mitigating the danger that more powerful participants will unfairly force others to alter their beliefs, interests, or preferences.

To some normative political theorists, the focus on understanding, criticism, and justification makes deliberative democracy an attractive ideal for plural polities. Because citizens are expected to understand others' situations and to justify their own political preferences, this model of democracy ideally checks majority tyranny.[10] Moreover, the inclusion of fair conditions for deliberation provides a ground for criticizing institutions and processes that silence oppressed minorities. Although I concur with the normative desirability of democratic deliberation for a plural polity, I believe that deliberative democrats, like normative theorists of pluralism, overlook the social, political, and institutional incentives that can encourage or undermine fair deliberation among diverse groups. In response, I attempt to clarify the conditions and institutions that can enable members of different collective identities to reach mutually acceptable collective decisions.

The normative core of my approach is a model of fair, plural deliberation. Supplementing this normative core are analyses of how collective identities are constructed and how different motivations and institutional incentives can aggravate or mitigate group conflict. This model and these analyses provide the basis for a detailed assessment of two types of institutions: electoral systems, and civil society and the public sphere. Clearly, this approach cannot address all the problems related to justice and stability in the United States, let alone in other plural polities. Indeed, by focusing on the institutions and processes through which collective decisions are made, I am unable to evaluate several substantive issues germane to a plural polity, such as affirmative action, immigration and naturalization, exemptions from general laws, and jurisdictional divisions between federal and state levels of government. However, this approach recommends itself in three ways.

First, by focusing on the processes through which a plural polity reaches collective decisions, this model facilitates a more flexible, context-sensitive approach to justifying specific remedies for group-related injustices. Several theories of justice between groups try to distinguish which groups deserve which measures, based upon excessively abstract distinctions between them. For instance, Will Kymlicka argues that national minorities deserve self-government rights, whereas ethnic minorities deserve rights to representation and exemptions from general laws. As I will argue in chapter 1, this method of justification disintegrates amidst more detailed accounts of how both types of groups are constructed. Instead of trying to match certain rights with certain groups, my deliberative approach focuses on the democratic processes through which the specific claims of different groups can be addressed fairly. Such democratic institutions and processes should not simply aggregate the existing preferences of citizens within a plural polity; doing so can leave minorities prone to majority tyranny. Instead, democratic processes must be deliberative: they must require participants to understand each other's situations and to justify and criticize each other's proposed measures. In this way, a deliberative theory seeks to ensure that the interests of members of diverse groups are granted a fair hearing within the process of collective decision-making.

But although this deliberative approach focuses on democratic processes, it is not a purely procedural theory. By this I mean that an outcome of a deliberative, democratic process cannot be taken as legitimate simply because the proper procedural rules were followed. The legitimacy of outcomes also depends on two types of substantive concerns. *Substantive outcomes,* like laws, policies, and jurisdictional divisions, must be contextually assessed in light of the claims and situations of members of different groups. Although I will not provide contextual analyses of specific laws or policies here, I emphasize that such case-specific work remains an important corollary to this project.[11] In addition, fair deliberation will require certain *substantive achievements* by participants within the democratic process. Fair deliberation depends not only on a fair distribution of resources within the democratic, decision-making process; it also requires certain dispositions and capacities among participants. Participants must possess equal voting strength and equal speaking allotments, and must also come to understand each other's positions prior to criticizing them. Achieving such understanding presupposes a disposition to try to understand the other, rather than simply retaining one's initial beliefs about the other. The failure to achieve understanding across group boundaries and to realize the deliberative dispositions underlying such understanding are some of the greatest obstacles to deliberative democracy in a plural polity.

The disposition toward understanding diverse participants, what I call *deliberative reciprocity,* can be encouraged or hindered by different motivations and incentives. This problem brings to light the second advantage of my deliberative, institutional approach. Deliberative democratic theorists, especially those influenced by Jürgen Habermas, ground deliberative reciprocity in moral psychology and a democratic political culture. Although such psychological and cultural motivations are necessary for deliberative reciprocity, they remain insufficient amidst the strategic dynamics of group conflict that can permeate plural polities. For this reason, my deliberative, institutional approach draws on empirical, social-scientific analyses of group conflict, in order to provide a more sophisticated account of the motivations and incentives that can encourage deliberative reciprocity across group boundaries. Specifically, I clarify how five strategic dynamics of conflict affect different groups in different ways, encouraging deliberative reciprocity across some group boundaries while hindering it across others. In addition, I suggest that certain measures can directly counteract the dynamics of conflict, whereas others can indirectly lessen their impact.

This careful analysis of the dynamics of group conflict leads to the third advantage of my deliberative, institutional approach. By combining a model of fair deliberation with attention to the dynamics of group conflict and the construction of collective identities, this approach permits a more detailed assessment of some of the key democratic processes and institutions through which a plural polity reaches collective decisions. Such a detailed assessment requires distinguishing three types of institutions. *Formal, decision-making institutions* are constitutionally established bodies within the democratic state, such as legislatures, executives, judiciaries, and administrative agencies. These institutions make collective decisions that legally bind all members of a plural polity. *Informal, deliberative institutions* are typically associated with civil society or the public sphere. They are not constitutionally established, although they are constitutionally protected by freedoms of speech, press, religion, and association. They cannot make legally binding collective decisions for the entire polity but primarily serve to communicate positions and ideas. *Quasi-formal, deliberative institutions* include temporary advisory commissions connected to formal, decision-making institutions. These institutions lack the power to make binding legal decisions and are not constitutionally established, but they do communicate deliberative insights to formal, decision-making institutions, like legislatures and administrative agencies.

Specifically, I examine how the electoral system, a type of formal, decision-making institution, and civil society and the public sphere, a set of informal, deliberative institutions, can enhance or obstruct fair deliberation across group boundaries. I focus on these institutions for two reasons. First, some deliberative theorists prefer civil society and the public sphere to the democratic state, contending that the lack of formal, decision-making power in the former frees participants from incentives to act strategically or the need to reach bargains. Although there is significant truth to this point, I argue that the public sphere is also a site for strategic action and aggregative bargaining. Recognizing the complexity of the public sphere undermines the primary reasons for eschewing deliberation within the state. Consequently, I examine how quasi-formal, deliberative institutions can house deliberation within the state. Second, electoral systems are important deliberative institutions because they connect public sphere deliberation to the legislative and executive bodies of the state. Moreover, they can be designed to redirect one of the strategic dynamics of conflict, in order to enhance deliberative reciprocity across group lines. My focus on the public sphere and electoral systems is not meant to dismiss other potential venues for deliberation; it only seeks to illuminate the specific prospects and limitations for deliberation across group boundaries within these important but sometimes misunderstood institutional settings.

CHAPTER SUMMARIES

In chapter 1, I use empirical accounts of collective identity construction to critique substantive theories of justice between groups. In arguing for or against group-specific policies, rights, or institutions, these theories commit three crucial oversights. First, they underestimate the internal diversity within groups, ignoring how subgroups may confront conditions that are significantly different from those of the broader group. Second, they overlook how group boundaries can shift over time and according to social, political, and economic circumstances. And third, their arguments for which groups, if any, deserve group-specific measures rest on spurious distinctions among different types of groups.

In order to illuminate the third problem, I distinguish four modes through which collective identities are constructed. The *interpretive-structural* mode shows how individuals inherit a collective identity that is culturally meaningful for them. The *interpretive-agency* mode portrays actors freely choosing a culturally meaningful collective identity. The *instrumental-agency* mode suggests that individuals choose a collective identity based on the expected costs or benefits associated with it. And the *instrumental-structural* mode holds that collective identities are imposed on individuals without their choice, usually to deprive them of material or other goods.

I then show how four normative theorists use a single mode of identity construction to argue for or against group-specific measures. Will Kymlicka argues that national minorities are interpretive-structural identities which, unlike agency-based ethnic minorities, deserve self-government rights. Yael Tamir argues that national self-determination is justified because it extends respect to the interpretive agency of individuals, who make constitutive choices about their identity. Russell Hardin argues against all group-specific measures because they reward the instrumental agency of self-interested individuals. Finally, Jeff Spinner defends group-specific measures for Black Americans because the instrumental-structural identity imposed upon them levies significant costs.

I focus on these four thinkers for two reasons. First, although they do not exhaust all possible normative approaches to pluralism, they do represent a broad cross-section of this field.[12] Second, and more important, these four thinkers provide powerful reconstructions of common moral intuitions about justice between groups. By arguing that Black Americans or French Canadians inhabit structural identities over which they exercise no choice, Spinner and Kymlicka make intuitively strong cases for the injustice of any unchosen inequalities suffered by these groups. Similarly, by claiming that collective identity reflects a deep, constitutive choice for individuals, Tamir provides a prima facie case for granting group rights as a way of extending respect to individuals. On the other hand, by portraying identity choices as instrumental and opportunistic, Hardin undermines the intuitive case for group-specific measures.

These thinkers powerfully reconstruct common moral intuitions about the justice of group-specific measures; however, their arguments become less compelling when confronted with empirical evidence. Consequently, I draw on empirical accounts of identity construction among Native Americans, Hispanic Americans, Asian Americans, and Black Americans, in order to illuminate all three oversights committed by the normative theorists in question. I argue that each group is internally diverse, that each group's boundaries have shifted over time, and that all four modes of identity construction are involved in the creation and maintenance of each collective identity. Because these empirical cases challenge substantive theories of justice between groups, I argue that the increased flexibility of my deliberative approach can better address problems of applying group-specific or group-neutral measures amidst a plurality of groups marked by internal diversity, shifting boundaries, and multiple modes of identity construction.

At minimum, a flexible, deliberative approach would require the careful and precise application of group-specific policies, such as affirmative action, in order to accommodate the internal diversity and changing boundaries associated with constructed collective identities. A deliberative approach to group-specific institutional arrangements presents a dilemma: inclusive deliberation may require guaranteeing the representation of groups within institutions, but this conflicts with the malleability of constructed collective identities. As a result, we must distinguish among formal decision-making, informal deliberative, and quasi-formal deliberative institutions. I suggest that group representation and flexible deliberation are compatible with informal, deliberative and quasi-formal, deliberative institutions because these institutions are more easily altered and do not directly reach collective decisions over conflict-inducing resource distributions. Constitutionally established, formal, decision-making institutions, which can be a source of group conflict, should not embody fixed group representation; rather, they should utilize electoral systems that simultaneously enable group representation and mitigate group conflict.

In chapter 2, I outline plural deliberation, a framework to judge the legitimacy of democratic processes and institutions that reach collective decisions among members of diverse and constructed identities. Legitimacy derives not from any single criterion, like rational consensus or consent of the governed, but from a complex assessment of four elements. First, legitimate institutions and processes should not restrict the scope of issues addressed, because the politics of a plural polity may involve epistemic disputes stemming from diverse social perspectives and world-views. Thus, we cannot limit deliberation to the testing of policy preferences, fundamental interests, or opinions about the common good, but must understand perspectives and world-views, so as to construct common grounds for testing preferences, interests, and opinions. Second, participants must accurately understand perspectives or world-views *prior to criticizing them,* so as to preclude stereotypical labeling rather than real deliberation. Wherever understanding is not fully attainable, criticism should proceed through a process of open-ended questioning that seeks to generate reflectivity among world-views. Such processes may occur through direct dialogue, mediated communication, or internal reflection. Third, deliberation must be adequately connected to democratic decision-making through workable decision rules, in addition to direct and indirect connections between the informal, deliberative institutions of the public sphere and the formal, decision-making institutions of the democratic state. Although multiple connections are possible, voting and elections are necessary, if not sufficient, means for connecting deliberation to democratic decision-making.

Finally, collective decisions must fulfill three fairness conditions: political equality, political autonomy, and political reciprocity. Because voting and elections are needed to connect deliberation and collective decision-making, these fair conditions must reflect distinct deliberative and aggregative dimensions. *Political equality* includes aggregative equality, understood as roughly equal voting strength among individuals, and deliberative equality, understood as the equal representation of diverse positions, regardless of their numerical strength. *Political autonomy* includes aggregative autonomy, the capacity to choose among multiple candidates, policy preferences, or political constituencies, and deliberative autonomy, the capacity to develop critical, reflective preferences under conditions of full information, nondeception, and noncoercion. *Political reciprocity* subdivides into aggregative reciprocity, symmetrical opportunities to bargain and coalesce with others over policy preferences, and deliberative reciprocity, the disposition to recognize others as deliberative partners, to understand others' world-views, perspectives, interests, and opinions, and to seek agreement on mutually acceptable collective decisions.

The substantive disposition of deliberative reciprocity is the most important condition of plural deliberation. However, there may be circumstances in which disadvantaged actors may withdraw deliberative reciprocity in favor of nondeliberative, agonistic challenges to political processes and institutions, challenges that eschew the robust attempt to understand across group boundaries and to seek agreement. I defend agonistic challenges but subject them to the following qualifications. First, agonists must justify their withdrawals from deliberative processes through the criteria of plural deliberation. Second, they must realize that plural deliberation's complex legitimacy must be assessed along a sliding scale: unless all four elements of plural deliberation are entirely absent, institutions and processes are likely to be more or less legitimate. Third, actors must use this framework to determine when, within which institutions, and with whom they should engage in plural deliberation. For instance, agonistic politics are unjustified between two disadvantaged groups that enjoy political equality and political autonomy in relation to each other. Finally, in order to fulfill its four elements, plural deliberation provides agonistic challengers with clear criteria for reforming or redesigning institutions and processes.

According to these qualifications, an agonistic challenge may best be described as a moral rejection of deliberative reciprocity; challengers justify their agonism through recourse to deliberative criteria. In this sense, justifiable agonism requires a temporary extension of deliberative reciprocity. The disposition of deliberative reciprocity is analytically associated with Habermas's idea of communicative action, which expresses an orientation toward understanding, as opposed to strategic action, which depicts an orientation toward goal-fulfillment. In this sense, even justifiable agonists act according to communicative action. However, empirical analyses suggest that five strategic dynamics of group conflict can undermine communicative action across group boundaries. Thus, in chapter 3 I outline these strategic dynamics of group conflict and examine whether deliberative motivations are necessary and sufficient to overcome them. The *resource dynamic* of conflict shows how groups compete for scarce economic resources; the *political dynamic* reflects group-based competition for political power; the *positional dynamic* portrays how groups compete for psychological status or esteem above other groups; the *information dynamic* illustrates how group-specific and mainstream media sources propagate inaccurate or stereotypical information about other groups; and the *security dynamic* shows how groups are led to engage in violent conflict through mutual distrust. Although actual violent group conflict is relatively rare and occurs only when the security dynamic permits, the other dynamics can hinder plural deliberation even in the absence of violence.

I then examine four motivations to deliberate across group boundaries. Moral psychology suggests that individuals want to justify norms consistently and impartially; modern cultural self-understandings ground a universalistic duty to recognize others beyond one's own group; publicity constraints show how appearing in public forces political actors to communicate in ways that a diverse public will accept; and the deliberative generation of trust suggests that the circulation of information about other groups can counter the information and positional dynamics of conflict. I conclude that these deliberative motivations are necessary but insufficient to support plural deliberation. Consequently, I argue that deliberative theorists should examine how strategic dynamics might, under some circumstances, encourage deliberative reciprocity.

To illustrate this last point, I provide a brief case study of how Black civil rights issues were taken up in the Jewish public sphere prior to the Second World War. Strategic dynamics encouraged the northern Jewish public to adopt deliberative reciprocity toward Blacks and their civil rights claims, while different strategic dynamics hindered such reciprocity in the South. This case leads me to make four suggestions for fostering plural deliberation amidst the dynamics of group conflict: (1) we must identify which groups are strategically positioned to adopt deliberative reciprocity across group boundaries, (2) those groups that are favorably positioned may wish to adopt the less demanding disposition of aggregative reciprocity as a precursor to deliberative reciprocity, (3) aggregative coalitions among favorably positioned groups should pursue policy goals that mitigate dynamics of group conflict, and (4) and these coalitions should try to reform democratic institutions, such as the public sphere and electoral systems.

The theoretical claims made in chapters 1–3 regarding identity construction, plural deliberation, and the dynamics of group conflict set the stage for the assessment of democratic institutions in chapters 4 and 5. In chapter 4, I examine civil society and the public sphere. Deliberative theorists influenced by the work of Habermas tend to favor this informal, deliberative setting for a variety of reasons. John Dryzek, for example, believes that the public sphere allows the widest possible participation of ordinary citizens and frees participants from strategic constraints; Seyla Benhabib, in turn, contends that civil society and the public sphere best realize conditions of egalitarian reciprocity, freedom of exit and association, and voluntary self-ascription. While acknowledging the indispensable role of the public sphere in a deliberative, plural polity, I simultaneously illuminate the dangers and obstacles in this realm by carefully examining the three primary public sphere actors: associations, social movements, and the media.

According to Mark Warren, associations can promote three democratic effects: *developmental effects* reflect how individuals evolve political capacities by participating in associational self-government; *institutional effects* show how associations can bolster the legitimacy of the democratic state by assuming certain state functions; and *public sphere effects* indicate how associations communicate their positions beyond their members to the public sphere. I argue that these democratic effects become more problematic when applied to group-based associations. Ethnic associations may cultivate political capacities, but whether they enhance deliberative reciprocity across group boundaries depends on whether the association includes more than a single group. Institutional effects may hinder deliberative reciprocity across group boundaries when group-based associations with control over resources encourage the resource dynamic of conflict. Finally, group-based associations take part in public sphere effects through the mass media and social movements, which themselves remain vulnerable to the dynamics of group conflict.

Social movements are quintessential public sphere actors; their primary activities (protests and civil disobedience) are effective only if they occur in public. However, social movements can fulfill specifically deliberative tasks only through the role of informal representatives, such as spokespersons, and only amidst certain strategic constraints and in conjunction with aggregative bargaining. These strategic and aggregative elements can be justified by plural deliberation; nevertheless they complicate the deliberative assessment of social movements. They also implicate social movements within the strategic dynamics of group conflict. I illustrate this problem through a brief analysis of three Black American social movements: the civil rights movement, the Black Power movement, and the movement to boycott Korean-owned stores in Brooklyn. I argue that the civil rights movement fulfilled the criteria of plural deliberation, albeit through the use of informal representatives, strategic action, and aggregative bargaining. Black Power did not fulfill plural deliberation's desiderata, although it can be seen as a justifiable form of agonism and noninstitutionalized, aggregative bargaining. The boycott movement cannot be justified according to plural deliberation, given the countervailing power relationships between the Korean merchants and the Black boycotters. However, it can be explained using the positional and information dynamics of group conflict in the mass media. This leads to an analysis of mainstream and group-specific media outlets according to the criteria of plural deliberation, the dynamics of group conflict, and the problem of identity construction. Whereas the mainstream media habitually violate deliberative equality and deliberative autonomy in their representation of racial perspectives, group-specific media can enhance deliberative equality and deliberative autonomy, but can diminish deliberative reciprocity across groups.

From my assessment of associations, social movements, and the mass media, I conclude that the public sphere remains a fruitful site for plural deliberation, especially because it facilitates the flexible representation of fluid and emerging collective identities. But because it remains vulnerable to the dynamics of group conflict, it is necessary to investigate alternative settings, such as the quasi-formal, deliberative institutions related to the state. It is also necessary to examine public policies that can support cross-group associations and improve the deliberative role of the media. But because the public sphere remains an informal institution, one that cannot be redesigned, I turn in chapter 5 to an analysis of electoral systems.

These formal, decision-making institutions are not usually perceived as sites of deliberation but as mere mechanisms for aggregating voter preferences. However, I argue that the aggregative functions of electoral systems can generate strategic incentives to encourage plural deliberation. If an electoral system requires candidates to seek votes across group boundaries, it generates strategic incentives that counter the political dynamic of conflict and encourage deliberative reciprocity.

For this reason, I contend that the proper, normative assessment of electoral systems requires recourse to plural deliberation's deliberative and aggregative criteria of fairness.

But before using plural deliberation to assess different electoral systems, I first examine problems in deliberative representation. Most important, I argue that deliberative models of representation place too much weight on deliberation between representatives and constituents, a relationship that typically violates deliberative autonomy. This problem requires rethinking deliberative representation and heightening the importance of descriptive representation. It also means that electoral systems must be comparatively assessed through five of plural deliberation's criteria, excluding deliberative autonomy.

I then assess four unfavorable electoral systems: the single-member district, plurality system used in the American House of Representatives; the multimember district, plurality system used in several American state and local elections; and open-roll and closed-roll reserved seats. While all of these systems fare poorly according to the criteria of plural deliberation, the single-member district plurality system can be improved in moderate but important ways. Following this, I assess four favorable electoral systems: party list proportional representation, the alternative vote, the single-transferable vote, and the cumulative vote. I conclude that the alternative vote and the single-transferable vote are far preferable to the other favorable systems because their ballot structure provides candidates with incentives to extend deliberative reciprocity across group boundaries.

However, I point out that altering electoral systems confronts five contextual problems: (1) whether the process of adopting a new electoral system itself exacerbates the political dynamic of group conflict, (2) whether the size of the jurisdiction requires using a simpler system, (3) whether an electoral system is deeply rooted in the polity's political culture, (4) whether the role and character of existing political parties can facilitate certain electoral systems, and (5) whether the populace will easily accept a new electoral system. Consideration of these contextual factors leads me to favor reforming the single-member district plurality system at the national level by increasing the number of districts and, perhaps, by introducing alternative voting. At the state and local level, institutional innovation faces fewer obstacles, allowing reformers to seek to replace multimember district plurality systems with the single-transferable vote. I conclude that adopting electoral reform may well rely on deliberative and agonistic political action by informal representatives in the public sphere.

SCOPE, METHODS, AND FOUNDATIONS

Before turning to my exposition of deliberative democracy in the plural polity, let me briefly discuss a few issues concerning the scope of the project, the methods of analysis, and the foundations for my deliberative, institutional approach. I have intentionally narrowed the scope of this project in three ways. First, I examine only problems concerning intergenerational collective identities, such as racial, ethnic, religious, or cultural groups. These groups include members of both sexes and enjoy greater ease in sustaining themselves through reproduction and socialization. As a result, I do not address problems related to gender or sexuality. I focus on intergenerational groups not because problems of sexuality or gender are less important than problems of race, ethnicity, or culture. Rather, intergenerational groups, given their capacities for reproduction and socialization, tend to raise certain distinct problems for political theory. In particular, problems of conflict and stability more directly arise in relation to these groups, which enjoy greater capacities to engage in destabilizing violence. To a lesser degree, the problems of identity construction and boundary maintenance are more pressing among these groups, although I admit that transgendered individuals complicate sexual divisions and the flexibility of human sexuality challenges essentialist distinctions between homosexuals and heterosexuals.

The scope of this project is also narrowed by its focus on intrapolity politics. Thus, I do not examine international or global political dynamics. Although I acknowledge that international and global factors can initiate, exacerbate, and mitigate intrapolity group conflict, I circumvent these issues for pragmatic reasons: looking at international and global dynamics would introduce a level of complexity to the argument that would obscure the many issues that I am already examining. Given that normative theories of pluralism already pay relatively little attention to problems of conflict, identity construction, and institutional design, injecting a more detailed discussion of these topics into normative debates is a sufficiently ambitious task. In addition, global and international pressures are somewhat less pertinent to the American case, my focus in this analysis. Although the problems of pluralism in the United States are affected by immigration, other common international and global influences, such as third-party intervention or cross-border irredentist movements, are decidedly less prominent.

This raises the question of why I focus only on the United States. Right away, I wish to abjure any claim that the American case is more important than other cases, along with any claim that American exceptionalism precludes instructive comparisons with other polities. Indeed, as I will discuss below, many of the analytical concepts associated with identity construction, group conflict, and institutional analysis have been derived from scholarship in the field of comparative politics. Again, pragmatic concerns drive my concentration on the United States: trying to conduct a sufficiently detailed account of deliberative democracy among several polities would be a much more demanding task, especially given that this project simultaneously raises questions of justice and stability. But beyond this pragmatic constraint, the American case also recommends itself on two further grounds.

First, the American racial order is often thought to mitigate problems of identity construction. Given that racial identities in America have largely been imposed upon minority groups by the majority White group, the impression is that these identities do not experience the same internal diversity, shifting boundaries, and multiple modes of identity construction common among ethnic identities in other countries. Collective identity construction might be a worthy topic in examining relations among European, African, or Asian ethnicities but not among America's fixed and imposed racial identities. As we shall see, there is considerable truth to this claim, especially regarding Black Americans. But even in that case, problems of internal diversity, shifting boundaries, and multiple modes of identity construction do arise. Consequently, if problems of identity construction can complicate justice among American racial groups, they are likely to do so among more fluid collective identities.

A second advantage to studying the American case is that both deliberative motivations and strategic dynamics of conflict permeate its politics. Although the United States has not witnessed civil wars among racial or ethnic groups, and although it is a wealthy, established democracy with the constitutional rights and democratic political culture that deliberative democracy presupposes,[13] it nevertheless remains vulnerable to most of the dynamics of group conflict. In addition, the rapid rise in America's Hispanic and Asian populations, to the point that non-Hispanic Whites are now a minority in California and Hawaii, raises the importance of interminority dynamics of conflict and deliberation. These factors suggest that the American case may be more generalizable than that of Canada, a common focus for normative theories of pluralism. Whereas the liberal pluralist, Will Kymlicka, claims that Canada's simultaneous recognition of itself as a multinational and multiethnic state improves the general applicability of his normative framework, Canada's rather genteel political culture need not be generalizable to countries that do not share its relatively small population, its high level of income, its protection by a friendly but militarily hegemonic neighbor, and its self-understanding as morally superior to that neighbor.[14]

So while pragmatic concerns have led me to focus on the American case, this case is not so idiosyncratic as to negate any extension of my analysis. And although I have narrowed my scope to the case of a single polity, I have broadened it beyond purely normative justification to include problems of identity construction, dynamics of group conflict, and institutional analysis. However, joining normative theory and empirical analysis can raise further questions about the foundations of my theory and the methods behind my empirical material. Although I doubt that I can resolve all dilemmas associated with these questions, there are grounds for allaying most concerns.

Much of deliberative democratic theory concentrates on providing foundations for deliberative principles and procedures.[15] This has resulted in a relative dearth in studies spelling out the implications of deliberative theory for actual or possible political processes and institutions, particularly under conditions of pluralism. For this reason, I have prioritized the application of deliberative theory to problems of pluralism. Nevertheless, I strongly believe that the elements of my model of plural deliberation are well grounded in the practices and intuitions of a democratic, plural polity. This claim is strengthened, I believe, by my inclusion of aggregative criteria, as contemporary democratic polities almost universally aspire to aggregative equality's equal voting power, aggregative autonomy's choice over alternatives, and aggregative reciprocity's symmetrical bargaining positions. Deliberative criteria, however, are typically more difficult to justify. The grounds for these criteria, I suggest, should be derived from a variety of philosophical and empirical sources, including the reconstruction of widespread political, social, and linguistic practices,[16] studies of intergroup communication,[17] and historical analysis. Moreover, all criteria of democratic fairness, be they procedural or substantive, aggregative or deliberative, should be seen as provisional and revisable in light of new experiences and practices.

In terms of methods, the most prominent problem is that scholars in the field of comparative politics (not American politics) have spearheaded the investigation of collective identity construction, the dynamics of group conflict, and institutions for a plural polity. This, of course, conflicts with the fact that my analysis focuses only on American cases. A second problem is that comparative research, especially quantitative studies of electoral systems, can overlook contextual features that strongly shape political processes on the ground. To solve the first problem, I have sought substantial American evidence of identity construction, dynamics of group conflict, public sphere deliberation, and, where possible, electoral systems. Of course, some electoral systems have not been used in the United States and thus American evidence remains partly unavailable. However, there is greater American innovation in electoral systems than is generally realized, and thus I have sought information about cases where they exist. In response to the second problem, I have augmented evidence from quantitative studies with more contextual studies of electoral dynamics on the ground.

Marrying normative and empirical research has, of course, required the inclusion of work from a variety of disciplines. Although my model of plural deliberation and the idea of the public sphere clearly stem from normative, deliberative democratic theory, the rest of my analysis has had to pull from a variety of empirical sources. For instance, my study of identity construction draws primarily on work in sociology and anthropology; the dynamics of group conflict and the analysis of electoral systems is informed by work in comparative politics, American politics, and American history; and the study of the public sphere relies on work in political theory, sociology, and media studies. Even though engaging in such broad, cross-disciplinary work taxes one's research efforts, I remain convinced that such work is essential for understanding what justice requires in a plural, democratic polity. I realize that I will not have the final word in our theoretical and practical discussions of this problem, but I hope to provoke further cross-disciplinary research aimed at combining the normative and empirical dimensions of democratic politics in a plural polity.

1

The Normative Consequences of Identity Construction

I was born to immigrants from South India. As a result, I was born White, am sometimes perceived as Black, and am presently Asian. The fact that I was born White is vouched for by my birth certificate, which identifies my parents' and my race as White. When I was born—in 1967—immigrants from the Indian subcontinent fell between the existing American racial categories and were designated as White. The fact that I am seen as Black most clearly manifested itself in April 1996, when I went to New York to visit a friend. Shortly before my trip, I had shaved my head. When I emerged from New York's Penn Station, I found myself unable to hail a cab. This surprised me, as I never had such difficulties before. The reason for my lack of success was revealed to me when a White man nearby sympathized with my plight, noting the unfairness of how cabbies avoid picking up Black men. The experience struck me not only as deeply troubling but also deeply ironic, because many of the cabbies who passed me by were clearly South Asian, perhaps even Indian. The fact that I am presently Asian reflects my response to job application forms and to the latest census. A recent employment document, for example, instructs individuals "having origins in the Indian subcontinent" to use the Asian/Pacific Islander category. These instructions stem from lobbying efforts by the Association of Indians in America (AIA), which sought to change the categorization of Indians from White to Asian in order to make them eligible for affirmative action benefits under the Small Business Administration Act.[1] All of these identity shifts occurred despite the fact that I actively try to identify myself as an Indian American, for instance by including my Indian middle name in between my rather Anglo-Saxon first and last names.

This personal anecdote illustrates some key factors in the construction and reconstruction of intergenerational collective identities. It reveals that groups can be

17

internally diverse (Asian Americans can be Indian, Chinese, or Korean); it reveals that group boundaries can shift (the boundaries of Asian and White shifted, extracting Indians from the latter and inserting them into the former); and it reveals that members of a given group can gain their identity through agent-based choices (like the collective lobbying by the AIA), or through the structural imposition of formal laws (census categories and equal employment policies), and informal perceptions (being perceived as Black). It also reveals that collective identities are important not only for their cultural meanings (like being associated with the historical legacy and cultural practices of the Indian subcontinent) but also for their instrumental benefits (eligibility for affirmative action) and costs (being unable to hail a cab).

My experiences, although not universal, are neither rare nor extreme. And although these shifts in identity do not reflect how I personally and authentically identify myself, they remain significant through their effects on the distribution of political, legal, and economic resources. Consequently, the construction of collective identity should be vitally important for normative political theories concerned with substantive justice between groups, because these theories typically try to assess whether group-specific measures are justified in order to achieve a fair distribution of resources or opportunities among members of different groups. However, I suspect that many political philosophers underestimate the importance of collective identity construction, given three common oversights within this literature.

First, many theorists underestimate the level of internal diversity within groups, ignoring how subgroups may possess cultural traits or confront social conditions that differ significantly from those of the broader group. Second, they overlook how group boundaries can shift over time and according to social, political, and economic circumstances. Instead, they assume that various collective identities are stable, without sufficiently examining how they came into existence, whether they will exist in the future, and under what circumstances they are or are not salient for the individuals marked by them.[2] Finally, some theorists use overdrawn distinctions among different types of groups to determine which, if any, deserve group-specific protections. For example, some theorists distinguish collective identities according to whether they are chosen by or are culturally significant to their members.

In this chapter, I argue that empirical accounts of collective identity construction complicate the ability of substantive theories of justice between groups to reach clear, determinate justifications for group-specific or group-neutral rights, policies, or institutions. I begin by discussing how collective identities are marked by internal diversity, shifting boundaries, and four modes of collective identity construction. I then argue that four normative theorists use a single mode of identity construction to identify which groups, if any, deserve group-specific political measures. Whereas relying on a single mode of identity construction is useful in reconstructing moral intuitions about justice between groups, I argue that the empirical evidence of collective identity construction complicates this picture. I make my case by examining the construction of the four most politically salient minority collective identities in the United States: Native Americans, Hispanic Americans, Asian Americans, and Black Americans. I consider these four collective identities to be most politically salient because they alone were subject to formal legal discrimination, unlike White ethnic identities that were subject primarily to informal prejudice.[3] The empirical accounts of these groups allow me to highlight the three oversights committed by normative theorists by revealing their internal diversity, shifting boundaries, and multiple modes of identity construction. This leads me to conclude that an adequate justification for group-specific or group-neutral measures must depend less on distinctions between different types of groups and more on contextually sensitive, deliberative processes that attend to problems of collective identity construction.

FOUR MODES OF COLLECTIVE IDENTITY CONSTRUCTION

Collective identity construction suggests that groups are internally diverse and that their boundaries can change. It further suggests that boundary changes can stem both from social structures and the choices of individual and collective agents, for instrumental and interpretive reasons. Donald Horowitz depicts internal diversity and group boundary shifts through a discussion of assimilation and differentiation.[4] Assimilation can occur through *amalgamation,* whereby two or more groups combine to create a third, new group, or through *incorporation,* whereby one group is incorporated into an already existing group. An example of amalgamation may be the initial creation of a common Black American identity from the diverse ethnic and linguistic identities of African slaves. An example of incorporation may be the assimilation of European immigrants into a unified, preexisting White American identity. Differentiation can occur through *division,* whereby one group is split into two or more new and distinct groups, and *proliferation,* whereby a smaller subgroup splits off from a persisting, more encompassing collective identity. Division can be exemplified by the increased salience of distinct regional, dialect identities from a unified Telugu linguistic identity following the creation of the separate Telugu-speaking state of Andhra Pradesh in India. Proliferation can be seen in the development in the 1980s in New York of a distinct West Indian identity out of a more encompassing and persistent Black identity.

Changing group boundaries through assimilation and differentiation can be an ongoing process. New collective identities that emerged through differentiation at one time may later become submerged through a process of assimilation. Individuals may choose distinct collective identities according to their relative salience at different times and in different circumstances. An individual who usually assumes an assimilated White identity may, on certain occasions, adopt a differentiated Italian identity. The capacity to change identification at different times depends upon whether others would recognize the asserted identification. Thus, identification with a group depends both on the agency of the actor and on structural factors, such as the informal perceptions of others and the formal categorization of laws and institutions.

Some normative political theorists acknowledge the complementary role of agency and structure in the formation of collective identity. Drawing on the work of George Herbert Mead, Charles Taylor depicts the creation of identity through individual assertion and recognition by significant others. However, his account tends to restrict the domain of significant others to relatively depoliticized settings, where assertion and recognition of identity are purely a matter of negotiating commonly shared cultural meanings and values.[5] Collective identity, however, can also develop under more politicized contexts, where recognition also involves and affects the distribution of political, social, and economic resources. As a result, the construction and reconstruction of potentially changing collective identities occur through processes of agency and structure, for reasons related both to instrumental interests over resources and interpretive concerns regarding cultural meanings and values. In order to clarify the processes through which collective identity may develop, let us refer to the following analytical framework in Table 1.1.[6]

I distinguish two ways that collective identities can be significant for individuals. They can have *interpretive significance,* when individual members share cultural meanings, values, symbols, practices, or cognitive frameworks. A language community may have interpretive significance because a common language provides a cognitive framework that enables members to express and communicate meaningful statements. Religious communities share meanings regarding the importance of human life, the morality of certain actions, and practices and symbols for commemorating and interpreting events in life, such as marriage, divorce, the birth of children, aging, and death. Collective identities can also have *instrumental significance,* if possessing a collective identity has positive or negative consequences for individual members, such as increasing one's chances of getting a grant or decreasing one's chances of getting a job. Thus, collective identity may be something that an individual would be willing to change, depending on the opportunity and the consequences involved. However, the capacity to choose collective identities can vary greatly among individuals, which prompts analysis of the sources of collective identity.

This dimension of collective identity formation shows whether individuals choose their collective identity. To the extent that a collective identity results from agency, individuals can choose whether to join or remain within one. This need not imply any idea of an atomized or essential self prior to all collective identities, and it is compatible with the notion that individuals are socialized into collective identities prior to any choice. Rather, agency assumes that individuals can choose whether to retain their inherited collective identity or to adopt a new one. Additionally, room for agency emerges if individuals are members of multiple groups and thus can choose which identity they find most salient or valuable, for either interpretive or instrumental reasons. Alternatively, they can experience collective identity as a social structure over which they exercise little or no choice. One may

Table 1.1. The Sources and Significance of Collective Identity

Significance of Identity	Source of Identity	
	Agent	Structure
Instrumental	e.g., Ethnic Interest Groups	e.g., Racial Identities
Interpretive	e.g., Symbolic Ethnicity	e.g., Language Communities

inhabit a collective identity simply by birth and socialization, as in the case of children raised within a language community, or one can be ascribed a collective identity in adulthood through formal legal categorization or informal perceptions. The perception of African immigrants as Black fits the latter case as these individuals were likely born and socialized into a much more specific national identity (e.g., Nigerian) or subnational identity (e.g., Yoruba). Using these two dimensions to distinguish the sources and the significance of collective identity, let me now outline four analytical modes through which collective identities are constructed.

Instrumental, Agent-centered Collective Identity

In this mode, individuals choose their collective identity for instrumental reasons, such as economic or political gain. Thus, collective identities are akin to interest groups.[7] Individuals identify with a collective identity to secure instrumental interests, and they may alter their identification or drop group affiliation entirely, depending on the economic and political incentives. Once identified with a group, individuals can then exercise collective agency to lobby, protest, or fight for their interests.

Instrumental, Structural Collective Identity

Under this mode, individuals either inherit a collective identity or are ascribed to one by others, who may or may not be members of the group in question. Race is the paradigmatic example of an instrumental, structural collective identity. Members of racial groups need not share common cultural symbols, languages, or practices but are simply ascribed racial membership by others. Racial ascription need not rely on any biological claim about racial descent; formal laws or informal perceptions can impose racial identities without recourse to discredited racial science. Nevertheless, strong racial social structures can impose racial identity as rigidly as any putative biological trait.

Interpretive, Agent-centered Collective Identity

This mode reflects how some individuals can choose their collective identities based on the meaningfulness of a group's beliefs, practices, symbols, or values. Additionally, these individuals may use interpretive agency to select which cultural beliefs and practices they consider central to that group's identity. Consider the idea of "symbolic ethnicity," a term associated with White ethnic groups in the United States. Because intermarriage among European immigrants provides a variety of ethnic roots to their descendants, the latter enjoy a variety of "ethnic options." And because choosing an ethnic identity bears no costs or benefits for White ethnics, their choices merely reflect the values or practices associated with a given ethnic group. In addition, White ethnics can often choose what beliefs or practices they consider central to their ethnic identity. Because few Italian Americans can speak Italian, retaining the ancestral language may be less central to their ethnic identity than is appreciating Italian cuisine.[8]

Interpretive, Structural Collective Identity

Under this mode, individuals do not choose their collective identity, and yet it remains culturally significant. Paradigmatic cases of this mode are linguistic communities, in which children are socialized into a "mother tongue" that they may experience as the natural medium through which to interpret the world. Only through great efforts of learning and immersion can such individuals come to inhabit a new language with the same ease and comfort that they experienced in their native tongue. National cultures might also exemplify this mode; individuals born and raised in them may take the practices, lifestyles, and beliefs of that culture as almost natural, even if they are aware of and have even lived in other national cultures.

These modes of identity construction reflect analytical, not empirical, distinctions. This means that a single act of identity construction may embody two or more of the modes outlined here. For example, one actor may exercise agency in creating a group boundary that excludes another actor, who would then have been passively categorized in a structural manner. Consequently, the examples provided are only illustrations of the mode in question, not categorical distinctions between different types of groups. Empirical evidence suggests that collective identities are often constructed through multiple modes. Instrumental agency by political actors can forge linguistic identities, whereas interpretive agency can imbue racial groups with common cultural practices. I introduce these analytical modes to reveal how certain normative theorists deduce substantive conclusions about justice among groups from narrow conceptions of collective identity formation. As we shall see, these thinkers use these modes not simply as analytical tools but as empirical referents that distinguish groups and their claims.

MODES OF IDENTITY CONSTRUCTION IN NORMATIVE THEORY

Normative political theorists concerned with substantive justice among groups often make a strong link between a type of group and the strength of its claims to group-specific rights, policies, or institutions. In this section, I argue that four political theorists—Will Kymlicka, Yael Tamir, Russell Hardin, and Jeff Spinner—use one of the four modes of identity construction to argue for or against group-specific measures. As I mentioned in the Introduction, I focus on these four thinkers for two reasons. First, they provide a fairly broad if not exhaustive survey of normative arguments regarding relations among ethnic, racial, national, or cultural groups. Second, by concentrating on a single mode of identity construction, these thinkers compellingly reconstruct common moral intuitions about the fairness or unfairness of group-specific measures aimed at realizing equality among members of diverse collective identities. Using a single mode can plausibly reconstruct moral intuitions regarding which groups, if any, deserve specific protective measures, but empirical accounts challenge this approach, because multiple modes are involved in the four most important minority groups in the United States.

Will Kymlicka: National Cultures as Interpretive, Structural Collective Identities

Will Kymlicka's theory of minority cultural rights distinguishes between national minority groups (depicted as interpretive, structural collective identities) and immigrant, ethnic minority groups (depicted as interpretive but agent-centered). This distinction justifies national minorities' claims to self-government rights, while limiting the "polyethnic" rights of immigrants to group representation or exemptions from general laws. Kymlicka's focus on cultural pluralism leads him to emphasize interpretive significance: collective identities are important to individuals because their cultural content provides meaning to their lives and the choices they make. In the modern world, the collective identities most able to support meaningful individual agency are societal cultures, which "tend to be territorially concentrated and based on a shared language" and which are unified not only by "shared memories or values but also common institutions and practices."[9] One's own societal culture enables one to choose not simply among various instrumentally functional economic or social roles but among meaningful life-plan options that foster dignity and self-worth. Indeed, individuals may make instrumentally irrational decisions in order to protect their societal cultures, such as expending extra resources to educate their children in a native language. Whether such instrumentally irrational costs are justified depends on whether one has chosen to inhabit a minority collective identity.

Members of a minority culture can claim the "right" to protect that culture if their identification with it is involuntary. Kymlicka's distinction between the rights of national versus ethnic minority cultures depends on this. Members of national minorities who were born into and raised in their societal culture did not choose the minority status they now inhabit. This contrasts with ethnic minorities, immigrants, and their descendants, who have voluntarily left their native societal culture and thus have negated any substantive claims to state support in re-creating their native culture in their new society. As a result, ethnic minorities can lobby for educational policies that enable their children to retain their native languages, but they "have no *right* to such policies" (emphasis in original).[10] Conversely, national minorities do have the right to govern themselves and to protect their language, because presumably they have been raised speaking that language and have not voluntarily chosen to exit the community within which it is spoken. Thus, national minorities, as opposed to ethnic minorities, suffer "unchosen inequalities," which distributive justice should remedy through self-government rights.[11]

According to the framework of collective identity construction, the minority status of a national identity is structurally induced, whereas the minority status of an ethnic identity results from agency. In each case, individual members were involuntarily socialized into a certain minority societal culture that is presently threatened by the majority culture. However, the minority status of an ethnic collective identity is a chosen inequality, created by the voluntary decision to vacate a native societal culture and to inhabit a foreign one. Conversely, the minority status of the national collective identity is an unchosen inequality, created by the structural, numerical relationship between the societal cultures within a specific state. Both forms of collective identity may be equally meaningful: indeed, ethnic minority cultures may have even greater meaning for their members. But because the inequalities of ethnic minorities result from voluntary decisions, substantive justice supports relatively weak measures to protect them.

Kymlicka's argument has been subject to enormous criticism, and I do not wish to reproduce all aspects of this debate here.[12] I do, however, wish to take issue with his claim that national identities are interpretive and structural, that they are significant primarily for the meaning that they provide to their members, and that those members exercise little agency in creating them. As James Johnson pointedly notes, Kymlicka "thoroughly depoliticizes" national identity by overlooking how individuals can strategically manipulate cultural meanings in order to further their own individual, instrumental interests in economic or political goals.[13] In a similar vein, Brian Barry notes that Kymlicka's interpretive emphasis on national identity neglects the fact that many national movements have little or no cultural content. The primary characteristic they share is not a distinct societal culture bound by language, history, or territory but the political goal of controlling the collective affairs of those individuals who populate the nation. Thus, Scottish nationalism can persist despite the fact that most Scots speak English.[14] For both Johnson and Barry, Kymlicka's theory fails because national cultural identity is often of instrumental, not interpretive, importance. Political or economic interests can lie at the heart of national collective identity, a possibility that Kymlicka's approach seems to deny by definition.[15]

Yael Tamir: National Cultures as Interpretive, Agent-centered Collective Identities

Whereas Kymlicka's theory of distributive justice among groups requires a sharp distinction between the agency associated with ethnic minority status and the structural character of national minority status, Yael Tamir's theory of liberal national-ism blurs this distinction. For her, all collective cultural identities can justly claim substantive protections precisely because they reflect individuals' free "constitu-tive" choices, those choices that grant meaning to an individual's life. Thus, inter-pretive agency justifies a variety of protections for culturally based collective identities. Tamir agrees with Kymlicka that a national culture is a precondition for the exercise of individual autonomy and that immigrants exercise choice in moving into a new one. Where they differ regards those who do not choose to migrate, with Tamir arguing that remaining within one's original national culture is itself an autonomous act of affirmation: "Choice is not to be identified with change."[16]

Yet if individuals choose their national cultural identity, why would it be unjust for the state to impose penalties upon those whose cultural practices conflict with state law? Indeed, if national membership is chosen, distributive justice and even distributive efficiency might justify requiring an individual to identify with the majority national culture. Tamir's response is that individuals affirm their mem-bership within cultural minorities through interpretive, not instrumental, agency. Thus, she infuses her portrait of individual constitutive choices with the language of cultural meaning. For Tamir, "national self-determination has little to do with civil rights and political participation" but expresses individuals' "desire to live in a meaningful environment" and "to be ruled by institutions informed by a culture they find understandable and meaningful."[17] The meaning attached to national membership also extends from the individual to other members, those "significant others" who recognize the individual's actions. Such recognition grounds the "nationalist belief that every action taking place within the boundaries of a national entity is endowed with additional meaning."[18] The ties of shared national meaning also affect the duties that individuals bear toward each other, creating "associative obligations" among compatriots that take precedence over, but do not negate, oblig-ations toward nonmembers.[19]

For Tamir, justice requires compensation for inequalities not because they are unchosen but because they result from constitutive choices. In contradistinction to Kymlicka, she eschews the language of group rights and declares "the right to na-tional self-determination as an individual right, contingent on a willed decision of individuals to affiliate themselves with a particular national group and to give pub-lic expression to this affiliation." And whereas Kymlicka draws a sharp distinction between the claims of national and ethnic minorities, Tamir believes "the right to national self-determination is merely a particular case of the right to culture."[20] This leads to some important conclusions. First, Tamir locates cultural claims on a con-tinuum that must consider pragmatic as well as moral considerations. Second, she justifies self-government rights for atypical national groups, like diaspora Jews, who lacked the contiguous territory and living language that typify Kymlicka's societal cultures. Finally, she distinguishes two types of rights to self-determination: the right to an autonomous public sphere within which to preserve one's national cul-ture versus the right to territorial self-government.[21] She elevates as a right only the first cultural definition of national self-determination, which entails not a separate state but only culture-preserving institutions like civil society associations. This allows her to avoid Kymlicka's somewhat arbitrary distinction between "national" cultural groups, which have a right to territorial self-government, and "ethnic" cultural groups, which have rights to representation and exemptions from certain general laws.

Although Tamir's reliance on agency grants her greater flexibility than Kymlicka has, she nevertheless fails to confront two important problems. First, like Kymlicka, she bears the burden of demonstrating that interpretive and not instrumental significance is central to national identity. If individuals autonomously identify with a national culture on instrumental grounds related to economic or political resources, then her justification for national self-determination fails. Second, she must contend with interpretive cultural beliefs that are morally repugnant. She recognizes that creating subjective, national sentiments "involves a conscious and deliberate effort to lessen the importance of objective differences within the group while reinforcing the group's uniqueness vis-à-vis outsiders."[22] However, she does not consider that this process could illegitimately constrain internal diversity in order to intensify contrasts with other groups. And whereas contrasts with other groups might remain benign, they might also embody the positional dynamic of group conflict, which I will discuss in chapter 3. The positional dynamic shows how individuals rank their own collective identity above that of other groups, thereby providing a deep psychological source of prejudice.[23] If political elites encounter political or economic incentives to heighten group conflict, they may enhance positional dynamics through a variety of means. In this light, Tamir's reliance on interpretive agency seems almost naïve, once we attend to the dangers of prejudice and power politics.

Russell Hardin: Ethnic Groups as Instrumental, Agent-centered Collective Identities

Power politics lies at the heart of Russell Hardin's approach to collective identity. Whereas Tamir and Kymlicka emphasize the interpretive characteristics of collective identity, Hardin emphasizes instrumental agency in asserting that individuals will tend to identify with those groups best able to provide material resources.[24] And although he acknowledges that agency over identity can be constrained by sex, skin color, language, or culture, he maintains that overlapping identities grant individuals the capacity to choose which identity to emphasize in a given situation.[25] Consequently, Hardin depicts the national or ethnic groups Kymlicka and Tamir see as interpretive as interest groups created by instrumental agency. Indeed, he sees ethnic or national groups as particularly effective interest groups because they can overcome collective action problems through selective cultural incentives, like food, fellowship, language, or traditional practices. They enhance their effectiveness by providing cheap information, leading members to equate their individual interests with the interests of the group. Moreover, as intergenerational communities, their members tend to have deeply sunk costs with respect to membership in the group. For example, members raised speaking a community's language will have already devoted substantial time and energy to learning that language and thus will have strong incentives to protect it through collective mobilization.[26]

Collective identity, then, results from the agency of individuals, and its significance is largely reduced to instrumental interests. From this model, Hardin develops an explanatory account of group conflict and a normative critique of group-specific norms. For Hardin, all norms are consequentialist social rules that have positive, negative, or neutral effects upon actors. Universalistic norms "apply universalistically to more or less all members of a society" and thus affect all groups similarly. Group-specific norms, conversely, benefit "members of a more or less well-defined subgroup within a larger society."[27] Hardin finds universalistic norms more morally defensible than group-specific norms, partially through a commitment to impartiality, but primarily through an explanatory account of group conflict. Because group-specific norms provide benefits to group members alone, individual members have strong incentives to enforce them. Conversely, universalistic norms lack such self-reinforcing motivations because all individuals benefit equally from them. When group-specific norms predominate over universalistic norms, individuals will tend to act for the good of the group, even if this means violating universalistic norms—like proscriptions against violence—that protect nonmembers. Should the state, the primary enforcer of universalistic norms, be weakened, violent conflict can ensue. The result is a consequentialist, utilitarian argument in favor of universalistic norms that relies on an explanatory account of group conflict.[28]

Hardin provides a compelling critique of group-specific norms created by and benefiting actors who exercise instrumental agency. If we make the plausible extension from abstract, group-specific norms to more concrete, group-specific rights, policies, or institutions, then Hardin's argument provides a realistic counterweight to the naïveté of Kymlicka and Tamir. However, this counterweight slights the fact that individuals do not exercise agency over their identities equally. At times Hardin seems to acknowledge this problem. For instance, he admits that group-based mobilization is sometimes necessary to create universalistic norms within racist societies, as exemplified by Black social movements against segregation in the United States and apartheid in South Africa.[29] Yet his critique of group-specific norms renders even these group-based mobilizations suspect, should they persist after universalistic norms and policies have been enacted. Thus he implicitly condemns postsegregation, African-American mobilization in service of group-specific policies like affirmative action and race-conscious districting. However, his argument falls into the same trap that snares Tamir and Kymlicka: its normative consequences flow from a one-sided account of collective identity. Instrumental agency clearly plays a role in collective identity construction, and it may undermine the substantive justice claimed for group-specific policies and norms. Yet such normative conclusions exceed the reach of his account, as individuals often exercise unequal levels of agency in choosing their collective identities.

Jeff Spinner: Racial Groups as Instrumental, Structural Collective Identities

Contra Hardin, Jeff Spinner realizes that individuals may have unequal opportunities to choose their collective identities. He contrasts the interpretive agency exercised by members of White ethnic groups with the instrumental, structural imposition of racial identities. Like Kymlicka, Spinner categorizes voluntary immigrants and their descendants as ethnic, but he argues that the descendants of White immigrants can continue to choose whether to emphasize their ethnic identity according to social situations and in light of cultural practices. Whereas an Irish American can choose to identify as Irish simply to connect to Irish history or to celebrate St. Patrick's Day, members of nonWhite racial groups are "defined from without."[30] Race is structurally imposed; ethnicity stems from interpretive agency.

Spinner deemphasizes the interpretive significance of racial identities. He cites the life of Cornelius May, a Black African, who internalized the cultural traits of his father's European foster parents but was never accepted as European. For Spinner, this case demonstrates that "race does not strictly map onto culture."[31] Members of a racial group may develop a common culture that comes to have great personal significance for them, but racial identities initially and primarily are imposed by others and reflect less shared cultural meanings than hierarchical social relations.[32] Thus, racial identities have only instrumental significance: dominant groups create them to cement their power over other groups. Spinner emphasizes this point by noting that some ethnic groups, like Italians, were initially considered nonWhite but were incorporated into a White racial identity only when their numbers posed a threat to Anglo-Saxon political dominance.[33]

Spinner's account corrects Hardin's focus on instrumental agency by recognizing that individuals enjoy different levels of agency over their collective identities. He views the difficulties faced by racial groups as unchosen inequalities that demand substantive state remedies. Specifically, the state should financially support historically Black colleges and Black businesses, promote the teaching of Black history and culture, and increase Black representation through racial gerrymandering. Unchosen racial inequality also justifies some Black separatism within civil society, in the form of increased Black business ownership in Black neighborhoods. This change should augment Black social power, which in turn should encourage Black integration into the broader society.[34] Spinner's defense of Black separatism does not seek to protect Black culture in the manner that French Canadians seek to protect Quebecois linguistic culture, because the terminology of culture obscures the social inequality suffered by Blacks as a racial group.[35] Instead, Black separatism seeks only to enhance Black economic and social equality in order to foster integration. Inequality through an instrumental, structural collective identity requires instrumental, not interpretive, responses.

Yet the sharp distinction that Spinner draws between the interpretive agency of ethnic groups and the instrumental-structural character of racial groups may not always hold, even among nonWhite groups. Spinner briefly acknowledges the indeterminate position of Asian Americans who, like European immigrants, may become ethnic groups through intermarriage and economic mobility. Yet he fails to discuss Hispanic Americans, urban-dwelling Native Americans, or multiracial Americans, collective identities that fit uneasily within the sharp dichotomy between race and ethnicity. And even if we remain focused only on Black racial identity, Spinner's model falls short in a number of ways. For instance, he inadequately examines the position of Black immigrants. He acknowledges that West Indians often identify as Caribbean Americans rather than as African Americans because they are not descended from American slaves and may retain distinct cultural practices.[36] However, he does not consider whether Caribbean Americans might have distinct political interests that require distinct political representation, nor does he consider whether they experience economic or social situations that might require different public policies.

Returning to the situation of African Americans, Spinner's framework has other shortcomings. Although he recognizes that African Americans have used interpretive agency to create a common culture in the United states, he occludes the role of interpretive agency in generating the cultural resources underpinning Black social movements.[37] Indeed, Black separatism to enhance Black economic power is historically linked with the Black Power movement, which used interpretive agency to cultivate and protect Black cultural traits.[38] Finally, Spinner's unwillingness to think through the role of agency in the maintenance of Black racial identity allows him to sidestep a crucial question: If members of racially defined groups come to exercise significant agency over their collective identity, do they themselves undermine the legitimacy of group-based racial mobilization? Whereas Tamir's justification of cultural rights on the basis of interpretive agency can affirm such mobilization, Spinner's formulation logically cannot.

EMPIRICAL CASES OF IDENTITY CONSTRUCTION

Although each of the above thinkers helps to clarify moral intuitions regarding group-specific measures, empirical evidence limits the applicability of their insights. These limits are apparent in the fact that all four modes of collective identity construction are involved in the four most politically salient American minority identities: Native Americans, Hispanic Americans, Asian Americans, and Black Americans. As I mentioned earlier, these four collective identities are politically most important because they were the most prone to formal legal categorization and discrimination. But even such instrumentally structural identities exhibit multiple modes of construction. These identities even exhibit mixed modes of construction. An act embodying one mode might prompt a response through a second mode, or a single act of identity construction might simultaneously embody two or more different modes, depending on the perspective taken. Moreover, these four collective identities also exhibit internal diversity and shifting boundaries, further complicating the picture. Given that some political theorists seek to draw strong, substantive conclusions from models of collective identity, the presence of internal diversity, shifting boundaries, and multiple modes of identity construction should bear some important normative consequences upon the justification or criticism of group-specific remedies. This does not mean that collective identity is inconsequential, but it does mean that the justification or rejection of group-specific measures must rely on context-sensitive deliberation. Before elaborating on this conclusion, let me flesh out the empirical picture.

Native Americans

Native Americans and other indigenous groups are clearly among the national minorities that should embody Kymlicka's interpretive-structural mode of identity construction. According to Kymlicka's logic, indigenous persons are born and socialized into cultures characterized by a common language, possession of territory, and a social order based on values and institutions. Such cultures thus have interpretive significance; the structural character of socialization justifies self-government rights in order to circumvent unchosen inequalities. Prima facie, this argument is viable: many tribes do have a fixed territory, share a common language, and possess institutions, such as tribal governments. However, closer inspection reveals internal diversity, shifting boundaries, and multiple modes of identity construction.

Internal diversity is clearly manifest in the hundreds of indigenous tribes occupying different territories, speaking different languages, and using different institutions. However, this diversity remains compatible with Kymlicka's framework, which would require separate self-government rights for each tribe. A less amenable type of internal diversity stems from what Stephen Cornell calls the tribal, subtribal, and supratribal levels of Native-American identity. The tribal level reflects individual attachments to formal tribes that possess land, government, and usually a language, and it coheres easily with Kymlicka's justification for self-government. However, the subtribal level fits less well; it has attachments to smaller, more localized kin structures that lack a separate language, governing institutions, or formal control over territory. That Kymlicka's justification for self-government rights would exclude the subtribal level seems ironic, given that this interpretive identity is historically prior, culturally more distinct, more deprived of resources, and more resistant to social and economic integration than are tribal identities.[39] Individuals who identify with all other Native Americans at the supratribal level also fit uneasily within Kymlicka's framework. Although this indigenous identity developed only in the twentieth century, it remains significant to urban dwellers, now the majority of Native Americans.[40] Notably, political tensions exist among urban, tribal, and subtribal Native Americans: tribal Native Americans often feel that urban Native Americans possess disproportionate political power but have lost touch with reservation interests, perspectives, and world-views; subtribal Native Americans level similar charges against tribal leaders.[41]

Shifting boundaries also complicate Native-American collective identities through high rates of exogamy, either between members of different tribes or between Native Americans and White, Black, Hispanic, or Asian Americans. The mixed offspring of intertribal and interracial unions can fall into a type of identity limbo: their personal identification may not map onto official tribal or federal criteria, which may require tribal residency, formal tribal recognition, or a certain proportion of tribal ancestry or "blood quantum."[42] Such boundary shifts might fit Kymlicka's framework if they develop through structural sources that maintain the interpretive significance of collective identities. However, it is clear that multiple modes of identity construction contribute to alterations in Native-American identity boundaries.

Interpretive agency contributes in two ways. On the supratribal level, those urban Native Americans who voluntarily left their tribal societal cultures are now, like voluntary immigrants, minorities in a new societal culture; on a tribal level, several native languages had fallen into disuse and, like modern Hebrew, regained use only through active linguistic renewal. In both scenarios, only Tamir's theoretical paradigm could justify group-specific measures to aid Native Americans; however, she would then have to confront the possibility that individuals might use instrumental agency to claim Native-American identity in order to secure preferential treatment in jobs, grants, or university admissions.[43] Hardin might cite such instances of instrumental agency to criticize group-specific measures, but he would have to recognize that Native Americans have been subject to discriminatory formal laws, continue to face informal social discrimination, and are categorized as a separate race by the census. Thus, Spinner might respond that Native Americans have an instrumental, structural identity that justifies group-specific, remedial measures.

The picture becomes even more complex when we recognize the existence of mixed modes of identity construction. Recall that the four modes of identity construction are analytical categories and not empirical referents, even though some normative theorists base substantive conclusions upon them. As analytical categories, two or more modes of identity construction can manifest themselves in a single empirical act. On the one hand, Native individuals can use agency to respond to an identity boundary imposed on them by the state, for example when they react to federal census categorization, tribal recognition, and assimilation policies. On the other hand, the same act of identity construction can represent different modes when viewed from different Native standpoints, as when tribal leaders grant or revoke tribal membership.

Let us consider the first type of mixed mode, in which Native individuals use agency to respond to federal impositions of collective identity. With respect to the census, self-identification has limited the federal government's capacity to impose racial identities upon individuals. But whereas Black Americans tend to exhibit little variation in racial identification on the census, Native-American racial identification seems to vary by geography. In the Southwest and the Plains states, where demographics render Native identity politically salient, there is a greater tendency to choose "Indian" as a racial category; in areas where Native-American identity is less politically salient, individuals exhibit greater flexibility over Native racial identity. Additionally, the number of individuals identifying their race as "Indian" rose from 792,730 in the 1970 census to 1,364,033 in 1980. Because this increase cannot be explained through immigration or natural increase, Joane Nagel attributes this to increased voluntary racial identification.[44] Individuals who formerly identified as White came to identify themselves as "Indian." This is not to say that structural factors played no role in this increase, as changes in the American social and political environment reduced the stigma attached to American-Indian identity. However, this reduction in stigma primarily functioned to increase individual agency over Native-American racial identification.

Agency also plays a role in the federal recognition of tribes by the Interior Department's Bureau of Indian Affairs (BIA). Because federal recognition is a prerequisite for federal funding, it becomes a valuable and scarce resource over which recognized and unrecognized tribes compete. It is not that tribal identity is simply concerned with gaining resources; several unrecognized tribes struggle to maintain their distinct identities amidst extraordinary costs. Yet recognized tribes also fear encroachment upon their resource base and fight the recognition of other tribes. Consider the 1979 federal court decision in Washington State, in which recognized tribes fought to have the Samish and Snohomish tribes declared extinct, in order to exclude them from Indian fishing quotas.[45] Such legal action reveals tribes not only as structurally imposed entities recognized by the federal government but also as collective agents that can act for instrumental reasons.

Finally, even assimilation policies generated agent-based responses that altered Native-American identity in unintended ways. From 1945 to 1969, the federal government rejected tribal sovereignty in favor of the termination policy, which withdrew federal recognition of tribes and transformed tribal land and assets into financial trusts for individual members. These members were then relocated to urban areas, where their assimilation into mainstream society would be fostered by separating them from other Indians and training them for jobs in an industrial economy. This assimilationist goal also animated federal Indian education policy, which undermined tribal attachments by emphasizing English language acquisition in reservation schools and Native-American boarding schools.[46] Although policies regarding Indian education, termination, and relocation shared the goal of assimilating Native Americans, these measures unintentionally fostered a supratribal identity. Educated Indians came to share English as a lingua franca, allowing them to communicate across tribal lines. Similarly, urban relocation broke down tribal attachments only to foster cross-tribal connections among urban Indians.[47] As a result, policies aimed at incorporating Native Americans into American society instead amalgamated distinct tribal attachments into a supratribal identity.

In this way, interpretive agency undermined an attempt to impose a new identity through instrumental, structural means. Indeed, despite instrumental incentives favoring assimilation, many urban-relocated Indians educated in English never came to understand themselves as White. But because their attachments to tribal identities had been undermined, they were left to construct a common Indian identity among those with whom they shared greater similarities.

In the above cases, federal officials exercised agency in enacting policies that Native Americans experienced as structural impositions to which they had to respond. Yet when tribal governments decide on tribal membership, Native Americans fall on both sides of the agency–structure divide. From the standpoint of laypersons, tribal membership is structurally granted or withdrawn; from the standpoint of tribal officials, it results from collective agency in service of instrumental or interpretive purposes. For example, the Santa Clara tribal council acted to grant tribal membership to the children of tribal men who married outside the tribe but not to tribal women who did so. As a result, the children of Julia Martinez, a full-blooded Santa Clara Pueblo tribal woman who had married a Navajo man, were denied tribal citizenship, could neither vote in tribal elections nor hold office in tribal government, and could not live on the reservation after her death. That Martinez's children "were raised on the Santa Clara reservation, spoke the Tewa language, and lived on the reservation as adults"[48] demonstrates that they experienced Santa Clara tribal identity as interpretive and structural; yet this did not prevent the tribal government from using collective agency to impose an unchosen inequality upon them.

A similar example involves the Seminole Nation of Oklahoma. In the nineteenth century, refugees from tribes fleeing White settlers migrated into Spanish Florida and came to be known as the Seminoles, a term derived from *cimarron,* the Spanish word for "runaway." African slaves fleeing American plantations eventually joined the Seminoles, and descendants of these slaves lived as and intermarried with members of the Seminole Nation. When the United States acquired Florida from the Spanish, the federal government moved most of the Seminole Nation to Oklahoma.[49] Then, in the summer of 2000, full-blooded Seminoles voted to strip the Black Seminoles of their membership.

Different reasons are given for this decision. Jerry G. Haney, the Seminole chief, argued that this decision was cultural and political, not racial. Contemporary Black Seminoles had ceased to identify culturally as Indians, unlike their ancestors, who adopted Seminole dress and language. Black Seminoles contend that they were stripped of their membership in order to exclude them from a federal land compensation payment worth forty-two million dollars.[50] Interior Department officials and Seminole leaders together initiated the idea of expelling the Black Seminoles, but the actual decision to do so remained with the tribe.[51] Thus, tribal members acted as collective agents to strip the Black Seminoles of their membership, either for the instrumental reason of the federal payment or the interpretive reason of Black Seminole cultural changes. As a result, the Black Seminoles find their collective identity structurally ascribed for them by tribal leaders, who exercised agency to exclude them.[52]

Some leaders restrict tribal membership in order to prevent individuals from identifying with a tribe simply to become eligible for affirmative action or tribal benefits. Although this concern appears justifiable, the power to withdraw tribal membership seems morally questionable in the cases of the Seminole Nation of Oklahoma and the Santa Clara Pueblo. Even when individuals less rooted in a tribe than the Black Seminoles or the Martinez children seek tribal membership, one cannot simply dismiss their claims, as they might be exercising interpretive agency, the same mode of identity construction behind some tribes' efforts to renew dead tribal languages.

Hispanic Americans

Kymlicka adroitly recognizes that Hispanic Americans straddle the interpretive-structural and interpretive, agency distinction: Puerto Rico exemplifies his idea of a national, societal culture with a common language, territory, and governing institutions, whereas Hispanic immigrants more closely resemble ethnic minorities.[53] Yet even if we set aside the case of Puerto Rico, Hispanic immigrants and their descendants face situations that do not map easily onto Kymlicka's framework because Hispanic identity in many ways functions as an instrumental-structural racial category, akin to that of Black Americans. Apart from this, Hispanic identity is marked by internal diversity, shifting boundaries, and multiple modes of construction, which together complicate a determinate, normative response to their condition.

Ethnic and racial differences among Hispanics can reinforce differences in socioeconomic conditions and political interests. Hispanic immigrants from Cuba, Colombia, and Nicaragua often enjoy higher levels of education and income than do those from Mexico, El Salvador, Guatemala, and the Dominican Republic.[54] Divergent political interests also generate divisions among Hispanics. In New York City, Central and South American immigrants come into conflict with the politically dominant Puerto Rican community; the latter are born with American citizenship and thus often overlook the legal and political concerns of immigrants.[55] Similarly, in Los Angeles, the politically dominant Mexican community tends to overlook the economic and legal concerns of Central Americans, who are often poorer or undocumented.[56] In addition, racial differences distinguish social conditions, with Black Hispanics often facing greater levels of racial discrimination than others.[57] In each case, internal diversity hinders generalizations about the Hispanic condition and any normative response to it.

Racial diversity also fosters boundary shifts among Hispanics. If, to American eyes, the child of a Hispanic immigrant appears to be Black, she is more likely as an adult to incorporate into the preexisting Black American identity. Conversely, a Hispanic child who appears White may incorporate into the preexisting White identity, especially if he loses his Spanish surname through intermarriage. Alternatively, those of mixed Spanish and indigenous heritage, who appear neither White nor Black, are more likely to amalgamate into a distinct, quasi-racial Hispanic identity. In addition, boundary shifts are likely to occur through multiple modes of identity construction. Instrumental-structural sources include formal laws regarding census classification and affirmative action, informal perceptions of a common Hispanic identity, and identity perceptions along the Black-White dimension. Agency manifests itself through interpretive attempts to foster political solidarity and the instrumental use of identity for social or economic advancement.

For the census, Hispanic identity is not a racial category but a blanket ethnicity, which can include members of any of the four racial groups—White, Black, Asian, or American Indian. Prima facie, this structure makes sense, given that Latinos may be White, Black, American Indian, or even Asian, as in the famous case of Peru's former President, Alberto Fujimori. Yet this census structure renders Latino ethnic identity different from the ancestral ethnicity tied to a specific nation, as Hispanic identity binds together people from multiple nations, solely through ties to the Spanish language. Thus, while a non-Hispanic individual would indicate the ancestral ethnicity of her two parents (e.g., English and Irish), a Hispanic individual would be expected to indicate ancestral ethnicity (e.g., Peruvian and Colombian) as well as Hispanic ethnicity. As a result, Hispanic census identity seems quasi-racial, encompassing less than race but more than national ancestry.[58] This quasi-racial character becomes more explicit in equal employment documents, which use Hispanic identity in the same manner as the four racial categories. Indeed, prior to the 2000 census, the Census Bureau itself sought to create a discrete Hispanic racial category, one that would function parallel to the other racial categories, thereby requiring respondents to identify exclusively as Hispanic.[59]

Instrumental-structural aspects of Hispanic identity also derive from informal perceptions regarding connections to the Spanish language, as indicated by a surname, given name, accent, or language.[60] Skin tone and phenotype are unreliable markers, given the amount of intermarriage in Latin American countries. Indeed, the denial of color-related class differences among Spanish-speaking individuals prompted one of the first steps toward a unified, instrumental-structural Hispanic identity. Although intermarriage was widely practiced in Spanish America, a gradated racial hierarchy nevertheless existed, with unmixed Europeans occupying the highest status. Early White settlers in nineteenth-century Texas, New Mexico, and California recognized this distinction, but later, poorer White settlers overlooked it and instead treated all Spanish speakers, regardless of color and class, as a unified and subordinate racial identity.[61]

Hispanic identity also assumes a more racial, instrumental-structural character when it trumps individuals' interpretive identities and exacts instrumental costs upon them. Suzanne Oboler's fieldwork with garment workers illustrates both of these points. First, all of her interviewees, when asked to identify themselves, referred to the country from which they emigrated and rejected the term *Hispanic.* Second, when asked to explain the significance of the term *Hispanic,* almost all of the respondents referred to its subordinate position within the American racial hierarchy. From these observations, Oboler concludes that Hispanics have been racialized, collectively ascribed to a common identity that imposes instrumental costs upon them.[62]

Thus far, it might appear that Hispanic identity is an instrumental-structural identity that deserves the remedial measures advocated by Spinner. The problem, however, is that a racialized Hispanic identity also cuts across the more entrenched racial lines of Black, White, Asian, and American Indian. Hispanics may be descended from any of the above racial groups, and most have mixed racial ancestry. In addition, the more fluid, multitiered racial structure of Latin American countries enables Hispanic immigrants not only to cross the American racial system but also to assert an alternative position within it. As a result, some experience the imposition of a second level of instrumental-structural identity, whereas others exercise a certain amount of interpretive and instrumental agency over their racial identity.

In terms of instrumental-structural identity, many Black Hispanics feel perceived as Black, even if this contradicts the identity they would choose through interpretive agency. Oboler documents the case of a Garifuna, a member of a group of Afro-Caribbeans who settled on the coast of central America, intermarried with indigenous peoples, and developed a language that mixes English and indigenous words. This individual resented being seen as Black; he valued his distinct ethnocultural identity and perceived the negative social status of Blacks in the United States.[63] A Dominican man interviewed by Clara Rodriguez similarly resented being perceived as Black because such labeling disregarded his own perceived identity. Nevertheless, he found himself going along with this ascription because it was too hard to explain his identity constantly.[64] Also notable is the case of an Afro-Panamanian immigrant who, while appearing Black to interviewers and expressing pride in her African heritage, refused to identify as Black on the census. She took this stance because she did not identify culturally with African Americans and because she had once experienced xenophobic animosity from an African-American woman.[65] Alternatively, some White Latinos resent being identified as Hispanic rather than as White, an identity their physical appearance and social class would have granted them in their homeland.[66]

Yet despite the instrumental-structural identities that often confront them, on at least some occasions Hispanic individuals can exercise some agency over their identity. Puerto Rican and Chicano nationalist movements of the 1960s exercised interpretive agency by using common cultural symbols to foster a unified Hispanic political identity.[67] Additionally, Hispanics arguably use interpretive agency to resist American racial categories. For example, forty percent of Hispanics in 1980 and forty-three percent in 1990 chose the census's "other race" option, one chosen by less than one percent of non-Hispanics.[68] Although "other race" responses do inversely correlate with education and time spent in the United States, controlling for such factors still reveals a much higher proportion of Hispanics than non-Hispanics choosing this option. Those who speak Spanish at home are more likely to choose the other race option because they retain the interpretive, cognitive framework of Latin American color categories. As a result, the other race response might be an interpretive, agent-centered means of resisting American racial identities in order to affirm their own self-perception as a racially diverse linguistic and cultural group.[69]

Hispanic individuals can sometimes exercise instrumental agency over their identity. Some of Oboler's interviewees were cognizant of the potential benefits of identifying as Hispanic when applying for jobs or educational admissions. One of Rodriguez's interviewees consciously used his Black and Hispanic identities in order to improve his chances at university admissions. On the other hand, one of Oboler's subjects mentioned that she consciously identified herself as White when applying for jobs or loans, perceiving the social costs of a Latino identity in these instances.[70] Hardin might critique the instrumental use of collective identity in the first two cases; however, the interpretive-structural costs implied by the last case mute the power of this critique. Being perceived as Hispanic might well hurts one's chances of getting a loan, even if it helps one get into college.

Asian Americans

In many ways, Asian Americans resemble non-Puerto-Rican Hispanics. Both groups are descended from immigrants who exercised agency to inhabit a new societal culture, and both also confront unchosen and imposed instrumental-structural identities. Yet even amidst such racialization, Asian Americans can exercise interpretive and instrumental agency to construct their identities. This stems partly from Asian internal diversity, which exceeds that of Hispanics through the absence of a common language or a dominant religion. Consequently, Asian Americans experience dynamic boundary shifts, leaving them suspended between being "forever foreigners" and "honorary Whites."[71]

Asian-American internal diversity results from its multiple national ancestries, which can reinforce socioeconomic differences. Thus, the image of the Asian model minority primarily (but only partially) reflects the situation of ethnic Japanese, Chinese, Koreans, and Indians, not that of most Vietnamese, Hmong, and Filipinos. Such internal diversity can generate numerous Asian-American boundary alterations. On a legal level, the present amalgamation of most Asian nationalities into a unified Asian group was preceded by separate ethnic categories or by the incorporation of some Asians into the White racial category. On the level of informal perceptions by non-Asians, assimilation usually takes the form of the amalgamation of Chinese, Japanese, Vietnamese, and Koreans into one unified category, with South Asians and Arabs in another. Notably, differentiation can occur among Asian Americans: Filipinos acted to proliferate into a separate category in California and even considered incorporating into the Hispanic category.[72] Such boundary shifts typically reflect agent-based, Asian responses to the instrumental-structural imposition of identity.

Several types of laws have imposed a common identity upon Asian Americans: discriminatory laws, citizenship laws, census categories, and affirmative action and welfare policies. Although early discriminatory laws, like the Chinese Exclusion Act, targeted specific Asian nationalities, later laws prevented all Asian immigrants from working in certain sectors, owning land, or becoming naturalized citizens. Indeed, Japanese internment during World War II was almost unique in targeting only a specific Asian ethnic group. Citizenship laws and census categories have less consistently grouped Asians together. Laws enacted prior to World War II restricted naturalized citizenship to White Americans; they excluded East Asians and South Asians through distinct, yet equally dubious, legal doctrines on race. In 1922, the U.S. Supreme Court used racial science to conclude that a Japanese immigrant, whose skin color was whiter than that of most Europeans, was nevertheless not genetically White. Hardly a year later, the Court withheld Whiteness and citizenship from an Indian immigrant, even though racial science ascribed both Scandinavians and South Asians to the same Caucasian race. In this case, the Court relied on social perceptions of Indians as nonWhite. Census guidelines also distinguished South Asians from East Asians. Censuses from 1920 until 1940 enumerated South Asians using the religious term Hindu, even though a majority of them were either Sikh or Muslim.[73] However, censuses from 1950 until 1970 dropped the Hindu category and had South Asians check off the "other" race category and then write in their nation of origin. Census enumerators would then categorize South Asians as White in their final tabulations.[74]

Welfare and affirmative action laws enacted following the civil rights movement and the war on poverty did lump Asian ethnics (excluding Indians) together by identifying Asians as a disadvantaged minority eligible for group-specific programs.[75] Unlike earlier, punitive forms of Asian categorization, welfare and affirmative action policies did spur instrumental, agent-based responses by Asian ethnic groups. As I mentioned earlier, the Association of Indians in America (AIA) lobbied to have Indians reclassified as Asian. This was done to qualify them for affirmative action programs, especially minority set-aside, contracting quotas for federal projects under the Small Business Act. Citing the Supreme Court ruling that Indians were not White, the AIA succeeded in having them categorized as Asian.[76] Conversely, Filipinos used instrumental agency to resist Asian categorization. For instance, they resented the dominance of Chinese and Japanese workers in pan-Asian welfare organizations. Although these workers had more training and experience, they were statistically unrepresentative of the Asian community and remained less able to serve clients of other ethnicities, due to linguistic and cultural differences.[77] In addition, the statistical overrepresentation of socioeconomically advantaged ethnic Indians, Chinese, Japanese, and Koreans meant that poorer Asian ethnic groups could not access affirmative action benefits. As a result, Filipino activists lobbied the California Assembly to tabulate Filipinos separately from Asians, allowing them to reap affirmative action benefits separately from the general Asian-American population.[78]

In each case, welfare and affirmative action policies using pan-Asian categories led to instrumental, agent-centered responses: Indians sought to enter the Asian group; Filipinos and Southeast Asians sought to exit it. Assessing the validity of these responses is difficult. The case of Filipinos and Southeast Asians may be justifiable, given their disadvantaged socioeconomic status, but the Indian case appears less so, given their above-average income. At least in the Indian case, Hardin's critique of group-specific policies seems more applicable than Spinner's defense. However, a different picture emerges in cases involving the instrumental-structural imposition of a common Asian identity through violence.

The perceived physical similarities among members of different Asian ethnic groups can lead non-Asians not only to group diverse individuals together but also to practice pan-Asian discrimination. More strikingly, it can lead to situations where members of one ethnic group are harmed because they are mistaken for members of another ethnic group. On June 19, 1982, Vincent Chin, a Chinese American, was brutally bludgeoned to death in a Detroit suburb by two White autoworkers. These workers blamed Japan for the ailing U.S. auto industry and misperceived Chin as Japanese. Although they were convicted of manslaughter, they were sentenced to only three years probation, a $3000 fine, and $780 in court fees. In addition, both were later acquitted of federal civil rights charges.[79] In a similar incident, Jim Loo, another Chinese American, was pistol-whipped to death by two White brothers in a North Carolina bar in 1989. The men were angry that a third brother had been killed in the Vietnam War, and they mistakenly took Loo to be Vietnamese. Both men were convicted of second-degree murder in a state trial, and one of them was also convicted of federal civil rights violations, the first such conviction involving a crime against an Asian American.[80] In both cases, Chinese Americans were attacked because they were mistaken for members of another Asian ethnicity, toward which certain non-Asians held animosity. In the eyes of the White perpetrators, Chinese ethnics were indistinguishable from Japanese or Vietnamese persons and thus became targets for violent hate crimes.

In response to these crimes, Asian Americans from various ethnic backgrounds mobilized to protest the lenient state sentencing in the Chin case and to lobby for federal civil rights prosecution in both cases. Although in each instance Chinese Americans spearheaded the mobilization efforts, members of various Asian ethnic groups donated time, money, and professional expertise. Correctly perceiving that such hate crimes threatened not only Chinese Americans but also other Asians, they created pan-Asian organizations like the American Citizens for Justice (ACJ) to protect their safety. However, pan-Asian mobilization faltered among immigrants from South Asian countries such as India, Pakistan, Bangladesh, and Sri Lanka, because these individuals bore few physical similarities to Chinese, Japanese, Korean, or Vietnamese ethnics. Consequently, these groups contributed to the ACJ only after that organization began to investigate hate crimes specifically targeting South Asians.[81] Perceived distinctions between South Asians and other Asians has recurred in the hate crimes following September 11th, with South

Asians perceived as Arabs. This raises the possibility of a reactive amalgamation of Arab and South Asian groups.

When instrumental agency is employed in response to violence, Spinner's theoretical approach seems more appropriate than Hardin's. Yet both of these approaches underestimate the level of interpretive agency involved in Asian-American collective identity. Certain Asian-American groups, especially American-born Chinese and Japanese ethnics, enjoy relatively high levels of income, residential integration, and intermarriage. Moreover, because these individuals were born and raised in the United States, they primarily speak English and only selectively practice ethnic pastimes, customs, and holidays. Consequently, they resemble White ethnics, whose symbolic ethnicity reflects the interpretive agency to select which practices are central to ethnic identity.[82] However, this interpretive agency retains certain intra-Asian racial dynamics. For instance, although ethnic exogamy rates are high, there is an increased tendency to intermarry with other Asian ethnics rather than with Whites.[83] Intra-Asian exogamy stems partly from fears of racism, but it also reflects the comfort shared among American-born Asians. Notably, this comfort level is not shared with Asian immigrants, whose customs and norms are insufficiently American to produce it.[84] Instrumental-structural racism can still separate Asians from Whites, even as interpretive agency makes them resemble White ethnics.

Yet Asians sometimes resemble White ethnics in less attractive ways, specifically the tendency to use instrumental agency to distance themselves from other groups. Mia Tuan documents the tensions and resentments between middle-class Asian families and working-class Hispanics.[85] More troubling is the case of the Mississippi Chinese. While Chinese Americans are among the largest and most established Asian ethnic groups in the United States, a rigid and binary, Black-White racial framework greeted a small group of Chinese immigrants to the Mississippi delta in the late nineteenth century. This framework allowed no room for a third Asian category, so Whites and Blacks alike perceived the Chinese as Black. Early in their stay, the Chinese saw themselves as temporary sojourners and thus were willing to accept the indignities they suffered as Blacks. But when they foresaw a permanent existence in Mississippi, they became unwilling to bear the costs of segregation and distanced themselves from Blacks by mimicking White behavior, touting their economic success, and excluding Chinese who married or socialized with Blacks. Because their small numbers never threatened the status of Whites, their distancing strategy succeeded. By the 1950s, most Chinese children could attend White school systems, while Chinese drivers held licenses with a "W" on the race line.[86] Like the Irish in the nineteenth century and the Jews following World War II,[87] the Mississippi Chinese could whiten themselves by accepting the dominant racial system and distancing themselves from Blacks.

The future of the instrumental-structural Asian identity is uncertain. On the one hand, the increasing rate of anti-Asian violence suggests that Asians will remain a group solidified by the informal perceptions of others. On the other hand,

Asians' relatively high mean income and rates of intermarriage with Whites suggest that, like the Mississippi Chinese, some Asians may whiten themselves, perhaps at a cost to Black Americans. A clear example of the relative whitening of Asians comes from the 1996 Washington state elections. During that campaign, the media often referred to Ron Sims, an African-American candidate for King County commissioner, as an inner-city politician, despite the fact that he grew up in a White neighborhood in Spokane. This tag never followed Gary Locke, the Chinese-American gubernatorial candidate, who grew up in a Seattle public housing project. Locke went on to become the state's first Chinese-American governor, after soundly defeating Norm Rice, Seattle's African-American mayor, in the Democratic primary. The conclusion that Rice drew from the election was that, when presented with a choice between an Asian and an African-American candidate, most voters in this overwhelmingly White state would prefer the Asian.[88]

Black Americans

The capacity for the Mississippi Chinese, the Jews, and the Irish to whiten themselves through instrumental agency depended upon a crucial common fact: the existence of a Black identity group from which to distance themselves. A despised Black identity provided a social referent against which other groups could contrast themselves, in order to display the social virtues that grounded their acceptance by Whites. The position of Blacks at the bottom of a racial hierarchy was the structural foundation upon which other groups could exercise instrumental agency, and thus Black identity remains the most instrumentally structural of all American minority identities. This creates a strong prima facie case for Spinner's framework. Nevertheless, internal diversity, boundary shifts, and multiple modes of identity construction complicate his normative justification for group-specific measures aimed at Blacks.[89]

Internal diversity was initially the norm among the slaves brought to North America from Africa. In fact, one cannot really speak of *internal* diversity because these involuntary migrants did not share a collective identity until their amalgamation into a common Black identity in America. A separate, mixed-race, slave identity did develop in parts of the South, especially New Orleans and Charleston, but following emancipation, this group was incorporated into a unified Black identity through the establishment of the one-drop or hypo-descent rule, which defined as Black all persons with any known African ancestry. The hypo-descent rule also incorporated children of mixed unions involving Blacks and either Asians or Native Americans, along with Black immigrants from Africa and the West Indies.[90] Strikingly, this rule is unique in two ways: it only exists in the United States, and it only applies to Blacks.[91] Thus, individuals whose genetic composition is less than half African are identified as Black, resulting in oxymoronic terms like "light-skinned Black."

More recently, however, a boundary shift of differentiation has emerged within the Black identity group, primarily through the proliferation of West Indian and multiracial identities. This has enhanced internal diversity, given the occasionally divergent socioeconomic conditions and political interests among these groups. For instance, multiracial Americans have conflicted with African-American politicians and activists over the addition of a separate, multiracial category to the 2000 census.[92] And although West Indian success stories like that of Colin Powell are statistically unrepresentative, these immigrants do differ from native-born African Americans through higher rates of labor force participation, particularly among workers with little education and few skills. This difference results from the fact that West Indians more effectively utilize group-specific social networks to gain employment, are self-selected immigrants who assess wages according to the lower monetary standards of their impoverished homelands, and are perceived by White employers as more industrious than native-born African Americans.[93] The result is that West Indians are often preferred over African Americans when White employers seek to fill employment positions governed by affirmative action policies.[94] Finally, we should note that in New York City, West Indian political interests diverged from those of African Americans, most notably when some West Indians supported Ed Koch's 1985 mayoral campaign and when African-American Democratic party leaders refused to support West Indian political candidates.[95]

The relative salience of boundary shifts and internal diversity within the Black American collective identity stems from multiple modes of identity construction. Clearly, the instrumental-structural imposition of a common Black identity has been and remains the most important mode. Whites undermined African ethnic identities and imposed a common racial identity by selling slaves as individuals, thereby separating ethnically unified groups and even families; by discouraging ethnic identification and linguistic unity, in order to minimize the threat of slave rebellion; and by imposing the one-drop rule, which allowed White males to exploit female slaves and mistresses without harming the status of their legitimate offspring.[96] Of course, all of these measures supported White economic privilege and gained support from racial science.

Yet Blacks also exercised interpretive agency in maintaining a common Black identity through "kinship systems, religion, customary practices, and forms of expressive culture such as music, song, and storytelling."[97] The personal significance of this identity was most powerfully manifested in the unwillingness of some light-skinned Blacks to assimilate into White society, despite being willing and able to "pass" as White for purposes of employment.[98] Its political significance was demonstrated by the role that cultural solidarity played in overcoming collective action problems during the civil rights movement.[99] Finally, the personal and political significance of interpretive agency revealed itself in Black acceptance of the one-drop rule, indicated by the statistically stable rates of Black identification even after the 1960 census adopted racial self-classification.[100] Such manifestations of Black interpretive agency lead some scholars to argue that they are not simply a structurally induced racial group but also an agent-centered ethnic group, somewhat akin to White ethnics.[101]

In turn, instrumental agency was clearly manifest when Black, Asian, Hispanic, and American Indian organizations resisted adding a multiracial category to the 2000 census. Their primary concern was that such a category would reduce the number of individuals within their groups, thereby weakening their political clout.[102] This type of sentiment was nicely expressed fifty years ago by a Black politician's dismissal of a race-neutral census: "How am I supposed to bargain for the Negroes if I can't prove how many there are?"[103] A similar dynamic of instrumental agency was at work in New York City in 1982, when politicians from the Coalition for Community Empowerment (CCE), a predominantly African-American faction within the New York City Democratic party, discouraged West Indian candidacies in predominantly West Indian districts. Instead, the CCE favored either African-American candidates or White candidates allied with them.[104] Yet in each case, recognizing the instrumental agency of African-American politicians must be balanced by recognizing how White politicians simultaneously used agency to levy instrumental-structural constraints upon them. White politicians in New York were more than willing to encourage West Indians to mobilize separately from African Americans, in order to divide their opposition.[105] Similarly, conservative White Republicans, like Newt Gingrich, quickly perceived the advantages of a multiracial category and thus supported it wholeheartedly.[106] But while the actions of White politicians might provide some justification for the instrumental agency of African-American politicians, the constraints levied upon the interpretive agency of West Indian and multiracial individuals should not be overlooked.

Notably, the capacity of West Indians in New York to exercise agency in asserting a distinct identity depended upon three structural conditions. First, the restriction of colonial immigration to Britain in 1962, combined with the relaxation of race-based American immigration restrictions in 1965, spurred West Indian immigration to New York. Second, because these immigrants arrived during and after the civil rights movement, they enjoyed greater access to housing markets outside of traditionally Black neighborhoods, allowing them to create distinct ethnic neighborhoods. Finally, the decline of the manufacturing sector and the rise of the service economy in New York decimated many Black neighborhoods, eliminated the professional niches that West Indians once filled, and created many low-wage jobs that appealed more to immigrants from impoverished West Indian countries than to African Americans.[107] These three conditions separated West Indian immigrants from African Americans at home and at work, while enabling the former to retain their ethnic foods, festivals, and patois within public settings. In response, West Indians exercised greater interpretive agency in developing a distinct ethnic and cultural identity, which manifested itself in a benign sense of comfort with other West Indians and in a more troubling sense of cultural superiority and stereotypical prejudice toward African Americans.[108] West Indians also exercised instrumental agency to distinguish themselves from African Americans, by using social networks to establish distinctly West Indian ethnic employment niches and by maintaining ethnic markers, such as intentionally intensified accents.[109]

Finally, one should note that West Indians and African Americans are separated by an interpretive-structural factor: the different racial systems into which they are socialized. West Indian countries have a more fluid racial hierarchy than the United States, such that having money and adopting European cultural traits can "whiten" African-descended individuals.[110] And because European-descended individuals are in the minority in West Indian countries, they may subtly try to block the social advancement of Blacks in economic affairs but are unlikely to use overt racial threats. The distinct racial dynamics in West Indian countries can lead West Indian immigrants to differ from African Americans in two crucial ways. Because they expect racism at work but not where there are no tangible resources at stake, they tend to feel relatively comfortable around Whites in social settings. In addition, they expect economic success to bring improved social status, providing an additional psychological incentive to work hard. White employers perceive this comfort and this work ethic and thus prefer West Indian to African-American employees, thereby imposing another instrumental-structural division between the two groups.[111]

Although a distinct West Indian ethnic identity has emerged in New York, instrumental-structural factors, particularly informal social perceptions, may limit its long-term persistence. Until verbal communication is exchanged, most Whites perceive West Indians as African Americans. Thus, West Indians remain vulnerable to interpersonal racism, from overt racial slurs to being falsely suspected of shoplifting.[112] It also makes them vulnerable to racial violence, as when Michael Griffith, a Trinidadian immigrant, was chased by a White mob onto a highway, where he was killed by oncoming traffic. West Indians do not expect and are often unprepared for such experiences, which erode their comfort with Whites.[113] Furthermore, the Griffith killing prompted improved political relations between West Indians and African Americans,[114] a reactive amalgamation similar to the pan-Asian mobilization following the Vincent Chin and Jim Loo killings. Similarly, the police killing of African immigrant Amadou Diallo and the police assault of Haitian immigrant Abner Louima might strengthen political solidarity among New York's Black immigrants and African Americans.

Interpretive-structural dynamics may also erode a distinct West Indian identity among the children of immigrants. Because they are socialized into a racial structure wherein both Blacks and Whites accept the one-drop rule, second generation West Indian adolescents are more likely than their parents to identify as Black or African American. It is noteworthy, however, that class differentiates second-generation adolescents in this respect. A majority of the middle class adolescents interviewed by Mary Waters identified as West Indian rather than as Black or African American, as opposed to only twenty percent of working class adolescents. Many who identified as West Indian adopted their parents' negative views of African Americans and had lower fears of interpersonal racism. Conversely, many of those who identified as Black accepted American racial categories, tended to embrace African-American culture, and resisted their parents' negative views of African Americans.[115]

THE NORMATIVE CONSEQUENCES OF IDENTITY CONSTRUCTION

At the outset of this chapter, I argued that many normative approaches to justice between groups commit three oversights: they underestimate the internal diversity within groups, they pay insufficient attention to shifts in the boundaries of collective identities, and they fail to acknowledge that these boundary shifts can occur through multiple modes of identity construction. This last oversight is most problematic for theorists like Kymlicka, Tamir, Hardin, and Spinner, whose arguments for or against group-specific political or legal measures rely upon a single mode of identity construction. While these theorists plausibly reconstruct certain moral intuitions regarding the justification of group-specific measures, I have argued that empirical evidence complicates their justifications immensely.

Consider Kymlicka's position. Native-American tribal identities, which should exemplify the interpretive-structural mode of identity construction associated with national minorities, are in fact constructed through multiple modes. In addition, nonWhite immigrant groups, associated with interpretive agency, often have identities imposed upon them in an instrumentally structural manner. Whereas one can argue that Asian, Hispanic, and West Indian immigrants voluntarily enter American societal culture,[116] Ronald Schmidt rightly notes that these groups are involuntarily incorporated into "racialized minority" identities.[117] As a result, both nonWhite immigrants and Native American tribes suffer unchosen inequalities.[118]

This insight would seem to validate Spinner's approach; however, problems of internal diversity, shifting boundaries, and multiple modes of identity construction complicate his justification for and application of group-specific remedies. For instance, group-specific affirmative action policies should distinguish Southeast Asians and Filipinos from other Asians, and West Indians from African Americans. Group-based political representation might require distinguishing West Indians from African Americans in New York, while distinguishing Central Americans from Puerto Ricans in New York from Cubans in south Florida, and from Mexicans in California and Texas. On the other hand, the combination of informal perceptions and collective violence suggests that hate crimes legislation might require assimilating West Indians with African Americans, South Asians with Arabs, and various Southeast and East Asian ethnicities.

These examples reveal the difficulties in identifying the targeted group in group-specific measures. Boundaries within groups can shift according to the issue or problem involved, and group-specific policies will have to shift along with them. Such shifts become more complex when we consider the increasing number of multiracial individuals in the United States. Unless we wish to formalize rigid boundary markers like the one-drop rule, it will become increasingly difficult to identify the category to which a mixed-race individual belongs. The need for boundaries, and the role of instrumental agency in negotiating such boundaries, challenges the very value of group-specific policies.

Perhaps we face a dilemma between creating loose group boundaries that enable opportunistic identification through instrumental agency and creating rigid boundaries that limit agency in both its interpretive and instrumental modes. If this were the case, perhaps Hardin would be right to advocate group-neutral policies. The difficulty with this approach is that many group-neutral policies, from plurality electoral systems to harsher penalties for using crack versus powder cocaine, often have group-specific results. Moreover, as the origins of supratribal identity suggest, even when instrumental incentives encourage incorporation into one identity, interpretive factors can lead to the amalgamation of another.

This brings us to Tamir's interpretive, agent-centered approach to pluralism. By affirming individual agency over the interpretive, cultural content of collective identities, and by locating group claims on a continuum that considers pragmatic concerns and eschews untenable distinctions among groups, Tamir may be able to address problems of internal diversity and shifting boundaries. Presumably, individuals can claim cultural rights in order to express the interpretive agency that they exercise in affirming their fluid and changing collective identities. Indeed, interpretive agency is perhaps the ideal to which democratic societies should strive, so that collective identities result from individual choices over interpretive values, not from structural impositions or instrumental choices over expected utility. Yet Tamir's theory fails to address the less-than-ideal conditions confronting most plural polities, where identities can be structurally imposed and where individuals manipulate identities for personal or collective gain. Her approach also overlooks the negative characteristics of some interpretive identities, especially those that gain their meaning primarily by demeaning other groups.

Notably, the problems of internal diversity, shifting boundaries, and multiple modes of identity construction also plague Iris Marion Young's more complex theory of social perspective. To her credit, Young affirms both the interpretive dimension of collective identity by recognizing the "affinity" of shared cultural meanings, ways of life, or historical experiences, and the instrumental dimension by defining justice among groups as the negation of oppression and domination.[119] Furthermore, she acknowledges both agency and structure as sources of collective identity by arguing that social structures position individuals, who then use agency to formulate their own individual and collective identities.[120] Finally, she helpfully eschews the strong distinctions between groups endorsed by Kymlicka and Spinner, instead locating group claims on a continuum.[121] However, Young too quickly dismisses the capacity to exercise instrumental agency over social group identity.[122] As a result, her theoretical framework tends to overlook how individuals can opportunistically claim Native-American identity for employment or educational benefits or how Indian lobbyists can seek incorporation into an Asian identity to access preferential contracting policies. Moreover, she too quickly employs the identity markers of Black, Asian, Latino, and Native American in applying the idea of group perspective to her theory of social oppression and her defense of group-representation. Doing so occludes problems of internal diversity in that these identity markers can overlook the specific differences between, for example, West Indians and African Americans or Puerto Ricans and Central Americans.[123]

On occasion, Young does recognize problems of internal diversity. For instance, she admits that Black Americans can come from a variety of nationalities.[124] And in concluding her discussion of social perspective, she rhetorically asks whether there is a single Native-American perspective. The proper response, I believe, is that at times, for some people, a common, supratribal, Native-American perspective is politically relevant, but at other times, for other people, diverse tribal and subtribal perspectives are salient. Similarly, circumstances and settings will distinguish the relative salience of a unified Black perspective from diverse African-American, West Indian, and multiracial perspectives. Now, I think Young may be on to something. Some individuals might share a social perspective that differs from that shared by others, and I will revisit this issue in chapter 2. But for now, let me simply point out that Young does not provide adequate institutional or political measures to address problems of internal diversity and shifting boundaries among perspectives. As a result, her theory of social perspective, though an improvement over the one-dimensional theories of Kymlicka, Tamir, Hardin, and Spinner, nevertheless confronts difficult problems amidst constructed collective identities.[125]

These problems force us to face the normative consequences of identity construction, manifest in problems like internal diversity, shifting boundaries, and multiple modes of construction. If constructed collective identities have the complicating characteristics that I have documented, how should normative political theory address problems of justice among groups? Does recognizing identity construction mean that justice can only inhere among individuals and not groups? Or can concerns about justice among groups remain a focal point for normative political inquiry? My contention is that justice among groups can remain an important concern, but only by incorporating three revisions.

First, substantive justice among groups cannot rely on abstract distinctions between different types of groups. Instead, we must engage in context-sensitive analyses that more carefully specify the groups to be targeted, the content of their claims, and the likely positive and negative effects of the measures advocated. Second, contextual analyses of substantive justice must be augmented by contextual analyses of the legitimacy of democratic processes through which a plural polity responds to the substantive claims of groups. Such processes will require fair deliberation among members of diverse and constructed collective identities.[126] Finally, recognition of identity construction and the realization of fair deliberative processes requires distinguishing between different types of democratic institutions, according to their ability to respond to internal diversity, shifting boundaries, and multiple modes of identity construction.

Joseph Carens best exemplifies the first revision regarding contextual sensitivity.[127] Instead of tying the validity of group-specific measures to different types of groups, Carens examines specific cases, the specific claims raised, the specific collective identities involved, and the pragmatic constraints confronting possible political responses. Where his approach fails to satisfy is in its insufficient analysis of democratic processes.[128] It is Carens the contextualist political philosopher, not ordinary citizens or their representatives, who investigates the problem and justifies a response to it. This is ironic because Carens argues that a political community's commitments must be articulated in a democratic manner.[129] Yet his analysis primarily provides substantive answers to specific problems, rather than assessing the democratic processes through which citizens and their representatives can reach such conclusions. Carens's exploration of issues like affirmative action, immigration, toleration for religious minorities, and aboriginal self-government are compelling; yet, as he admits, they are not "definitive" and thus could legitimately be rejected by a democratic process. Consequently, his investigations should be understood as powerful contributions to democratic deliberation over pluralism but not as necessary solutions to these questions.[130]

This leads to the second revision. Problems of internal diversity, shifting boundaries, and multiple modes of construction require that justice between groups, and any group-specific or group-neutral measures to combat injustices among groups, be realized through context-sensitive, democratic deliberations that include as many perspectives as possible. Participants in such deliberative processes must recognize that individuals may attach interpretive significance to their collective identities, and thus they must seek to understand the perspectives and world-views of their interlocutors. However, this deliberative process must also enable criticism across group boundaries, as group claims may reflect instrumental opportunism, and interpretive identities may embody morally troubling beliefs, practices, or prejudices. According to this approach, the theorist can contribute to deliberation not only by proffering substantive suggestions about which measures might realize justice among groups; the theorist can also suggest what procedures, conditions, and institutions would enable inclusive deliberation to proceed fairly. In chapter 2, I will provide a deliberative model for assessing the legitimacy of such political processes. This model incorporates both substantive and procedural elements. The legitimacy of deliberative democratic processes depends not simply on the realization of certain procedural rules; it also depends on the substantive resources, capacities, and dispositions of the participants within the process. Consequently, deliberative democratic processes in a plural polity must embody a complex form of legitimacy that incorporates a wide variety of elements.

The third revision to understanding justice among groups requires a more careful distinction among different types of democratic institutions. Internal diversity, shifting boundaries, and multiple modes of construction require that institutions aimed at realizing fair deliberation among groups remain as flexible as possible, in order to respond to the specific conditions and changing boundaries of various groups or subgroups. Consequently, a deliberative approach attuned to problems of identity construction requires a distinction between different types of institutional settings: formal versus informal and decision-making versus purely deliberative.

Formal institutions are those that are part of the constitutional democratic state. Formal, decision-making institutions include legislatures, executives, judiciaries, and administrative agencies. These are the least amenable to group-specific provisions for two reasons. First, their formal, constitutional status gives them a level of fixity that renders them less able to respond to problems of internal diversity, shifting boundaries, and multiple modes of identity construction. Second, they are prone to the political dynamic of conflict, one of the five dynamics of group conflict to be analyzed in chapter 3. As Jack Knight and James Johnson point out, constitutional choices about institutions are among the most conflict-inducing political phenomena.[131] At least part of the problem is that constitutionally entrenched decision-making institutions establish the rules of the game for political competition, thereby structuring payoffs for political groups long into the future.[132] Furthermore, in most plural polities the individuals creating such institutions are often parties to group competition and thus may be motivated less by an interest in stable and fair institutions than by an interest in gaining an advantageous position over other groups.[133] Thus, vulnerability to conflict and a level of fixity incompatible with the recognition of identity construction render formal, decision-making institutions ill-suited to group-specific measures, like group-based representation.

Yet if a context-sensitive, deliberative approach to pluralism is to embody fairness, it must include all relevant group perspectives, and this will likely require some degree of group-based representation. If group-based representation is incompatible with formal, decision-making institutions, how can collective decision-making be both inclusive and yet compatible with the problem of identity construction? Two responses are germane. First, formal, decision-making institutions should not constitutionally enshrine group-based representation, but they can be designed to enable group-based representation in a flexible manner. The key mechanisms for this are electoral systems, the topic for discussion in chapter 5. Second, although group-based representation is incompatible with formal, decision-making institutions, it may be more compatible with quasi-formal or informal institutions that are purely deliberative and lack decision-making power.

Quasi-formal, deliberative institutions include advisory panels, which influence but do not control collective decision-making within formal, decision-making institutions. Such advisory panels are incorporated into the institutions of the democratic, constitutional state but are not constitutionally established and indeed are usually only temporarily convened. Moreover, they are purely deliberative; they can influence but cannot have a direct impact on collective decision-making. As a result, they can include group-based representation without unduly exacerbating problems of identity construction or group conflict. The key informal, deliberative institution is the public sphere, the loose network of public communication that lies outside the constitutional state and is housed by the associations of civil society. As an informal, purely deliberative institution, the public sphere embodies a level of fluidity that enables flexible responses to problems of identity construction; it can serve as a flexible site for group-based representation. However, although the informal status of the public sphere distinguishes it from the constitutional state, its viability depends upon the protection of certain rights (like freedoms of speech, press, and association), and its capacity to mitigate other dynamics of conflict depend upon certain policies. The policies, rights, and forms of representation that enable context-sensitive deliberation within deliberative institutions like the informal public sphere and quasi-formal advisory panels will be the focus of our attention in chapter 4. Assessing the public sphere and electoral institutions will require adducing a model of fair deliberation among diverse collective identities and outlining the dynamics of group conflict, the respective tasks of chapters 2 and 3.

2
Plural Deliberation and Complex Legitimacy

THE ELEMENTS OF PLURAL DELIBERATION

Deliberative democracy in a plural polity is a complex matter. Members of diverse and constructed collective identities must come together democratically in order to address matters of common concern, issues over which different groups conflict, or problems particular to one group that require a collective response from the entire polity. Reaching legitimate collective decisions in a plural polity will require members of these diverse groups to participate in democratic processes of deliberation and decision-making that all can accept as fair. Unfortunately, fairness in the democratic process will remain difficult to achieve for a number of reasons. The problem of collective identity construction may complicate attaining inclusiveness within the democratic process because different collective identities may gain or lose salience under different circumstances. Moreover, participants must attend both to the interpretive and the instrumental significance collective identities have for their members. For these reasons, fair democratic processes require more than mere procedural rules in order to reach legitimate collective decisions; fair processes also require substantive achievements among participants in the form of specific capacities, dispositions, and understandings.

I doubt that the full requirements of fair deliberation for a plural polity can be distilled into a neat package; however I propose a provisional model for judging such fairness. This model recommends itself for a number of reasons. It entwines procedural rules, such as those regarding the scope of deliberation, with substantive concerns, like those regarding how participants can understand and criticize each other fairly. It also tries to spell out, as precisely as possible, the conditions of fairness that govern deliberation among diverse and constructed collective identities. These fairness conditions incorporate both deliberative and aggregative characteristics, for bargaining and voting may be needed to reach collective decisions in a plural polity. But perhaps most important, this model tries to clarify its own limits by identifying when participants can legitimately eschew deliberation in favor of more intransigent, agonistic stances. Citizens themselves must ultimately judge when the limits of deliberation have been reached; this model provides clear guidelines for such judgment. In addition, it provides criteria that can guide future reforms of the democratic process. I call this model *plural deliberation* and its way of assessing democratic processes *complex legitimacy.*

Plural deliberation is a framework for assessing the legitimacy of the democratic processes and institutions through which members of diverse and constructed collective identities reach collective decisions. Central to this framework is a critical process that induces participants to reflect upon and potentially to revise their preferences, interests, opinions, perspectives, and world-views. Collective decisions may include the choice of broad constitutional frameworks and specific policies or candidates.[1] Like many deliberative formulations, legitimacy remains central within plural deliberation. But unlike many formulations, legitimacy derives from a complex assessment of four elements: the scope of deliberation, the relationship between understanding and criticism, the link between deliberation and decision-making, and conditions governing the deliberative and aggregative fairness of institutions and processes.

First, institutions and processes are legitimate to the extent that the scope of contributions is not limited prior to deliberation itself. Thus, plural deliberation conflicts with formulations that limit deliberation to the neutral boundaries of an overlapping consensus among reasonable comprehensive doctrines.[2] Because political disputes among divergent collective identities may involve not only specific political values but also epistemic frameworks, political processes should not circumscribe deliberation to the testing of preferences, interests, or opinions through recourse to commonly shared political values. Plural deliberation instead requires understanding comprehensive doctrines, or better, perspectives and world-views, in order to construct a common basis for deliberative criticism. As a result, reasonable pluralism becomes an outcome of, rather than a precondition for, deliberation.

Second, deliberation is legitimate to the extent that the criticism of perspectives or world-views follows their understanding. Critique prior to accurate understanding is more akin to stereotypical labeling than real deliberation. Wherever understanding is not fully attainable, criticism is possible only through a process of open-ended questioning, a process that generates the reflectivity among world-views associated with reasonable pluralism. Such critical, deliberative processes will likely include direct dialogue, indirect communication, and internal reflection.

Third, collective decisions are legitimate to the extent that they are secured through processes that adequately connect deliberation with actual democratic decision-making. This requires the identification of feasible decision rules, along with direct and indirect connections between the informal, deliberative institutions of the public sphere and the formal, decision-making institutions of the democratic state. Possible decision rules include rational consensus, weaker but more workable agreements, anonymous public opinion or societal consensus, and deliberative voting. Possible connections between the public sphere and the state include elections, the resonance between public opinion and state policy, and direct interactions between citizens and representatives within quasi-formal, deliberative institutions. I conclude that, although other connections are possible, deliberative voting and elections remain indispensable links between deliberation and collective democratic decision-making.

Finally, legitimate collective decisions must occur under fair conditions, which include both procedural and substantive aspects. But because the linkage between deliberation and collective decision-making cannot dispense with processes like voting and elections, fair conditions must include distinct deliberative and aggregative dimensions. Thus, I propose assessing the conditions of deliberative collective decisions through three criteria—political equality, political autonomy, and political reciprocity—each of which includes aggregative and deliberative dimensions.

THE SCOPE OF PLURAL DELIBERATION

As stated above, plural deliberation is a model for assessing the legitimacy of democratic processes and institutions that secure collective decisions among members of diverse and constructed collective identities. Because these identities can have deep interpretive significance for their members, plural deliberation must include a wide scope of communicative contributions. It cannot simply concern the common interest because multiple and conflicting common interests may exist among diverse collective identities.[3] It also cannot ignore the deeper epistemological or normative frameworks that undergird interests; these may be essential to understanding and accommodating the interests of minority or subordinate collective identities. However, plural deliberation also cannot uncritically accept the positions of narrow interests or epistemological or normative frameworks, which may be morally or pragmatically unacceptable to members of other groups. Thus, plural deliberation requires a wide scope of contributions, all of which must be subject to potential criticism. In order to clarify these types of contributions I propose the following, nonexhaustive set of concepts: preferences, interests, opinions, perspectives, and world-views.

Collective decisions are made among alternative preferences over policies, laws, political candidates, or even constitutional frameworks. Interests and opinions may inform preferences. Interests are individual or group ends that lie beyond political activity itself,[4] and may or may not cohere with the common interest of all participants.[5] Opinions are fallible assessments of what would be in the common interest of all participants and thus may conflict with interests.[6] Perspectives and world-views, in turn, inform interests and opinions. Perspectives correspond to politically relevant positions within a society.[7] Women and men within a modern, industrialized society are likely to approach questions of reproductive rights from divergent perspectives, as women alone have the capacity to bear children. This means only that women will form their preferences and interests regarding reproductive policy from the perspective that they are more directly and intimately affected by reproduction, not that all women share the same preferences, interests, or opinions on this issue. World-views reflect the cultural, ethical, and epistemo-logical frameworks within which individuals understand the world and order the entities within it.[8] Perspectives and world-views may overlap or cut across each other. Religiously based opponents of abortion may share an epistemological and normative framework regarding the origins of life, yet men and women within this world-view may nevertheless have distinct perspectives on the issue. Similarly, two women may share a perspective on reproduction, while holding divergent world-views that shape their interests, opinions, and preferences on abortion.[9]

Although collective decision-making is ultimately about preferences, the capacity of interests, opinions, perspectives, and world-views to shape preferences suggests that plural deliberation should seek to generate reflection on all of these entities. Consequently, plural deliberation would find illegitimate models that in some way constrain the scope of deliberation. Take Adam Przeworski's claim that deliberation is primarily over means (what I call preferences) and not goals (which roughly correspond to interests or opinions). Clearly a great deal of important polit-ical deliberation concerns preferences regarding the means to ends, and yet this hardly exhausts deliberation's scope. Consider the trivial example Przeworski him-self provides: "The large part of political discussion concerns not goals but means, not the question whether motherhood is good but whether the best way to promote motherhood is indeed to throw mothers and children on the street."[10] Although many people do think of motherhood as good, there are clearly many questions regarding the conditions under which women should adopt motherhood. Do people agree that lesbians should have the same opportunities to become mothers as het-erosexual women? Is motherhood really good for a woman on welfare or a teenager in high school? Do we want to promote motherhood in overpopulated countries? And, perhaps most important, under what conditions should women become moth-ers? Should they be forced into motherhood because of the inaccessibility of birth control or abortion rights or should they have significant choice over this impor-tant, life-transforming event? Quite clearly, when it comes to motherhood, much of our deliberation is about goals, not just means.

Such disagreement regarding goals is also apparent in deliberation over issues related to ethnic, racial, or cultural groups. Disputes over self-government rights, affirmative action, or group representation involve not only the means to achiev-ing predetermined goals but also conflicts over the goals themselves. In particular, they concern different conceptions of equality: Should equality be sought among individuals or among groups; should it be understood as material equality, cultural equality, or equality of opportunity? Again, this is not to say that deliberation over means is unnecessary: it is only to say that disputes over means usually do not exhaust the scope of deliberation in a plural polity.

Plural deliberation seeks to induce reflection on interests, but it does so without precluding self- or group-interests from deliberation ex ante. Instead, it forces participants to justify their interests through appeals either to the common interest or to reasons that others in the general public are free to accept or reject.[11] In other words, it subjects the defense of interests to publicity constraints. Given that preferences justified through appeals to common interests are more likely to gain acceptance, publicity constraints will tend to hinder self-interested claims within deliberative settings. However, it is important that plural deliberation not preclude self-interested claims from deliberation; disadvantaged groups historically have suffered from having their particular interests (e.g., resource redistribution) ignored in favor of putatively common interests (e.g., national security).[12] This danger is exemplified by the Democratic party's temporary elimination of minority caucuses, for fear of appearing to be the party of special interests.[13] Measures that enhance self- or group interests require their advocates to justify them through common interests or other reasons before an unconstrained public that remains free to accept or reject such justifications. But the problem of group-related injustice within a plural polity requires that such self- or group-interested proposals not be excluded prior to deliberative testing.

Regarding opinions, plural deliberation primarily tests whether they are accurate and sincere. These two tasks can be interrelated. For instance, should a participant justify a policy preference, like a tax cut, by claiming that it would stimulate the economy, plural deliberators would examine whether that claim is empirically true. In addition, they could also examine the extent to which the sponsor of the tax cut also benefits from this proposal so as to determine the sincerity of the justification. This places burdens of proof on participants who would try to justify self-interested policies as publicly interested opinions. Should the tax cut be proven only to benefit the sponsor without having a salutary effect on the economy, the sponsor's credibility within deliberation would be undermined.[14]

The role of perspectives within plural deliberation is more complex. In chapter 1, I expressed my ambivalence about Iris Marion Young's idea of social perspective. On the one hand, I believe that it more adroitly accommodated multiple modes of identity construction, but on the other hand I fear her application of this term to well known identity groups neglects problems of internal diversity and shifting boundaries. Seyla Benhabib develops a similar but more thoroughgoing critique of Young's theory of social perspective. Like me, she fears that Young's catalogue of social perspectives too easily maps onto the common group identities found within identity politics, such as gender, sexuality, and various racial and ethnic groups. But beyond this, Benhabib claims that the concept of perspective, which originates in phenomenology and refers to unified structures of consciousness, is misapplied as a form of empirical sociology. As a result, Young ascribes essentialist identities to the various social groups, neglecting the contentious debates within each group about its identity.[15]

I clearly concur with Benhabib's first criticism. However, I am willing to grant credence to the claim that members of different collective identities may perceive the world differently than do members of other collective identities. This is not a necessary situation, nor is it generated by any unified structures of consciousness among members of that group. Rather, members of some collective identities might be more likely to share certain experiences or vulnerabilities than members of other collective identities. For instance, Black American males are more likely than Indian American males to experience difficulties hailing a cab in New York City. In this way, a probabilistic concept of social perspective has some purchase, even if Young's association of it with common racial or ethnic groups underemphasizes the internal diversity of perspectives within a constructed collective identity.

Still, the probability of sharing an experience is not the same as necessarily sharing it. And when one combines the probabilistic ground of perspective with the recognition of internal diversity and shifting boundaries, social perspective becomes a highly contestable concept. Consequently, when citizens or representatives claim to share a perspective with others, these claims must be critically tested. Young's own reflections seem to suggest that perspectives are not open to criticism: she argues that all perspectives are legitimate because they only reflect social positions in a plural polity.[16] This seems to imply that social perspectives are not really open to deliberative criticism. There is some initial plausibility to this. To return to an example discussed earlier, women and men have divergent perspectives on reproduction. While the preferences, interests, or opinions derived from these perspectives would clearly be open to criticism, it is hard to see how the perspectives themselves would be. This is because a perspective represents an ontological status shared among several individuals, a status grounded in common experiences, vulnerabilities, or problems.

But while an ontological status itself is not open to criticism, individual claims to share an ontological status with others clearly are. In addition, claims that a given ontological status is politically relevant are also open to critical testing. Height and eye color are also shared ontological statuses, yet they are not recognized as politically significant. Or to take a historical example, the common ontological status of male sex, age, and traceable bloodlines grounded the shared perspective of patriarchs, but this perspective is not considered politically relevant today.[17] More pertinent to plural deliberation would be the claim that subgroups within larger, more socially recognized collective identities share distinct experiences and vulnerabilities that are also politically relevant. If West Indian immigrants claim a distinct perspective from that of African Americans, or if Filipinos claim a distinct perspective from that of more prosperous Asian ethnicities, these claims affect our assessments of whether all relevant perspectives are represented within plural deliberation. Thus, deliberation about perspective involves claims to share a politically relevant ontological status, and such claims are clearly open to criticism and may require justification.[18]

While including interests, opinions, and perspectives distinguishes plural deliberation from constrained models of deliberation, the inclusion of world-views most emphatically marks its difference. Constrained models require collective decisions to be justified through public reasons, those shared by members of a plurality of comprehensive doctrines or world-views. These must be reasonable, such that their epistemological and normative premises are compatible with modern rationality, democratic equality, and liberal freedom. This "reasonable pluralism" constrains the domain of public reasons that can justify collective decisions. This restricted domain of justifications thereby constricts the acceptable range of collective decisions that a deliberative democracy could possibly reach, as certain collective decisions, such as the restriction of religious liberty or expressive freedom, could not possibly find justification amidst reasonable pluralism.[19]

There is considerable merit to this approach. Collective decisions based on controversial world-views not shared by the entire polity are intuitively illegitimate. However, this framework relies on two tendencies that should trouble pluralists. First, as Benhabib points out, constrained models demonstrate less a process of deliberative reasoning than a regulative principle constraining the domain of publicly acceptable reasons.[20] Constrained models do not show how individuals engage in the give and take of exchanging justifications and criticisms but instead present the domain of reasons that could possibly support collective decisions. Indeed, this rather staid model might include little in the way of public debate as long as elected representatives act according to publicly shared reasons. Second, constrained models rely excessively on a background condition of reasonable pluralism. Collective decisions must find justification within public reasons, which inhabit an overlapping consensus among a plurality of world-views. But to avoid the danger that this overlapping consensus may be stretched by world-views that deny modern scientific reasoning, espouse hierarchical beliefs, or deny individual liberty, the overlapping consensus of public reasons must preclude unreasonable world-views.

Yet what is to be done with individuals or groups who espouse unreasonable world-views? Joshua Cohen provides several reasons reasonable pluralism is unlikely to disappear, but he does not clarify what to do with proponents of unreasonable world-views.[21] Presumably, they should be tolerated but should not contribute to deliberative collective decisions, or at least to those that deal with constitutional essentials. But this response does not clarify how we engage unreasonable doctrines within normal democratic deliberation. Moreover, to exclude unreasonable doctrines might also be deeply unjust; groups with apparently unreasonable world-views may be and often are disadvantaged economically, socially, or politically. For instance, some New Mexico Pueblo tribes have world-views that include hierarchical beliefs, but it would be a travesty to preclude members of such groups from the deliberative forum ex ante, given their history of military, political, and economic subjugation.[22]

Alternatively, one could seek to use deliberation to undermine such beliefs, under the assumption that they are likely to fail critical tests of justification. Such deliberation would be subject to publicity constraints, so that participants would remain prone to the judgments of an unrestricted public. But such publicity con-

straints differ from deliberation constrained by public reason. In the latter, participants are enjoined from contributing positions that lie beyond the pale of reasonable pluralism; in the former, participants remain free to introduce positions from
their world-views that may lie beyond the bounds of reasonable pluralism, but these
contributions are subject to criticism from an unlimited public. Publicity constraints
thus enable interlocutors and the public to reject contributions that strain their tol-
erance without precluding these contributions prior to deliberation itself. This does
not mean that publicity constraints are always benign: indeed, in chapter 3 I will
examine how they might unfairly discriminate against contributions from members of disadvantaged groups. Nevertheless, they provide a flexible means for
including diverse world-views within plural deliberation without requiring their
uncritical acceptance or accommodation.

However, proponents of constrained models correctly contend that democratic deliberation will remain incompatible with at least some world-views. If a
world-view rejects participation within collective decision-making, is unwilling
either to proffer justifications or accept criticisms, or resorts to violence rather than
discussion, plural deliberation is unlikely. But short of these limits, deliberative
democrats will do better to explore how critical processes can generate reflectivity among even unreasonable world-views, such that reasonable pluralism becomes
an outcome of, rather than a precondition for, plural deliberation.[23]

THE CRITICAL PROCESS OF PLURAL DELIBERATION

For reasonable pluralism to be an outcome of plural deliberation, more is needed
than simply the inclusion of a wide variety of contributions within public communication. The generation of reasonable pluralism implies that participants come
to reflect upon their world-views and perspectives, along with the opinions, interests, and preferences derived from them. Reflection need not result from all forms
of communication. For instance, actors can communicate to share information or to
signal their intentions, simply to enable the aggregative tasks of building alliances
or bargaining with opponents. To generate reflection, plural deliberation requires
a more robust communicative practice whereby participants actually or at least
potentially criticize each other's contributions. Aggregative bargaining and alliance-
formation play a role in a plural polity, but they do not suffice for generating a critical, deliberative process.

Unfortunately, deliberative criticism among diverse world-views or perspectives is a difficult task among participants who differ in their experiences, epistemological beliefs, or normative values. The key question is how plural deliberation
can legitimately generate reflectivity and reasonable pluralism among diverse perspectives and world-views. John Dryzek and James Johnson include world-views
within the scope of deliberation but envision engaging them only through contestation and critique.[24] But a plurality of perspectives and world-views assumes dis-

tinct epistemological and perceptual frameworks, and so critique must be preceded by attempts at understanding. As the history of intergroup relations in the United States and elsewhere has shown, critique unmoored by understanding is the ground of stereotypical labeling.

Understanding begins with the assumption that another perspective or world-view is, in principle, capable of being understood. Participants cannot assume that their world-views are hermetically sealed chambers of meaning: rather, they must assume that they are more like distant but open horizons, understandable through vigorous interpretive effort.[25] Ideally, understanding develops through actual encounters, not through empathy, whereby one vicariously experiences the feelings, thoughts, and experiences of the other, or through transposition, whereby one claims to know the other's intentions and motives.[26] Both empathy and transposition risk encouraging the imaginative projection of one's own prior beliefs, fantasies, and prejudices about the other onto the other. In a brilliant illustration of this danger, Iris Marion Young relates how able-bodied people in Oregon perceived being disabled as worse than death. Disabled people disagreed. Young concludes that the projection of one's prior prejudices about the other fundamentally closes off any genuine dialogue through which participants could truly learn each other's perspectives.[27] Understanding demands that members of different cultures actively engage each other in real dialogue, listen to what the other says, and reach partial agreements about the meanings communicated.[28] In this way, understanding occurs gradually, in incremental steps, based on mutual agreement.

At this point, we must recognize that this ideal portrait of understanding across perspectives and world-views has important empirical and ontological limitations that may require relaxing or altering its requirements. One empirical limitation reflects how constraints of opportunity, time, energy, effort, and skill may limit one's capacity to understand another perspective or world-view. Absent an unlimited communication community,[29] such limitations are ubiquitous within a large, plural polity where the scarcity of time and resources constrains deliberation involving multiple groups. Nevertheless, it is important to examine the extent to which empirical limitations can be overcome in order to assess the extent to which criticism is valid. Some participants may overcome these empirical limitations more than others. Take, for example, a minority group that constantly encounters the majority culture through the news media, forms of mass entertainment, or policies and laws enacted by majority rule. Should this be the case, it is possible (though not necessary) that members of the minority culture, to a greater extent than members of the majority culture, will overcome the empirical limitations to understanding and more validly engage in criticism.

While empirical limitations chasten the belief that understanding can develop quickly or easily, they do imply that perspectives and world-views can be fully understood, given sufficient time, skill, and effort. More daunting are two ontological limitations on understanding. The first reflects the fact that perspectives and world-views can change over time. As a result, if one seeks to understand a perspective or world-view in which one does not regularly participate, one's understanding may become outdated or inaccurate. On a more complex level, the content and even the boundaries of a culture may change as it encounters other cultures. For example, the Native American supratribal consciousness cited in chapter 1 developed only after members of diverse tribes came into repeated contact with each other and with Whites. This led them to discount cultural differences among themselves and emphasize shared values that distinguished them from Whites.[30] Similarly, Americans of South Asian descent may emphasize distinct religious or linguistic identities in their interactions with each other but then emphasize shared social mores or culinary tastes in environments dominated by White Americans. In either case, individuals may give greater salience to different values or cognitive beliefs when placed in different contexts. And as the discussion of supratribal consciousness in chapter 1 suggests, we cannot reduce such changes solely to instrumental agency aimed at protecting individual or group interests. While instrumental agency remains a part of identity construction, interpretive significance clearly affects the shape and character of collective identities as members seek to maintain a perspective or world-view for its cultural or symbolic significance. How these interpretive changes complicate understanding should neither be underestimated nor dismissed.

A second ontological limitation results from the possibility that certain beliefs or practices can only be understood through lived experience.[31] For instance, it seems unlikely that men can fully understand the experience of giving birth. Similarly, it may remain impossible to understand completely certain Black perspectives regarding racial equality in America. Recall the problems I had hailing a cab in New York City after I had shaved my head. With hair, I looked South Asian. Although South Asians are subject to certain stereotypes, they generally do not invoke the images of crime and violence associated with Black Americans. Without hair, I looked Black and thus became associated with Black stereotypes, even in the eyes of South Asian cab drivers. Deliberation with Blacks could have allowed me to gain some cognitive understanding of these types of problems, but nothing hit home quite as hard as the lived experience of this type of discrimination. When we consider the prevalence of other, more costly forms of discrimination, we might more clearly understand why Lee Sigelman and Susan Welch conclude that "Blacks and Whites inhabit two different perceptual worlds."[32]

Given these deep ontological and empirical limitations to understanding, what can we expect from plural deliberation? I contend that empirical and ontological limitations need not completely preclude understanding: rather, they preclude only *complete* understanding. Participants must acknowledge that a final and comprehensive understanding of another perspective or world-view is unlikely, but partial, provisional understandings remain possible. Thus, acknowledging the limitations to understanding need not lead one uncritically to accept statements like, "You wouldn't understand anyway." Rather, acknowledging these limitations should prompt participants to expect to learn something from the other, as any prior assumptions are only partial, finite, and incomplete.[33] My understanding of another world-view might become outdated, and certain lived experiences, while communicable, might not be fully comprehensible. Nevertheless, the generous recognition of another's beliefs and experiences can enable partial understandings, even as the depth of such differences illuminates the finitude of one's own understanding. Recognizing the empirical and ontological limitations to understanding reconfigures plural deliberation as part of an ongoing process that can come to partial conclusions but can never reach a final resting point.

Ontological and empirical limitations to understanding clearly limit the capacity for valid criticism; one can validly criticize only what one understands. However, these limitations need not preclude criticism in its entirety: rather, they might require that we transform its method and aims. According to a deductive method of criticism, understanding a perspective or world-view is the basis for criticizing the preferences, interests, and opinions derived from it.[34] Alternatively, a questioning method allows for criticism even where full understanding is unattainable. From her analysis of limitations to understanding, Young concludes that interlocutors will probably end up engaging in questioning when they do not fully understand each other's perspectives.[35] When portrayed in this way, questioning remains part of the process of understanding. However, coming to know what one does not know should remind us of Socratic wisdom. Although Socratic questioning was, at least ostensibly, motivated by his admission of ignorance, it also enabled criticism of the values and beliefs of his interlocutors by drawing on their own answers and inconsistencies. This method of criticism is most evident in the aporetic dialogues, where neither Socrates nor his interlocutor arrives at any firm conclusion about the topic in question.

When we adopt the open-ended manner of questioning, the aims of intercultural criticism also change. The deductive method brings substantive criticisms to bear on the preferences, interests, or opinions derived from perspectives and world-views; the model of aporetic questioning achieves the more modest goal of promoting reflectivity among perspectives and world-views. In this approach, it is hoped that participants will realize the contingency and finitude of their perspectives and world-views, thereby opening them to possible changes on their own.[36] Thus, when we present criticism as open-ended questioning, its aim shifts: participants seek only to encourage each other to experience their perspectives and world-views as limited, contingent, and open to revision.[37] In this way, critical questioning sets the stage for further deliberation, wherein the partial agreements that ground deductive criticism may be attained.[38]

Yet even open-ended questioning confronts a second empirical limitation: the problem of scale. Direct deliberation cannot but exclude the great majority of citizens within a large-scale, modern democracy, and thus understanding across perspective or world-view must be mediated or internal. Mediated deliberation requires representation, either within the informal, deliberative institutions of the public sphere, like associations, social movements, and the mass media, or within the formal, decision-making institutions of the democratic state. Internal deliberation occurs within the minds of individuals who on their own reflect upon the communication that they have experienced either directly or in a mediated form. Because I will examine mediated deliberation in chapter 4, I wish now to focus on internal deliberation.

Robert Goodin argues that internal-reflective deliberation can supplement direct deliberation in two ways. First, it enables listeners to reconstruct the logic of a speaker's utterances, as deliberators rarely communicate in fully formed syllogisms. More problematically, it enables individuals to imagine themselves in the situations inhabited by others, the very type of transposition that plural deliberation ideally eschews.[39] Given that the scale of modern democracies will limit the extent of direct deliberation, internal-reflective deliberation may be a necessary concession in order to include more than just a select few within the deliberative process. At minimum, however, participants must check their internal reflections through direct, deliberative ratification, so as to avoid the misunderstanding and projection so feared by Young.[40]

John Dryzek rejects Goodin's approach precisely because of the need to include a direct, deliberative check on internal reflection. Instead, he proposes overcoming the problem of scale by portraying deliberation as a contestation of discourses within the public sphere, arguing that this approach enables an "indeterminate" number of individuals to participate in deliberation. Taking the environmental movement as an example of such a discourse, he argues that the number of people participating in the movement may ebb and flow over time, sometimes involving only a few, sometimes involving many.[41] The problem with Dryzek's response is that it does not do away with the need for internal-reflective deliberation. Even when a social movement involves a large number of participants, it still does not include all those who may engage its views. For instance, a clear goal of the civil rights movement was to shape White public opinion nationwide.[42] In order to achieve this goal on a mass scale, it was crucial that the mass media communicate the situation and struggles of Blacks in the South to other parts of the country where listeners, viewers, and readers could internally assess the validity of their claims of injustice. In this way, a democratic social movement and its discourse invoked the participation not only of the protestors but also of the general citizenry, who learned of the movement through the media and who then used internal-reflective deliberation to respond to its claims.

Goodin is not wrong to perceive a clear role for internal-reflective deliberation, especially as he acknowledges the need for direct or mediated deliberative correction. His error lies in the tendency to circumscribe the focus of internal deliberation to the logical and imaginative understanding of others. Whereas internal reflection can play an important, if insufficient, role in understanding, perhaps its greatest role is critical. As Simone Chambers points out, we are less likely to accept cogent criticism while we are directly engaged in deliberation with others because we do not like to admit publicly that we are wrong. Rather, we are more likely to accept the validity of criticism between conversations, in a gradual, piecemeal fashion, on our own.[43] This is especially the case when one's world-view is challenged. An individual is less likely to accept a full-scale revision of an epistemological or normative framework while in the midst of direct deliberation, even when acknowledging that one's partner has understood this framework accurately. Rather, one "reevaluates fragments of one's worldview" over time, in between direct, deliberative encounters.[44]

Let me conclude by illustrating plural deliberation through the civil rights movement, an example I will revisit in chapter 4. Although participants face epistemological limits in trying to understand a world-view or perspective, some participants, such as members of a minority group, might develop a greater understanding of the majority world-view through their greater exposure to it. This grants the minority greater validity in criticizing the majority world-view. Part of the success of the civil rights movement was the understanding its leaders had of the egalitarian world-view espoused by American political culture and its ability to communicate to White America the Black perspective that the ideals of this world-view were not extended to them. White public opinion, in turn, was swayed by the gradual realization that Black reality did not match up with American ideals. This realization did not occur at once, within direct deliberation, but unfolded over time through mediated and internal deliberation. Internal-reflective deliberation, in turn, enabled White Americans to realize the contingency and finitude of their perspective on American society and the need to criticize the partiality and hypocrisy of the supposedly egalitarian world-view that they espoused.

PLURAL DELIBERATION AND COLLECTIVE DECISION-MAKING

Plural deliberation can articulate the process through which the understanding and criticism of perspectives and world-views can proceed. Its aim, however, is not simply to enable fair criticism but to secure collective decisions that incorporate the reflective preferences generated by such criticism. This requires addressing two interrelated issues: the identification of a decision rule, a mechanism for ending deliberation and arriving at collective decisions; and the relationship between the informal, deliberative institutions of the public sphere and the formal, decision-making institutions of the state. Regarding decision rules, deliberative theorists have proffered four alternatives: rational consensus, weaker but more workable agreements, broader public opinion or societal consensus, and deliberative majority voting. Consideration of these decision rules will involve a concurrent consideration of the relationship between the public sphere and the state.

Rational consensus requires that participants agree on a collective decision for the same reasons. Jürgen Habermas arrives at this decision rule in order to distinguish between agreements reached through pure rational communication and agreements reached through strategic bargains or compromises. As Habermas states, "Whereas parties can agree to a negotiated compromise for different reasons, the consensus brought about through argument must rest on identical reasons able to convince the parties *in the same way*" (italics in oridinal).[45] Rational consensus thus has the advantage of placing justification at the heart of collective decisions: we must agree on a plan of action because we also agree on the justification behind it. This grants rational consensus a level of impartiality not found in strategically negotiated bargains. Unfortunately, as a number of sympathetic commentators have noted, rational consensus is rarely feasible as a rule for making collective decisions.[46] It is difficult enough for multiple participants to reach agreement on a collective decision without requiring them also to reach agreement on the justifications behind it. Habermas might respond that we cannot distinguish between deliberation and bargaining unless we require agreement on both justifications and outcomes.[47] Bargaining allows parties to agree on an outcome for divergent reasons, for instance when a labor contract secures the assent of management for its preclusion of work stoppage and the assent of unions for its generation of higher wages.

This reply overlooks two other ways of distinguishing bargaining from deliberation: deliberation's preclusion of threats and rewards and its inclusion of critical reflectivity. If deliberation requires participants to reflect upon their preferences, interests, opinions, perspectives, and world-views, and if reflectivity occurs under conditions that preclude threats and rewards, then deliberation can distinguish itself from bargaining without the need for agreement on the reasons behind collective decisions. In this way, deliberation can reach collective decisions through more feasible "workable agreements" rather than through rational consensus. For example, an environmental policy aimed at reducing factory emissions can garner the assent of area residents for its reduction of emissions, of management for public relations reasons, and of company engineers for the technical interest of devising new production processes.[48]

Although workable agreements are clearly more feasible than rational consensus, they remain problematic for two reasons. First, they are possible only in settings with relatively small numbers of participants, where direct, unanimous agreement can be achieved without majority voting or heavily mediated representation.[49] Second, unanimity on a proposal, even absent consensus on its justification, risks favoring the status quo by providing a virtual veto for an entrenched minority.[50] For these reasons, several theorists turn to broader public opinion as the ground for securing legitimate collective decisions. Earlier formulations of this thesis argued that some form of rational consensus could be reached through the "anonymous," "subjectless," and "decentered" communicative processes that create public opinion. Such public opinion would, through a network of extended deliberation, reach a deep and broad consensus not on specific collective decisions themselves but on the procedures through which specific collective decisions were made.[51] Thus, deliberatively generated public opinion grounds but does not replace the electoral, legislative, and administrative institutions and procedures of the constitutional, democratic state.[52]

If we interpret procedures broadly so as to include not only the rules whereby decisions are made but also the substantive standing of individuals within such procedures, there is much to recommend this approach in a plural polity. For instance, public opinion research demonstrates that the greatest effect of the African-American civil rights movement was to alter public opinion on racial equality. White public opinion in the 1940s strongly supported the belief that Black Americans were inferior to Whites, but this shifted in favor of racial equality during and especially after the civil rights movement.[53] Indeed, as I will discuss in chapter 3, the norm of racial equality now functions as a publicity constraint within deliberation. As a result, public sphere actors, like the civil rights movement, were able to change public opinion over the long term, thereby altering the standing of Black Americans within the formal and informal institutions through which collective decisions are secured in this country.

But on the other hand, this portrait can be criticized as too vague, too anonymous, and too procedural to represent the popular sovereignty needed to create legitimate collective decisions.[54] If deliberation only affects collective decisions in this oblique way, then members of divergent collective identities may end up acquiescing to a political process within which they exercise little influence. For this reason, John Dryzek suggests an alternative model of how specific collective decisions, such as policies, can be deliberatively achieved. Policy discourses compete with each other within the public sphere, leading to resolutions in the form of workable agreements within public opinion. These agreements are then communicated to the state through extraconstitutional measures, such as rhetorical communication. State policy must then "resonate" with these workable agreements in order to be legitimate. Resonance, while vague, can be measured through a three-pronged social scientific analysis: an identification of the different discourses within the public sphere, a measurement of the relative weight or success of the competing discourses in order to determine public opinion, and a measurement of the similarity between state policies and public opinion.[55]

Dryzek admits a clear problem with this formulation of deliberative collective decision-making: it substitutes "social science for democratic process."[56] While provocative, this conclusion remains unsatisfactory: thoroughly nondemocratic states can pursue policies that seek to resonate with public opinion. Marc Lynch argues that by severing ties with the West Bank and supporting Iraq in the Gulf War, state policy resonated with public opinion in monarchical Jordan, "an authoritarian system which is relatively open to public deliberation but retains executive power."[57] Dryzek's own interest in how public opinion shapes the decisions of transnational authorities, which lack clear channels of electoral representation, mirrors this situation. Thus, resonance between public opinion and state policy may, on its own, reflect the deliberative legitimacy of decisions, but it hardly guarantees their democratic legitimacy.

A second and related problem with Dryzek's resonance formulation is that, although more concrete than Habermasian "subjectless" communication, it still cannot identify who is accountable for passing laws that fail to resonate with public opinion. In an excessively vague fashion, Dryzek seems to identify only the monolithic state as the responsible party, not specific officials within it. This, of course, reflects the applicability of the resonance model to nondemocratic states. But in a democratic state, the resonance between public opinion and state policy should distinguish those officials who uphold public opinion from those who violate it. Moreover, because public opinion is typically vague and political circumstances often change, officials might justifiably contradict public opinion. Given these problems, electoral campaigns, at least as much as social-scientific analysis, should be used to assess who specifically violates or upholds public opinion and whether specific violations can be deliberatively justified.

For this reason, deliberative democrats are right to incorporate voting and elections into their models through the idea of deliberative majorities. In an influential presentation of this approach, Bernard Manin suggests that the legitimacy of collective decisions stems from the free participation of all within a deliberative decision-making process that ends with a majority vote. The majority vote simply reflects what reasons have convinced the most people during the deliberative process. Its legitimacy stems from the fact that the minority's reasons were considered during the deliberative process prior to the election, may be reconsidered during procedures of parliamentary questioning, and may again be considered and potentially incorporated into a new majority through a later election.[58] But although the incorporation of majority voting provides deliberative models with a realistic manner of reaching collective decisions, it renders them vulnerable to the social choice criticism that voting mechanisms can create arbitrary outcomes through ambiguity and instability.

Ambiguity reflects the fact that voting outcomes can differ, depending on the method chosen for aggregating votes. Instability reflects the possibility that voting cycles can allow one or a few powerful individuals to determine an outcome by setting the agenda.[59] Voting cycles can occur when three or more individuals vote over three or more alternatives when none of those alternatives is a Condorcet winner (an alternative that beats the other two in a paired comparison). Absent a Condorcet winner, any one of the alternatives can gain majority support, depending on how they are paired. Instability enables agenda manipulation when actors intentionally sequence the pairing of alternatives in order to enable their chosen alternative—one that is no more preferred than the other two—to win. Both issues are important for deliberative democratic decision-making, but I will begin with instability because the danger of agenda manipulation most clearly generates an undemocratic outcome. To meet the challenge of instability, we must examine the empirical likelihood of this problem and deliberative methods for mitigating it.

Gerry Mackie, in a magisterial critique of social choice theory, concludes that actual voting cycles are extremely rare. [60] By examining data on voting and citizen preferences over a variety of elections and legislative votes, he finds very few instances of voting cycles, and the few that do occur are typically minor ones involving cycles over lower preferences that cannot win in an election. In addition, Mackie argues that the historical examples of cycles cited by William Riker, the most vociferous proponent of social choice theory in political science, are in fact fabrications based on faulty historical evidence. Voting cycles simply do not occur very often in the real world.

In addition, deliberative democrats have proposed four ways that deliberation can mitigate instability by increasing the likelihood of a Condorcet winner. First, democratic deliberation can transform voter preferences, thereby enabling a majority to coalesce around a single alternative. Such an alternative is by definition a Condorcet winner, and the problem of voting cycles is eliminated.[61] Second, deliberation can reduce the number of alternatives. Voting cycles are less likely as the number of alternatives decreases—indeed, they are impossible when there are only two alternatives. While an ex ante restriction of alternatives would be democratically illegitimate, deliberation can legitimately restrict alternatives through critical testing, which could reveal certain alternatives to be unconvincing, immoral, or impractical.[62] Third, deliberation can reduce the number of preference rankings among voters, even when the number of alternatives remains constant. Should deliberation lead voters to rank certain alternatives at the bottom of their preference sets, even if these alternatives remain on the ballot, the likelihood of voting cycles again decreases. Finally, deliberation can clarify the dimensions along which different alternatives are to be evaluated. Voting cycles are more likely when alternatives involve different issues. For example, in a choice between building a prison, a mall, or a park, each of these three alternatives can win a majority when paired against another single alternative because each paired choice reflects a different issue dimension. A majority may prefer the park to the mall on an environmental dimension, another majority may prefer the mall to the prison on a lifestyle dimension, and a third majority may prefer the prison to the park on a crime prevention dimension. Deliberation can help participants distinguish the dimension on which they wish to base their decision, and then vote among the alternatives accordingly.[63]

Each of these deliberative methods emphasizes that voting cycles are a logical possibility, not an empirical necessity. But at the same time, these methods need not necessarily eliminate the empirical manifestation of voting cycles. For in each instance, reducing the chance of voting cycles depends upon a dynamic of convergence within deliberation. Deliberative participants converge on a Condorcet winner, on which alternatives to exclude, on which alternatives to rank lowest within their preference orderings, or on which dimension to assess alternatives. The problem is that deliberation that includes critique and preference transformation need not lead to convergence. Instead, it might undermine the support for a Condorcet winner, add new alternatives to the agenda, create more diverse preference orderings, or increase the dimensions along which alternatives are assessed.[64] The last issue is particularly vexing in the case of elections, where candidates often stand for multiple issues along multiple dimensions.[65] Thus, deliberation might equally mitigate or exacerbate the problem of voting cycles.

The inconclusiveness of any deliberative method for mitigating voting cycles requires that we more carefully examine the sources of deliberative convergence: the dispositions of the participants and the character of the decision-making institutions. Should participants be of the disposition that I call deliberative reciprocity, they will seek common grounds to construct shared principles or to minimize disagreement when such principles cannot be found.[66] As the previous discussion of the scope of plural deliberation and the process of understanding and criticism suggests, such common grounds need not exist prior to deliberation but can emerge through the process itself. I will examine deliberative reciprocity more carefully below, but for now note that it might enable participants to avoid voting cycles, although under conditions of inequality or coercion, participants might rightly eschew this disposition.

A second source of convergence is the character of decision-making institutions, which in a deliberative democracy will likely include voting or electoral systems. This brings us back to the problem of ambiguity, whereby different voting systems can lead to different outcomes. Social choice theory has used this problem to denigrate the capacity of democracy accurately to reflect a popular will. However, this conclusion gains credence only if predeliberative preferences are seen as sovereign. This clearly is an impoverished vision of democracy that utterly overlooks the role of deliberation in improving and critically testing preferences.[67] But whereas social choice theory incorrectly identifies predeliberative preferences as sovereign, deliberative democracy to some degree must view postdeliberative preferences as sovereign. If deliberation transforms preferences to create a deliberative majority supporting one alternative, we should not favor a voting system that eliminates the position held by that deliberative majority.

However, Mackie again provides substantial empirical evidence to demonstrate that ambiguity is less problematic than social choice theorists might suggest. Examining voting and preference data under a variety of electoral systems, he concludes that most systems overwhelmingly select the same Condorcet winner. Interestingly enough, the single-member district plurality system used in the United States consistently performs somewhat more poorly than the other systems studied, although even this system identifies the Condorcet candidate most of the time.[68] Consequently, there is relatively little ambiguity among electoral and voting procedures.

But even if we consider this small level of ambiguity significant, it does not leave deliberative democrats subject to the arbitrary workings of whichever system happens to be in place. Electoral and voting systems are likely to influence the deliberation that precedes voting by affecting the number of candidates and the campaign postures they adopt. If a system favors a few moderate candidates or parties over a larger number of extremist candidates or parties, that system will likely encourage campaigns that highlight broad consensual issues over narrow divisive ones. When we recognize the deliberative role of voting and electoral procedures, the problem of ambiguity becomes even less debilitating for deliberative democrats because they can assess voting systems not simply according to aggregative effects but also according to their effects on campaign styles. If one system is more likely to foster a campaign style that more closely accords with the conditions of fair, plural deliberation, then there are less ambiguous reasons for supporting that system than the sometimes arbitrary relationship between preferences and voting outcomes. Deliberative democrats might favor a system that encourages convergence under some circumstances; however, they might not if convergence comes only at the price of suppressing the domain of alternatives and positions within campaign deliberation. So when assessing electoral systems, deliberative democrats should ideally favor those that simultaneously encourage deliberative reciprocity and convergence while enabling a broad array of candidates and viewpoints.

Of course, a deliberative judgment of electoral or voting systems requires understanding campaigns as deliberative processes. In an earlier formulation Dryzek comes close to this position, holding that "election campaigns do provide one opportunity (among many others) for discursive transmission, and elections themselves constitute a reason for state actors to listen to the public sphere."[69] However, in a later formulation he seems to reject this position, suggesting that "elections themselves are not exactly deliberative affairs, even for those who do participate in them—deliberation often has to be subordinated to strategy in the interests of winning."[70] This latter stand depends upon identifying deliberation exclusively with Habermasian communicative action, as opposed to the strategic action of rational choice theory. However, Dryzek does not demonstrate that deliberative participants must be *purely* communicative actors. Indeed, it is hard to imagine that the participants in his contestation of discourses do not, to some degree, act strategically. I will revisit this issue in chapter 4, where I show how the African-American civil rights movement adopted not only communicative action but also strategic action in order to achieve plural deliberation across group boundaries. If my analysis is right, then rational choice theorists wrongly depict social movements in purely strategic terms, overlooking how they can enable understanding and criticism across perspectives and world-views, but Dryzek is also wrong to view them as purely communicative actors.

Voting and electoral campaigns, like a public sphere populated by social movements, can be understood as deliberative settings that employ both strategic and communicative elements. Campaign deliberation is not ideal, in terms of the conditions under which elections proceed. But whereas the "public sphere is not a formal institution and so cannot be designed,"[71] electoral systems are formal institutions, and thus their redesign can become a direct aim of deliberative democratic action within the public sphere. Accepting the strategic dimension to deliberation enables us to assess electoral systems according to the incentives they provide to foster plural deliberation. As Donald Horowitz cogently argues, some electoral systems can encourage candidates to appeal across group boundaries.[72] So though electoral incentives are certainly insufficient for achieving understanding and fair criticism across perspectives or world-views, they can support candidates who attempt to do so.

Dryzek claims that democracy "does not have to be a matter of counting heads—even deliberating heads . . . [L]egitimacy can be sought instead in the resonance of collective decisions with public opinion." Goodin claims that the "final show of hands is what is crucial in conferring democratic legitimacy on the decision."[73] In a plural democratic state, collective decisions must rely on both methods to augment their legitimacy. This means that the interplay between deliberation and collective decision-making must proceed through multiple channels. Deliberative theorists are right to identify the public sphere as crucial for deliberation, but it is not the only deliberative forum. In addition, the connection between the public sphere and the state should proceed through multiple channels: through extra-constitutional mechanisms, such as rhetoric aimed at changing the terms of political discourse;[74] through direct links between the administrative branch and citizens;[75] and through the constitutional mechanisms, like elections, that tie voters to their representatives.[76] And insofar as public opinion is transmitted to the state via elections, plural deliberation favors those systems that provide incentives favoring candidates who appeal across group boundaries.

THE CONDITIONS OF PLURAL DELIBERATION

To be legitimate, deliberatively generated collective decisions must be reached under fair conditions. Deliberative theories commonly identify and defend fairness conditions but rarely articulate them in deliberative and aggregative dimensions. But if we reach deliberative collective decisions through voting or elections, as is inevitable to some degree, then both dimensions are indispensable. Thus, I propose three fairness conditions (political equality, political autonomy, and political reciprocity), distinguishing their deliberative and aggregative dimensions. This renders six fairness conditions (aggregative equality, deliberative equality, aggregative autonomy, deliberative autonomy, aggregative reciprocity, and deliberative reciprocity), which clarify how plural deliberation assesses democratic institutions.

Political Equality

Although the concept of political equality is ubiquitous among deliberative theories,[77] most theories fail to distinguish between its deliberative and aggregative dimensions, and some seem to conflate the two.[78] Following Thomas Christiano, I define *aggregative equality* as the quantitatively equal distribution of political goods among individuals and *deliberative equality* as the qualitatively equal distribution of political goods among positions.[79] For example, aggregative equality would require the numerically equal distribution of votes among individuals, whereas deliberative equality would require the equal distribution of speaking time among viewpoints, regardless of the number of individuals supporting each one. Each dimension of political equality is governed by a distinct distributive principle because aggregation and deliberation serve distinct functions and adopt distinct stances toward preferences.

With respect to functions, deliberation is concerned with understanding and criticizing preferences, interests, opinions, perspectives, and world-views through the exchange of justifications and criticisms; aggregation is concerned with the collection and tabulation of preferences once deliberation has ended. Political preferences, taken in the form of votes, are aggregative and cannot be combined without diluting the weight of each preference. If you and I have identical preferences, we should nevertheless retain our separate votes; having us share a single vote would dilute the aggregative weight of our preferences. Conversely, justifications and criticisms have what Christiano calls "jointness of supply": two or more individuals can share a justification or criticism without its being diminished.[80] Thus, if you and I share a justification, and our friend holds a different justification, for us to share twenty minutes of speaking time while our friend keeps twenty minutes for herself will not violate deliberative equality. The primary concern is that all positions initially enjoy equal representation within discursive fora, although the process of deliberation will legitimately come to rule out some positions.

The status of preferences within deliberation and aggregation provides an additional basis for the divergent distributive principles governing each dimension of political equality. Within deliberation, preferences are not sovereign. Thus, exposure to diverse criticisms and justifications, even those with little support, must be granted equally, as their expression may lead others to alter their preferences, along with the interests, opinions, perspectives, and world-views that animate them. But within postdeliberative aggregation, preferences are sovereign: the process of tabulating votes should not alter votes. Whereas deliberation and aggregation are linked within many democratic decision-making processes, like elections, the character of the two dimensions should remain analytically distinct in order to assess how different institutions fare along each.

Both aggregative and deliberative equality have procedural and substantive aspects. Minimally, aggregative political equality presupposes the procedural requirement of one-person $\Leftrightarrow$ one vote/equal votes $\Leftrightarrow$ one value/equal value.[81] The first pair in this formula grounds the uncontroversial rejection of unequal voting power.[82] The second pair reflects the problem of "wasted votes" or vote dilution, where all votes do not have the same likelihood of supporting the election of a winning candidate. This common phenomenon in single member district plurality electoral systems hinders the ability of geographically dispersed minorities, be they ethnic or ideological minorities, to elect representatives proportional to their numbers.[83] The substantive aspect of aggregative equality reflects citizens' capacity to participate effectively. Individuals may differ in their access to information, and even when access is equal, they may differ in their capacities to process information, leaving them in a state of "political poverty."[84]

Deliberative political equality can assess procedural matters, such as the distribution of allotted speaking time discussed above. It can also assess institutions according to the number and variety of positions they represent. Deliberative theory has more trouble assessing how the sequencing of speaking assignments affects which justifications are found most convincing. If being the last speaker prior to a collective decision means that a speaker's justifications will stick in participants' minds when they make a decision, then sequencing may have undermined deliberative political equality.[85] Alternating or random sequencing of speaking opportunities, however, may mitigate this problem.

The substantive aspect of deliberative political equality assesses how effectively different justifications are conveyed within a decision-making forum. While deliberative equality grants equal representation to positions regardless of their numerical strength, it adds the substantive requirement that such representation be equally effective. Thus, deliberative political equality is undermined if a speaker is unable to convey his position effectively, due either to a lack of communicative capacities, such as cognitive and expressive skills, or to the ascriptive identity of the speaker.[86] Procedural measures like equal speaking time are useless if one is effectively mute.

Substantive aspects of deliberative political equality are, of course, very difficult to measure without recourse to outcome assessment, a vexing problem for a deliberative theory that perceives preferences as validly malleable. Nevertheless, it may be necessary to incorporate careful, contextual analysis of outcomes as part of a preliminary assessment of institutions. If certain speakers or groups of speakers are consistently found to lack discursive capacities, it may be within the spirit of deliberative equality to use procedural or other means, such as extra speaking time or information aids, in order to achieve a more substantive level of deliberative equality. A response to substantive deliberative inequality more clearly compatible with a deliberative institutional approach would involve investigating how certain institutions can enhance citizen capacities. In chapter 4 I will examine how certain types of associations can cultivate the substantive capacities needed to approximate deliberative equality.

Political Autonomy

Political autonomy presumes that citizens understand themselves as the authors of the laws under which they live and is thus associated with concepts of self-rule or self-determination. It is particularly important for deliberative (and participatory) theories of democracy, which seek more than the mere choice among competing sets of legislative and executive elites.[87] Mark Warren provides a sophisticated but ultimately problematic account of how political autonomy functions within deliberative democracy. For Warren, individual autonomy means that individuals "hold their interests with due consideration and are able to provide reasons for holding them."[88] This self-critical, reflective form of autonomy suggests that interests (and presumably preferences, opinions, perspectives, and world-views) must result from autonomous choice and affirmation, not from physical or emotional impulses or from blind adherence to propaganda or tradition. Political autonomy, in turn, requires that participants engage in deliberation in order for their public opinion to be reflective, critical, and therefore valid. Warren adroitly points out that individual and political autonomy are "co-determining." Autonomous individuals are constituted by critical social processes embodying reciprocal recognition; the critical social processes that enable political autonomy must presuppose rights protecting individual autonomy. But like many deliberative and participatory theorists who prioritize political autonomy, Warren must conclude that "agreement" is the culmination of democratic self-determination.[89]

Critics disparage as unrealistic the role of agreement within the conception of self-determination or self-rule at the heart of deliberative and participatory democratic theories.[90] However, this criticism is blunted for theorists like Dryzek and Warren, who focus on the public sphere as the site for democratic deliberation. More specifically, Warren seeks to show, with admirable detail and theoretical sophistication, how associations enable the individual and political autonomy that together provide a normative consensus grounding the legitimacy of the formal, decision-making institutions of the democratic state. Nevertheless, given the present focus for assessing deliberation not only in the public sphere but also in the state, we must seek a more flexible model of political autonomy that retains the core concern with critical reflection over preferences. To this end, I propose a conception of political autonomy as the capacity for collective choices to be made reflectively, from among a suitably wide range of alternative preferences and constituencies, under conditions suitably free of deception and coercion. This definition gives aggregative and deliberative dimensions to political autonomy. In each case I focus on the autonomous expression of preferences because collective decisions ultimately hinge upon them. Nevertheless, this formulation recognizes that preferences are informed by interests, opinions, perspectives, and world-views, each of which requires critical reflection.

Aggregative autonomy requires that collective choices enable citizens to aggregate their preferences across the widest workable set of alternatives. Recall that preferences can pertain to alternative policies (in direct voting), candidates (in elections), and constitutional provisions (in constituent assemblies). Aggregative autonomy thus reflects the common principle that democracy is incompatible with political processes that restrict the agenda of collective decision-making or the candidates and parties that can compete for election. On the other hand, I emphasize that the set of alternatives must be workable; at some point including more alternatives can actually hinder effective collective decision-making.

In conceiving of aggregative autonomy in light of the specific problems of a plural polity, one must also seek political processes that enable autonomous choice as much as possible, not only over alternatives but also over constituencies. Much recent scholarship is concerned with the validity of "descriptive" representation, where, for instance, Blacks represent Blacks and women represent women.[91] However, this debate incompletely examines the question of political constituency. For example, the debate over the validity of race-conscious districting is sometimes inaccurately depicted as primarily concerning descriptive representation, overlooking those instances where majority-Black districts have elected White representatives.[92] In fact, the creation of majority-Black districts more directly raises issues of political constituency: the collectivity deemed sufficiently politically relevant that it requires distinct representation. In a plural polity with diverse but constructed collective identities, citizens ideally should have some autonomy over which political constituency they prefer. The ability to enhance aggregative autonomy over constituencies, not simply the ability to enhance descriptive representation, commends the proportional and semiproportional electoral systems advocated by several scholars concerned with the political representation of racial and ethnic minorities.[93]

Autonomous choices over alternatives and constituencies, while not devoid of deliberative considerations, should be seen primarily in terms of aggregation. In each case, the availability of multiple alternatives mainly affects the capacity of citizens to aggregate their preferences in different ways. With respect to political alternatives, enhanced aggregative autonomy allows greater choice over the aggregation of preferences in terms of policies, candidates, or constitutional provisions. With respect to political constituencies, it allows for greater choice over the voting coalitions that individuals can enter to support political alternatives.[94] Still, deliberative benefits can result from enhancing aggregative autonomy: for instance, increasing the number of viable candidates may also increase the number of viewpoints included in campaign deliberation. But by including more positions, a political process can improve deliberative equality, not deliberative autonomy. As I will argue below, however, enhancing deliberative equality can, through the equal representation of opposing viewpoints, indirectly enhance deliberative autonomy.

Deliberative autonomy reflects Warren's concern that participants hold critical and reflective preferences. Procedurally, participants must engage in deliberation about preferences under conditions suitably free of misinformation, deception, manipulation, or coercion. Substantively, they must possess the "critical skills" needed to interrogate their own preferences and those of others.[95] The substantive criticism of others' preferences lies at the heart of any deliberative exchange of justifications and criticisms, but substantively criticizing and reflecting on one's own preferences is less intuitive. Nevertheless, such self-criticism is crucial for participants to avoid adaptive preferences whereby they come to prefer only those alternatives that appear likely to be satisfied.[96] By increasing the number of political alternatives, increasing aggregative autonomy seeks to counter adaptive preferences. Yet these preferences often stem from deeper sources, such as a lack of self-respect, a sense of inefficacy, or blind adherence to a world-view that hinders individual or collective aspirations. Sexist, racist, or hierarchical world-views exemplify this last problem when they teach subordinate groups to strive for less than those above them have.[97] In chapter 4, I will examine how some associations can expand their members' critical skills to interrogate their own world-views and develop deliberatively autonomous preferences.

A potential dilemma arises when a disadvantaged group has a sexist, racist, or hierarchical world-view. On the one hand, deliberative autonomy seeks the substantive criticism of self and other that can induce reflection upon such world-views; on the other hand, deliberative autonomy procedurally requires that the legitimate criticism of world-views proceed under conditions suitably free of misinformation, deception, manipulation, and coercion. This is of more than theoretical interest. For instance, several subordinate populations—like some aforementioned Pueblo communities in New Mexico—have world-views that appear and may well be illiberal and hierarchical. Dominant political actors, like the federal government, sometimes use such world-views to justify imposing new political structures upon them. Even if the federal government uses communicative methods to critique such world-views, and even if genuine understanding precedes such critique, power asymmetries between the parties will undermine the legitimacy of this process. Well-grounded criticism of even a prejudicial world-view remains less legitimate, though not entirely illegitimate, if its defenders are dominated within the deliberative process.[98]

The critical issue is to uncover and neutralize forms of power. Citizens can uncover power by realizing when they are being manipulated. In chapter 4, I will examine how certain associations may increase deliberative autonomy by educating citizens to realize when they are being manipulated. However, uncovering relations of power or potential manipulation can also lead them legitimately to eschew deliberation. Thus, in chapter 5 I will examine how voters avoid deliberating with their legislative representatives, as asymmetrical information renders citizens vulnerable to manipulation by legislators. This finding will reveal that deliberative autonomy is an unattainable and thus an inappropriate standard by which to assess competing electoral systems.

As is well documented, most deliberative theorists influenced by Habermas seek to neutralize within communication not only physical but also economic coercion, in the form of both threats and rewards. An alternative form of coercion emerges through the power that well-informed elites, such as policy experts, political officials, or mass media communicators, can exert over a lay public. Benjamin Page and Robert Shapiro suggest that deliberative equality among political elites can indirectly enhance deliberative autonomy by limiting the unilateral persuasive power that a single elite communicator can exert over a lay audience.[99] In chapter 4 I will illuminate how, unfortunately, the insufficient representation of Black perspectives in the media undermines deliberative equality and deliberative autonomy in the public sphere. On the other hand, I suggest in chapter 5 that one electoral system, the alternative vote, can improve deliberative equality without improving aggregative autonomy, by increasing the number of "elective" candidates and parties that contest but rarely win elections. Thus, the alternative vote improves deliberative equality by increasing the number of viewpoints in campaign deliberation, but does not improve aggregative autonomy because the number of candidates or parties likely to gain election does not increase.

More problematic are forms of power that permeate types of communication itself. Bohman points out that experts can exercise power over laypersons through their communicative styles.[100] More emphatically, Young suggests that argumentation embodies a form of cultural power that silences women and some minorities.[101] Young clearly raises an important point. Arguments are won not simply by the force of the better argument but also by the force with which one argues. Conversely, valid points can be overlooked simply because they are tentatively raised, whereas at the extreme, some individuals will be cowed into silence or false agreement because they are intimidated by argumentative speech. We must inquire into how actors can counter cultural power without constraining dialogue.

To do so, one might proscribe argumentative speech within plural deliberation, but this solution falters on two grounds. First, it may violate deliberative equality by excluding certain justifications because it is probably impossible to make a clear distinction between the content of speech and its communicative style. Sometimes, one's true meaning can only be conveyed in a specific way. Second, argumentative speech contributes to the process of criticism grounded in understanding: argumentation is clearly part of the deductive criticism of the opinions, interests, and preferences derived from understanding a perspective or world-view. A blanket condemnation of argumentation within plural deliberation is misguided.

A different response suggests that participants adopt putatively more inclusive modes of speech, such as greeting, rhetoric, narrative, and testimony.[102] There are real benefits to adding these modes of communication, and in chapter 4 I will discuss the role of rhetoric in the civil rights movement. However, these alternative forms of communication also levy certain costs through their monological characteristics. For instance, narrative and testimony could aid understanding by providing detailed portraits of others' perspectives and world-views. This, in turn, can ground the deductive criticism associated with argumentation.[103] However, narrative and testimony, as monological forms of speech, can also ground stereotypes and thus must be subject to the dialogical testing of content. Similarly, rhetoric can get an audience to listen receptively to a communicative contribution by fastening on turns of phrase or types of humor specific to that audience.[104] Yet again, the monological character of rhetoric raises troubling concerns because it typically depicts a relationship between an active speaker and a reactive audience. Young recognizes the well-worn danger that rhetoric can manipulate an audience by distracting it from the content of the speech, but she overlooks how the group-specific cues she admires can effectively exclude outsiders within the audience. Again, the danger of rhetorical manipulation and exclusion requires dialogical checks that allow outsiders and passive audiences actively to affirm or reject the speaker's contributions. Finally, Young advocates greeting as a form of public acknowledgment that welcomes interlocutors as active participants, not passive objects, within public deliberation. Yet, as she admits, greetings can become superficial formalities unless accompanied by deeper recognition within the dialogic exchange of communication. Moreover, given that the unilateral extension of a greeting puts the greeter in a position of vulnerability,[105] greeting becomes a monological submission to the other that generates a power asymmetry unless it is reciprocated.

In each case, including alternative forms of communication can generate potential benefits and costs, and the former will likely outweigh the latter only when the monological aspect of each communicative form confronts a dialogical response or check. Young correctly shows that theorists err by restricting deliberation to rational argumentation, but she herself errs by overlooking the monological characteristics of the modes of speech she advocates. Greeting, rhetoric, narrative, and testimony certainly can serve useful functions within plural deliberation, but the intracommunicative cultural power that undermines deliberative autonomy requires a more holistic and dialogical response. Such a response need not be restricted to formal argumentation, but it must invoke the spirit of political reciprocity.

Political Reciprocity

Political reciprocity is a necessity among participants within deliberative democratic decision-making. It reflects the motivation to exchange communication in order to reach mutually acceptable collective decisions. As a disposition, it cannot directly be generated by institutions, although institutional incentives can indirectly encourage it or at least lessen the obstacles to it. Like political equality and political autonomy, political reciprocity has deliberative and aggregative dimensions. Whereas most deliberative theorists emphasize only the deliberative dimension, aggregative reciprocity can also facilitate legitimate collective decision-making within democratic institutions. But before distinguishing between these dimensions, let me first articulate three characteristics shared by both.

Political reciprocity presupposes the recognition of others as free and equal agents.[106] Free and equal agency grounds the political character of reciprocity by excluding unequal relations like paternalism. The political character of reciprocity also affects the depth of recognition extended between free and equal agents. It must be deeper than the relatively superficial customary reciprocity found in greetings, and yet we cannot expect political participants to extend toward each other full reciprocity, wherein they seek to further each other's self-development.[107] Instead, political reciprocity requires an intermediate level of recognition: participants must acknowledge each other as free and equal agents capable of holding preferences, interests, opinions, perspectives, and world-views, which prima facie could be worthy of respect. Of course, deliberative testing will determine whether such respect is warranted.

Political reciprocity also presupposes that free and equal agents engage in some sort of proportional exchange of goods.[108] In its deliberative dimension, political reciprocity reflects the exchange of reasons that dialogically mitigates the monological dangers within greeting, rhetoric, narrative, and testimony. Yet exchange also manifests itself in the aggregative dimension by distinguishing reciprocity from the unilateral provision of goods in gift giving or the unilateral withdrawal of goods in theft or appropriation. Political reciprocity among free and equal agents additionally requires that such exchanges be proportional: participants give to each other to the extent that others give to them.

Finally, political reciprocity assumes an orientation toward agreement of some sort, whether it be a contract, bargain, understanding, or consensus. Where such an agreement is impossible, participants seek convergence, whereby they minimize the distance that separates them. The orientation toward agreement or convergence is governed by proportional exchange and recognition. Thus, when recognition is denied or exchanges are disproportional, a participant is justified in withdrawing the attempt to reach agreement or convergence. But even when recognition and proportional exchange are forthcoming, such withdrawal may still be justifiable if the institutional setting or relationship between participants does not embody political equality or political autonomy.

Whereas aggregative and deliberative reciprocity share the three characteristics mentioned above, they differ as to the type of recognition involved, the type of goods exchanged, and the type of agreement sought. *Aggregative reciprocity* demonstrates how agents recognize each other as strategically competent: they are not objects or fixed parameters but are intentional, rational actors able to formulate and pursue their preferences and to anticipate and react to the actions of others.[109] With respect to the goods exchanged, aggregative reciprocity requires a proportional exchange of political resources or favors. Such an exchange seeks to secure agreements in the form of contracts, bargains, or coalitions. As a result, aggregative reciprocity does not try to criticize or induce reflection upon agents' preferences, interests, opinions, perspectives, or world-views. Rather, it simply seeks fair conditions enabling actors to construct mutually acceptable contracts, bargains, and coalitions.[110] To the extent that actors do attempt to understand the interests of others, they do so only to gain information regarding whom to engage as allies or adversaries within bargaining and coalition processes.

Deliberative reciprocity focuses on inducing reflection on preferences and their bases through criticism and justification. Thus, with respect to recognition, agents recognize each other as communicatively competent: they are able to pursue preferences but can also reflect upon, justify, and potentially revise those preferences, along with the interests, opinions, perspectives, and world-views that inform them. With respect to the goods exchanged, deliberative reciprocity involves agents in the proportional exchange of criticisms and justifications.[111] Finally, the agreement sought can take the form of common understandings of perspectives or world-views, which can ground deductive criticism, or agreements on mutually acceptable collective decisions. Where such agreements cannot be secured, deliberative reciprocity seeks only critical questioning, convergence that limits disagreement, and mutual attempts to avoid voting cycles. It requires actors who can competently exchange justifications and, perhaps more important, are receptive to criticism.

Dryzek tries to circumvent the need for deliberative reciprocity through his conception of "reflective modernity," which contends that most discourses within late modernity are in crisis and thus open to deliberative critique. However, this claim reflects a dubious generalization from the specific case of environmental discourses. Given that environmental crises threaten the entire globe, cannot be addressed by piecemeal reform, and can be remedied by coordinated human action, environmental discourses are forced to be reflective and engage new inputs from alternative perspectives.[112] The problem is that this example is not necessarily generalizable to other discourses, or, better, to other world-views and perspectives.

For example, much of religious fundamentalism stems from a sense of crisis within late modernity.[113] What differentiates this crisis from environmentalism is that environmental crises reflect a common threat, whereas religious fundamentalism perceives crises imposed by specific threats. Jewish fundamentalists in Israel perceive specific threats from Islam, Islamic fundamentalists perceive specific threats from Judaism and Christianity, and fundamentalists from all three religious world-views perceive specific threats from modern secularism. Similarly, crisis discourses are prominent within ethnic social movements, but here again the threats are likely to come from specific groups rather than a common problem. Although the perception of a common external threat often facilitates interethnic accommodation, this is a contingent factor that need not be met in all plural polities. Common external threats have facilitated intergroup accommodation in the Netherlands and Belgium, but mutually exclusive external threats have exacerbated tensions in Northern Ireland, where Catholics feared the British and Protestants feared the Irish Republic.[114]

The problem of group conflict reveals an important presupposition shared by aggregative and deliberative reciprocity: a threshold level of trust among participants. Indeed, political reciprocity in both dimensions often requires what Jane Mansbridge calls altruistic trust: one party must unilaterally extend recognition, provide goods for exchange, or relax its initial position in order to reach agreement or at least convergence.[115] However, reciprocity further requires that this moment of altruism lead to a process of testing, to see whether the other reciprocates in a proportional manner. Should a proportional exchange not emerge, the initial provider is justified in withdrawing from the relationship, all other things being equal.

Although both dimensions of political reciprocity require trust, the threshold of trust can at times be lower in the aggregative dimension. This is especially so when participants seek only to share information or to signal their intentions to each other, without engaging in the robust process of understanding and criticism associated with plural deliberation. As I shall argue in chapter 3, aggregative reciprocity, in terms of information exchanges, can serve as an important precursor to plural deliberation, by allowing participants to signal to each other that they share common interests or concerns. Perceptions of shared interest can then generate the deeper level of trust needed to exchange justifications and criticisms.

Aggregative and deliberative reciprocity are also important in our judgments of the legitimacy of institutions; deficits in either form can undermine the legitimacy of collective decisions. For instance, aggregative reciprocity requires that individuals and groups experience relatively equal capacities to participate in the bargaining and coalition-building processes of collective decision-making. Should prejudice, resource deficits, or diminished capacities exclude individuals or groups from such processes, they might be fully justified in exiting institutional politics to engage in extrasystemic political action, such as protest or civil disobedience.[116] Similarly, when some actors are not recognized as communicatively competent, or when their justifications or criticisms are systematically ignored, it may be legitimate under plural deliberation for these actors to reject deliberation in favor of nondeliberative, agonistic challenges to the political system. For these reasons, I include both dimensions of political reciprocity in the fairness conditions of plural deliberation.[117]

Of course, measuring deficits in deliberative or aggregative reciprocity again remains difficult. Both dimensions require an equitable distribution of resources, such as communications media for deliberation or exchangeable resources for bargaining. Yet resources alone are insufficient to realize this principle, as some individuals or groups may be less able than others to utilize resources. Again, it is best to assess aggregative and deliberative reciprocity through recourse to capacities, for which some rough indicators are available.[118] In addition, a contextual judgment of outcomes can be used to assess "deliberative uptake," the ability of individuals or groups to have their communicated concerns addressed within the process of deliberation.[119] This could be paired with aggregative uptake, the ability of individuals or groups to have their exchangeable goods accepted by others.

Although measurement problems remain an important issue, the conditions outlined above help to clarify what plural deliberation requires. The disposition of political reciprocity, and perhaps especially deliberative reciprocity, will remain the most important requirement because it can correct for deficits in the other two conditions. However, deficits in political equality and political autonomy also qualify the extent to which political reciprocity is justified. They also clarify which actors bear the burden of remedying these deficits. For example, if certain actors enjoy superordinate positions with respect to political equality or political autonomy but still refuse the demands of deliberative reciprocity, then they bear the burden of justifying their recalcitrance. But if a subordinate group eschews deliberative reciprocity because it lacks political equality or political autonomy, then plural deliberation places a greater burden on more advantaged actors within the political process. If these more advantaged actors have failed to ensure that the process fulfills the deliberative or aggregative conditions of fairness, then they bear the burden of reforming the process in order to enable fair plural deliberation. Political reciprocity is perhaps the crucial condition of fairness; yet its insufficient realization does not mean that plural deliberation does not still exert normative duties upon actors within the process of collective decision-making. Even at its edges, plural deliberation seeks to identify who is more or less justified in rejecting deliberation and who bears greater or lesser burdens for remedying shortcomings in the deliberative process.

PLURAL DELIBERATION AND COMPLEX LEGITIMACY

The preceding discussion of political reciprocity and its limits reveals the dual face of plural deliberation. I introduced plural deliberation as a framework for assessing the legitimacy of democratic institutions that secure collective decisions among members of diverse but fluid collective identities. As such, it is simultaneously affirmative and critical: it clarifies what would count as legitimate democratic processes and institutions for securing collective decisions, but it also clarifies when existing democratic processes or institutions fail the test of legitimacy. In this way, plural deliberation is self-limiting: by clarifying when institutions or processes are illegitimate, it also helps to clarify when actors can legitimately eschew deliberation itself. Thus, the second, critical face of plural deliberation legitimizes nondeliberative practices, like agonistic or activist challenges to existing institutions or processes, wherein actors do not extend deliberative reciprocity to their interlocutors.[120]

Note, however, that plural deliberation justifies agonistic and activist challenges through recourse to its four elements. Nondeliberative challenges are legitimate if the scope of deliberation has been limited through ex ante stipulation, if criticism occurs without understanding perspectives or world-views, if democratic decision-making is not connected to deliberative input, or if deliberation and aggregation occur under unfair conditions. In this way, plural deliberation outlines a complex form of legitimacy, one that makes recourse not to a single criterion, like consent, rational consensus, voting, the resonance between public policy and public opinion, or the realization of fair conditions. Instead, the four elements of plural deliberation together ground judgments of the legitimacy or illegitimacy of institutions of democratic collective decision-making. Assessed through these four elements, complex legitimacy is likely to have four broad implications.

First, agonistic or activist challenges should be a reaction to the failure to realize plural deliberation. Thus, agonists and activists should first test whether plural deliberation is possible prior to withdrawing from deliberative democratic institutions and processes. And when agonists do eschew deliberation, they should retain just enough deliberative reciprocity to communicate why they are withdrawing. In effect, they should justify their withdrawal to those who continue to deliberate.

Second, there are likely to be trade-offs among the four elements of plural deliberation, and especially among the aggregative and deliberative dimensions of political equality, political autonomy, and political reciprocity. Institutions and processes may well satisfy one criterion only by sacrificing another. For example, group-specific associations may enhance the substantive achievement of deliberative equality and deliberative autonomy while undermining deliberative reciprocity across group boundaries. Similarly, some electoral systems may encourage deliberative reciprocity across group boundaries while potentially diminishing aggregative equality. As a result, judgments of legitimacy will fall along a sliding scale. Institutions or processes may fulfill some elements but not others, or some institutions may fulfill more of the elements than other institutions. What complex legitimacy requires are specific judgments of their relative legitimacy.

Such specific judgments lead to the third implication of complex legitimacy: actors must use this framework to determine when, with whom, and within which institutions they engage in deliberation animated by deliberative reciprocity. For example, members of different groups may engage each other deliberatively within those institutions that more fully realize political equality or autonomy, but in a more agonistic or activist fashion within less legitimately structured institutions. Furthermore, though members of disadvantaged groups might legitimately eschew deliberative reciprocity when engaging members of more advantaged groups, they less legitimately do so when engaging members of other disadvantaged groups.[121] The judgments of complex legitimacy that flow from the framework of plural deliberation suggest specific responses to specific situations, involving specific participants within specific institutions. Blanket rejections of deliberation as impossible or unfair within our racist, capitalist society do not sit well with plural deliberation;[122] specific rejections based on unfulfilled elements of plural deliberation are, however, compatible.

These three implications stem from the critical face of plural deliberation. A fourth implication flows from its affirmative face. Plural deliberation not only helps participants assess institutions and processes in light of complex legitimacy: it also provides specifications for reforming processes and redesigning institutions. Of course, the applicability of these criteria will depend upon many contextual questions. And of course, institutional reform cannot expect to fulfill all elements of plural deliberation. Plural deliberation is not a blueprint for utopia. However, it can provide challengers with clearer guidelines to what they seek to achieve and clearer responses to skeptics who resist their advocacy.[123] Hence, by incorporating affirmative and critical faces, plural deliberation can ground concrete political action aimed at securing greater democratic fairness among members of diverse but fluid collective identities.

3
Deliberative Motivations and the Dynamics of Group Conflict

COMMUNICATIVE ACTION, STRATEGIC ACTION, AND DELIBERATIVE RECIPROCITY

From the genocidal terror in Rwanda, to the secessionist wars in the former Yugoslavia, to the Hindu–Muslim riots in India, to the paramilitary battles in Northern Ireland, conflict among groups should chasten any naïve hopes that plural deliberation will be easy to realize. Although careful analysis reveals group conflict to be the exception rather than the norm,[1] its specter still haunts plural deliberation, the success of which depends upon the disposition of deliberative reciprocity. While deliberative reciprocity can ground the process of understanding and criticism, decrease the likelihood of voting cycles, and correct for deficits in the other fairness conditions of political equality and political autonomy, it also requires participants to recognize each other as communicatively competent, to exchange justifications and criticisms, and to seek agreement or at least convergence across differences in world-view, perspective, opinion, interest, or preference. Indeed, it requires a threshold level of trust that the threat of violent group conflict can easily undermine.

The tension between plural deliberation and the threat of group conflict intensifies when deliberative reciprocity is legitimately withdrawn, should democratic institutions, processes, or participants insufficiently realize plural deliberation's broad scope, critical process, connection to decision-making, or fairness conditions. Of course, plural deliberation requires individuals to justify their withdrawal of deliberative reciprocity, and different actors may bear different burdens of justification, depending on the extent to which they enjoy the fairness conditions or other elements of plural deliberation. Moreover, actors must withdraw deliberative reciprocity from specific institutions, processes, and participants. Nevertheless, such withdrawal can be justified via the model of plural deliberation itself.

When actors use the elements of plural deliberation to withdraw deliberative reciprocity and adopt agonistic or activist stances toward specific institutions, processes, or participants, these stances can be understood as deliberatively justified, moral rejections, based on the assessment that one or more of the elements of plural deliberation remains unfulfilled. Such a moral rejection of deliberative reciprocity contrasts with two types of nonmoral withdrawals: an *immoral* rejection reflects a situation in which actors intentionally and opportunistically eschew deliberative reciprocity; an *amoral* rejection reflects a situation in which they would like to extend deliberative reciprocity but are hindered by physical, social, economic, or political circumstances. I describe the second instance as amoral because deliberative reciprocity requires an initial moment of altruistic trust:[2] one actor or set of actors must unilaterally extend recognition, goods, or an orientation toward agreement, rendering them vulnerable to the other's willingness to reciprocate. Should circumstances render the extension of altruistic trust physically, politically, or economically threatening, then withdrawing deliberative reciprocity need not be criticized as immoral. But because the actors do not reject it intentionally, through justifications based on the elements of plural deliberation, this withdrawal is not moral either.

Immoral or amoral rejections of deliberative reciprocity are common problems in plural polities. As recent and widespread instances of group conflict amply illustrate, deliberative reciprocity is not always extended to actors who are perceived to belong to hostile or at least distant collective identities. Where group conflict is possible, some actors immorally reject deliberative reciprocity across group boundaries in order to further the political, economic, or psychological interests of their own or their group. Yet in polities marked by group conflict, some actors also confront situations where they would face real threats were they to extend reciprocity toward members of other groups. Such amoral rejections of deliberative reciprocity may be prompted by extreme situations of anarchy or violent threat or by milder constraints like incomplete information, political risks, or economic uncertainty.

Each type of rejection of deliberative reciprocity requires a distinct political response. An immoral rejection of deliberative reciprocity demands criticism of the opportunistic rejecter. Conversely, an amoral rejection requires not criticism of the rejecter but the reform of processes and institutions in order to lessen the obstacles to deliberative reciprocity. Finally, a moral rejection may require both criticism and reform: agonistic challengers can criticize those participants who fail to uphold the elements of plural deliberation while pressing for concrete reforms to democratic institutions and processes. The problem is to distinguish reliably whether any specific rejection of deliberative reciprocity is moral, amoral, or immoral. Someone might claim that he refuses to extend deliberative reciprocity across group boundaries for moral reasons, like the unfair structure of political institutions, or for amoral reasons, like the fear of physical, economic, or political reprisals, yet his rejection might really stem from immoral prejudices.

One might distinguish the different rejections of deliberative reciprocity through Jürgen Habermas's distinction between communicative and strategic action. Communicative action reflects the orientation toward mutual understanding between two or more actors who seek mutually acceptable agreements that can resolve their conflicts and enable them to pursue their individual preferences.[3] Strategic action reflects the orientation of actors who do not seek to understand each other but simply want to fulfill their individual preferences, while incorporating how others may strategically react to their own actions.[4] Given this distinction, communicative action could reflect how plural deliberators morally accept and agonists morally reject deliberative reciprocity, as such acceptance or rejection could be communicatively justified through recourse to the normative criteria of plural deliberation. This seems to be the position of Iris Marion Young, who defends the unruly and uncivil characteristics of agonistic or activist challenges but nevertheless grounds her approach in Habermasian communicative action.[5] Strategic action, in turn, could depict how actors immorally or amorally reject reciprocity, as such withdrawals do not incorporate communicative or deliberative justification.

However, using the communicative-strategic division to ground this distinction presents several problems. First, it does not deal well with forms of action that mix strategic and communicative characteristics. For example, aggregative reciprocity combines strategic recognition with normative regulations to ensure mutual recognition, proportional exchange, and an orientation toward agreement. Such normative regulations clearly require justification through communicative action and deliberative reciprocity, even though they govern only the aggregative and strategic characteristics of fair bargaining. Second, this distinction does not aid our assessment of institutions. Although some theorists try to associate communicative action with the public sphere and strategic action with the state or the economy, I will argue in chapter 4 that some public sphere actors, like social movements, engage in strategic action in order to deliberate with an extended public, and in chapter 5 I will suggest that electoral systems contain strategic incentives that can be assessed through deliberative criteria. Finally, this distinction does little to guide the institutional reforms necessary to respond to the problem of amoral rejections of deliberative reciprocity. Should circumstances endanger those actors who extend deliberative reciprocity across group boundaries, deliberative democrats would do better to harness or transform strategic dynamics in order to facilitate plural deliberation. Doing so requires recognizing that strategic action can foster plural deliberation, depending upon the institutional or social incentives. Communicative action's orientation toward understanding will remain necessary to achieve plural deliberation's understanding across perspectives and world-views, but it is hardly sufficient. For this reason strategic action and strategic incentives should augment communicative action in order to realize plural deliberation.

In this chapter, I clarify how strategic action can both hinder and enhance plural deliberation. I draw on empirical analyses of intergroup relations to identify five strategic dynamics of group conflict that encourage amoral or immoral rejections of deliberative reciprocity across group boundaries. I then argue that purely deliberative motivations, more closely associated with communicative action, cannot suffice to overcome such dynamics of group conflict. However, I provide an illustrative example to suggest that strategic dynamics can foster either group conflict or plural deliberation, depending on the specific institutional and contextual incentives. I conclude that attention to strategic dynamics can ground four recommendations regarding the means to encourage plural deliberation across group boundaries.

FIVE DYNAMICS OF GROUP CONFLICT

Various empirical analyses suggest that five strategic dynamics can foster conflict among intergenerational groups. The *resource dynamic* depicts group conflict over material goods; the *political dynamic* shows competition over political power; the *positional dynamic* reflects psychological incentives toward conflict based on competing assessments of esteem; the *information dynamic* traces conflict to distorted or incomplete information about other groups; and the *security dynamic* reflects threats of physical harm across group boundaries. Although I describe these incentives as dynamics of conflict, it is important to qualify this characterization in two ways. First, the initial four dynamics need not lead to violent conflict, which typically requires the security dynamic. But even in the absence of violent conflict, these dynamics can hinder deliberation across group boundaries. Second, the initial four dynamics could also foster cooperation among members of diverse groups, depending on how policies, institutions, or social environments structure the incentives facing them. Should these four dynamics be structured to encourage cooperation among groups, they may also support plural deliberation by removing obstacles to extending deliberative reciprocity across group boundaries. Before making this argument, I will first examine the five strategic dynamics of group conflict in greater detail.

The *resource dynamic* traces group conflict to competition over scarce material resources. Closely related to the instrumental, agent-centered mode of identity construction discussed in chapter 1, it assumes that individuals will identify with those groups through which they can secure sources of material goods, such as jobs, state funding, or economic niches. Ethnic or cultural groups are particularly capable of pursuing such resources; these groups are often preexisting and need not be created anew by individual actors. Consequently, ethnic or cultural groups function as especially effective interest groups.[6] However, individuals will act on behalf of such groups only if they overcome the collective action problems associated with the prisoners' dilemma. In a prisoners' dilemma, individuals are enticed to eschew long-term, collective benefits in favor of suboptimal, short-term, individual benefits. Actors most effectively surmount collective action problems when a prisoners' dilemma is transformed into a coordination game, whereby collective action is more strategically attractive than individual deviation from collective action.

The quintessential example of a coordination game is a traffic convention. Driving on the right side of the road in the United States, like driving on the left in Britain, is a self-reinforcing form of collective action. Deviating from this collective action, by driving on the left in America, will immediately lead the deviator to suffer a negative outcome, like a car wreck. Other drivers also have an incentive to enforce the driving convention because they too will suffer from any deviance. Collective action on behalf of racial, ethnic, or cultural groups can be transformed from a prisoners' dilemma into a coordination game through tipping phenomena, which can reflect either economically rational or arational incentives. One economically rational tipping phenomenon can be the presence of large numbers of individuals looting stores during an ethnic riot. This reduces the probability of any single individual being arrested and punished by the police. Another tipping phenomenon occurs when members of a group force other members to act collectively for the group. This makes it more costly to avoid collective action (thereby incurring the wrath of fellow group members) than to participate in collective action (despite its own costs in time, effort, and potential police punishment). One set of noneconomic, arational factors are the selective incentives associated with group membership, such as customs, food, or fellowship. Should an individual fail to act collectively for the group, other members may shun the deviant and withhold such arational, cultural goods. In this way, group coordination enables individuals to overcome collective action problems in order to act for group-specific goals.[7]

According to the resource dynamic, group conflict emerges when action on behalf of common interests shared by a particular group takes the form of a coordination game. This must then be followed by one of two additional scenarios. In the worst-case scenario, interactions with other groups take the form of a zero-sum conflict game, where the number of resources to be divided is fixed and one group can benefit only at the expense of the other. Here, cooperation is highly unlikely. Alternatively, collective action on behalf of common interests shared among groups—like mutually beneficial increases in the overall amount of resources to be divided—takes the form of a prisoners' dilemma, as compared to the coordination game of collective action for group interests. In this scenario, mutually beneficial outcomes are possible among groups, but are hindered by the specific incentive structure that renders collective action in favor of common interests less immediately attractive than collective action in pursuit of group-specific interests.[8]

Notably, proponents of the resource explanation of group conflict argue that a competitive dynamic over scarce resources transforms benign group identification into the chauvinistic attitudes associated with group conflict. Thus, prejudice is depicted as a result, not a cause, of group conflict. Conflict does not result from ethnic hatred and violence: ethnic hatred and violence result from coordination within groups and collective action problems or competition among groups. In this way, a peaceful, multicultural society like Bosnia can degenerate into a cauldron of violent group conflict.[9]

The related but distinct *political dynamic* shows how political elites, like leaders of political parties or social movements, strategically foster group identification and mobilization in order to gain political power. The associated goals may vary, from control over state-run resources to enhancing a group's symbolic status.[10] In any event, the political dynamic may manifest itself in at least three ways. In established, plural democracies, it may take the form of electoral competition among ethnically based political parties or candidates. Here, violence is often associated with electoral campaigns.[11] In transitional polities, it can shape how political elites bargain over alterations in political institutions, such as electoral constituencies or whole electoral systems.[12] Finally, in democratic or nondemocratic polities, the political dynamic may be based in ethnic social movements that seek to capture political power through secessions, armed revolts, or even peaceful, noninstitutionalized bargaining, a phenomenon to be discussed in chapter 4.

In each case, conflict results only if actors overcome collective action problems, like those associated with the resource dynamic. Also common to each case is the flanking strategy, whereby an ethnic party or movement may take a more extreme position along an ethnic political spectrum in order to capture support from a more inclusive party. This may be seen in the political competition between the Hindu nationalist BJP versus the more inclusive Congress Party in India. Alternatively, an extremist faction within a nonelectoral ethnic movement may outflank a more moderate wing, as often occurs among splinter groups aligned with both Nationalist and Unionist movements in Northern Ireland or different factions within the Basque separatist movement in Spain.[13]

The intensity of the political dynamic within electoral politics varies with the electoral system in use. For instance, the single member district plurality (SMDP) electoral systems found in the United States, India, and Great Britain can exacerbate the political dynamic because each constituency contains only one seat, creating a zero-sum competition dynamic among groups within each district. This contrasts with multimember district, proportional representation systems, which can mitigate this zero-sum competition dynamic. In addition, electoral systems that allow voters to choose only one candidate or party, like SMDP and party list proportional representation, increase the efficacy of flanking strategies: an extremist candidate can threaten a moderate's ethnic electoral base, forcing the moderate to adopt a more extreme ethnic position. Preferential voting systems can limit the efficacy of flanking strategies by providing greater incentives for moderate candidates to appeal across group boundaries. I will discuss these issues in greater detail in chapter 5, but for now let us note how electoral institutions can foster or mitigate the political dynamic of conflict.

Political and resource dynamics can clarify certain aspects of group conflict; however, they face two problems. First, each relies upon either a zero-sum conflict dynamic or the predominance of collective action for group interests over collective action in the service of common interests. Yet violent group conflict often results in negative-sum outcomes, whereby all groups are harmed through the destruction of resources or political institutions. Second, each of these dynamics tends to benefit elites disproportionately: ethnic elites tend to gain most from an ethnic group's capture of scarce resources, whereas ethnic political elites gain the power sought within the political dynamic. Thus, the political and resource dynamics do not explain why the followers follow the elites who stand to gain from group-based mobilization. As a result of these two problems, empirical accounts often explain why ordinary actors follow elites through recourse to other strategic dynamics, like the positional dynamic and the information dynamic.

Psychological theories of group conflict are grounded in the *positional dynamic,* which holds that individuals defend the esteem of their personal or collective identities by positioning themselves above the identities of others. For instance, individuals of European extraction may position themselves above those from Asia or Africa by attributing to themselves traits of rationality, civility, culture, or refinement. As discussed in chapter 1, this positional relationship manifests itself in the American racial order, which places Whites at the top, Blacks at the bottom, and Hispanics, Asians, Native Americans, and Jews somewhere in between. Donald Horowitz reveals that such positional relations are not limited to the United States or European countries but can also emerge among Asian and African ethnicities.[14] For present purposes, the most important point is that the positional dynamic provides four reasons followers would follow ethnic elites, even when doing so would be strategically counterproductive according to resource or political dynamics.

First, the positional dynamic locates the motivation for collective action internally, in one's identity, rather than in external goods. Action is motivated by the desire to attribute nonmaterial virtues and vices rather than to accumulate external goods. Second, the relationship between groups and individuals is not instrumental but intrinsic, through the psychological attachment of the individual to the group. Thus, the positional dynamic predicts the relatively easy generation of cooperation within groups and conflict between groups. Third, because gains accrue by positioning one's identity above that of others, there can be no mutually beneficial outcome that induces cooperation among groups. Conflict erupts not just through zero-sum or variable-sum competition over an external, absolute good, which one would seek regardless of the presence of others; rather, it results from a relative-sum interaction, whereby goods exist only to the extent that others are deprived of them. A group's attribution of some virtue to itself comes about only by attributing some relative vice to another group. The positional dynamic thus predicts group conflict and emotive antipathy whenever one group perceives that another threatens the status of its identity. Finally, experimental data suggest that groups acting according to a positional dynamic will prefer to forgo not only mutual gain but even group-specific absolute gains in material rewards, in order to maximize differential gains between groups. As a result, the threatened group will engage in the economically irrational behavior toward outgroups that leads to negative-sum outcomes.[15]

It is worth noting that whereas the resource dynamic is associated with the instrumental-agency mode of identity construction, the positional dynamic can derive from the interpretive modes of identity construction introduced in chapter 1. When someone associates her collective identity with certain cultural virtues relative to the cultural vices associated with other groups, her collective identity has interpretive, not instrumental, significance. So although an interpretive identity might seem morally superior to one valued only for its instrumental costs or benefits, this need not be the case. Consequently, we must reject any simple distinction between morally valid interpretive identities and morally questionable instrumental identities, while also recognizing that collective identities can have interpretive significance without positional rankings.

An alternative explanation for why ethnic followers follow ethnic leaders stems from the *information dynamic,* which suggests that elite and ordinary actors confront different incentives regarding the acquisition and promulgation of information. Ordinary, non-elite actors often confront high costs in acquiring accurate information and thus tend to rely on relatively cheap information. Conversely, because elite actors tend to benefit disproportionately from group-based mobilization, they have strong political and resource incentives to promulgate misleading and conflict-inducing information to non-elites. These divergent information incentives can manifest themselves in two forms.

Some scholars, typically those examining non-American cases of violent ethnic conflict, argue that the information dynamic more readily appears in forms of group-specific communication, like ethnic media or rumors. For instance, they document how Hutu hate radio explicitly encouraged violence against Tutsis in Rwanda, and how Sinhalese newspapers stirred up anti-Tamil sentiments in Sri Lanka. For these scholars, the absence of group-neutral information sources like the American mainstream media ignites the explosion of violent group conflict.[16] Other scholars, examining the information dynamic within the United States, proffer a less sanguine view of the mainstream media. For them, mainstream television, radio, and even elite newspapers like the *New York Times* intensify group conflict surreptitiously, without explicit appeals to violence. Robert Entman and Andrew Rojecki argue that media professionals are influenced by mainstream American culture, which largely rejects biological racism but nevertheless associates certain social problems, like crime, welfare, or poverty, with Black Americans. And because professional norms require journalists to appear politically neutral, they avoid providing contextual information on the causes of Black poverty, crime, or welfare dependency, for fear of appearing too liberal. Furthermore, market incentives lead media executives to seek sensational stories and thus to cover instances of racial violence or race-based policy conflict disproportionately, along with a tendency to use White characters in socially normal roles. Finally, political officials, who may be subject to the political dynamic of group conflict, shape news coverage, either through the content of their speeches or by pressuring newscasters either to cover or suppress certain topics.[17]

In both explicit, group-specific and implicit, mainstream cases, the information dynamic encourages each of the other dynamics of group conflict. It can aggravate the positional dynamic by disseminating positional stereotypes about groups. It can intensify the resource dynamic by emphasizing zero-sum, group-based economic conflicts, as when media devote greater coverage to conflicts over affirmative action than to class-based issues like health care. It can reinforce political dynamics, as when Indian political parties publicize instances of collective violence against groups who are important vote banks, while overlooking similar incidents against politically insignificant groups.[18] Finally, it can promote security dynamics by overemphasizing the potential for violent threats from other groups. In each case, the information dynamic thrives when contrary or disconfirming information is blocked. In the case of explicit, group-specific information dynamics, this occurs when group-specific media gain a monopoly on a group's information, for example when a minority language group is served by only one media outlet. In the case of implicit information dynamics in the mainstream media, contrary information is blocked out through the media's desire to appear neutral and objective, excluding supposedly controversial information that undermines widespread racial stereotypes.

The presence of strategic dynamics of group conflict need not lead to actual violence. Indeed, ethnic competition over resources or political power is often peaceful, even in the midst of information constraints or positional prejudices. The emergence of violent conflict usually requires the initiation of the *security dynamic* in one of two ways. A breakdown of the state's coercive apparatus may create a quasi-Hobbesian state of nature, wherein groups confront each other in a security dilemma. Peaceful interactions may be most beneficial for all groups, but fear of the coercive capacity of another group and the lack of a common police power may lead one group to make a preemptive strike and initiate violent conflict. Russell Hardin believes that this accurately describes the genesis of violence in the former Yugoslavia, where the death of Tito and the economic crises of the late 1980s weakened the coercive, peacekeeping capacity of the Yugoslav state.[19]

On the other hand, the security dynamic can prompt violence without the complete breakdown of the state. This occurs when some groups perceive, often correctly, that the coercive, peacekeeping apparatus of the state—the police force—is not impartial in its treatment of different groups. In this scenario, the disfavored group might choose between two options. Either it may take the law into its own hands by using nonstate means of coercive power, or it may follow the political dynamic to gain power over the state and, in turn, the police. The former strategy describes actions taken by Nationalists in Northern Ireland, whose peaceful civil rights movement turned to the IRA for protection when it appeared that the Royal Ulster Constabulary was favoring Protestants and indiscriminately attacking Catholics.[20] The latter strategy is often adopted by oppressed but numerically dominant caste groups in northern India.[21]

The strategic dynamics of group conflict have strong implications for the extension of deliberative reciprocity across group boundaries. Even if violent group conflict is the exception rather than the norm, these dynamics can undermine the deliberative reciprocity that enables plural deliberation's attempts to achieve understanding across group boundaries. However, most deliberative theorists addressing problems of pluralism rarely confront this problem. And to the extent that they do, they tend to focus only on the positional dynamic, given its resemblance to the American problem of racial prejudice. Although the positional dynamic clearly can promote violent conflict and undermine deliberative reciprocity among groups, examining this dynamic without considering the others can lead to misleading conclusions.

For example, Iris Marion Young attributes group conflict in Yugoslavia to the positional dynamic, or "difference as otherness." Yet her analysis fails to explain the genesis of this dynamic among groups which, she admits, were until recently relatively equal in terms of social power and had a weak sense of group identity.[22] Hardin's analysis of this case through recourse to the resource, information, and security dynamics provides a more thorough and convincing portrait.[23] Moreover, these dynamics of conflict are not only present in established but poor democracies, like India, or transitional societies, like the former Yugoslavia; they can also emerge in wealthy, established democracies like the United States. Of course, anarchic civil wars will be less likely in a wealthy, established state. But even absent full-fledged ethnic civil wars like those found in the Balkans, Sri Lanka, or Rwanda, conflict dynamics other than the positional dynamic can hinder plural deliberation across group boundaries.

The security dynamic can hinder plural deliberation and lead to violence when White police bias is exercised against racial minorities, as exemplified in the 1965 Watts riot and the 1992 Los Angeles riot.[24] Notably, problems of police bias can also occur among minority groups, for instance when Black police officers used excessive violence on Latinos in Compton, California, or Washington, DC.[25] Security dynamics can also intensify when police forces fail to step into areas of potential violence. The clearest example of this occurred during the 1992 Los Angeles riots, when the LAPD diverted its personnel from South Central, Pico-Union, and Koreatown in order to protect wealthy, predominantly White areas. When Korean storeowners realized that the police were not responding to their calls, they organized their own informal security networks to defend their property and lives against security threats leveled by predominantly Black and Latino rioters.[26]

As is well documented, a resource dynamic involving competition over manufacturing jobs provided incentives for immigrant Whites to riot against Black workers at the turn of the century.[27] Paula McClain and Joseph Stewart argue that resource competition in the United States can foster "some aspects of the discrimination experienced by minorities," along with hostility and distrust among working class minorities.[28] For instance, aggregate data suggest that Hispanics tend to suffer economically in cities with Black majorities or pluralities, although Blacks do not suffer in Hispanic-dominated cities.[29] This problem is illustrated through a detailed case study of Hartford, Connecticut, which revealed Puerto Rican resentment over African-American control over antipoverty and affirmative action programs.[30] Similarly, resource dynamic tensions emerged in Los Angeles over resistance to bilingual education among African-American leaders, who feared that emphasizing this problem would distract from struggles for school desegregation,[31] and in housing competition between Caribbean immigrants and Lubavitcher Jews in the Crown Heights neighborhood of Brooklyn.[32] Finally, Black resentment over Asian economic power emerged in Los Angeles both in opinion polling, where more Black respondents felt threatened by Asian than by White economic power, and in the targeting of Korean businesses during the 1992 riots.[33]

Political dynamics of conflict emerge on many levels. Perhaps most infamous are the electoral incentives that supported racial segregationists during the 1960s. In Georgia, elected school superintendents were more likely than their appointed counterparts to resist integration decrees.[34] In Arkansas, electoral incentives led Governor Orval Faubus, a man who once boasted of integrating government services and of sending his son to an integrated school, to adopt a militant segregationist stance in response to the flanking maneuvers of right-wing opponents during his third term.[35] Electoral incentives continue to foster anti-Black and anti-immigrant campaigns today,[36] but they can also encourage conflict among nonWhite groups. For example, aggregate data reveal that Hispanics suffer acute losses in political representation in cities with Black majorities or pluralities, a clear reflection of the political dynamic's key insight that SMDP elections can foster zero-sum competition over seats.[37] Cruz fleshes out this dynamic in his study of Hartford, where the fact that African Americans were "simultaneously powerful and oppressed" led to their political dominance over Puerto Ricans. Because African Americans had come to Hartford earlier and had a longer and more tormented history of suffering, African-American political elites felt justified in using their demographic strength to make Puerto Rican aspirants wait their turn for political power.[38] The drawing of electoral districts can itself foster the political dynamic of conflict, as exemplified in two Brooklyn cases involving Hasidic Jews. In one instance, Hasidim in the Williamsburg neighborhood contested the creation of a majority-Black district that divided the Hasidic population between two districts.[39] In a counterexample, Caribbean immigrants came to resent the creation of the majority-Lubavitcher Community Board 9 in Crown Heights.[40]

Finally, Los Angeles examples reveal surprising shifts in coalitions caused by political dynamics. In one case, African Americans and Mexicans fought for control of the ninth city council district, whose population was evenly split between the two groups. When an African-American candidate defeated a Mexican candidate for the seat, this ushered in a twenty-three-year period without Mexican representation in the Los Angeles city council.[41] More recently, the 2001 mayoral election revealed a curious coalition of African Americans, Asians, and White conservatives supporting James Hahn, a White candidate. This coalition was formed through Hahn's strong family ties to African-American struggles in the city and his political ads depicting the Hispanic candidate, Antonio Villaraigosa, as soft on crime. The potentially prejudicial ads attracted White conservatives and did not repel African Americans, but they did lead White liberals, especially Jews, to join Mexicans in supporting Villaraigosa.[42] Such Black-Hispanic political dynamics have even appeared in debates over possible reforms to the Los Angeles city council electoral system, with Hispanics favoring a proportional representation system to enhance their political clout and Blacks favoring the existing SMDP system in order to maintain the gains they achieved since the 1960s.[43]

Of course all of these dynamics, along with positional stereotypes, can be intensified by information dynamics within both group-specific and mainstream media. I will delay addressing American cases of this problem until chapter 4, where I discuss how the information dynamic of group conflict affected the public sphere in three cases: the 1990 "Red Apple" boycott of two Korean-owned stores in New York city; the 1991 shooting of a Black teenager, Latisha Harlins, by a Korean merchant, Soon Ja Du, in Los Angeles; and the 1991 Crown Heights riot involving Lubavitcher Hasidic Jews and Caribbean immigrants in Brooklyn. For now, I will simply point out that the presence of all five dynamics of conflict within a wealthy, established democracy like the United States should prompt greater concern among deliberative theorists. For even though these theorists realistically restrict the domain of deliberation to established democracies with institutionalized communication rights and a modern moral and political culture,[44] the dynamics of group conflict within such a democracy can nevertheless undermine plural deliberation. The fact that Bosnians negotiate with each other while Quebecers talk to each other is truly not a trivial difference.[45] But this difference may become blurred when we examine interactions among racial or ethnic groups in urban America.[46]

DELIBERATIVE MOTIVATIONS

The dynamics of group conflict provide strategic incentives which, even in the absence of violent conflict, can hinder robust plural deliberation. Nevertheless, one might argue that a strategic dynamic might instead motivate plural deliberation, as the costs of actual or potential conflict might outweigh the costs of deliberating with members of different collective identities. Clearly, calculations of such costs often prompt limited communication among groups, primarily in the form of aggregative bargaining processes. I will defend the real importance of such processes in the last section of this chapter. But as noted in chapter 2, bargaining processes require aggregative reciprocity, wherein actors reciprocally recognize only the strategic agency to formulate and pursue preferences and interests, seek only minimal agreements on mutually beneficial outcomes, and exchange only resources, threats, or information needed to build coalitions or confront adversaries. Aggregative reciprocity will not suffice to ground plural deliberation's robust process of understanding and criticizing preferences, interests, opinions, perspectives, and world-views. Instead, this process requires deliberative reciprocity and its recognition of communicative competence, its proportional exchange of justifications and criticisms, and its orientation toward agreement in the form of understanding, consensus, or convergence. Deliberative reciprocity thus requires distinct, deliberative motivations. Deliberative theorists have outlined four of these: moral psychology, cultural self-understandings, publicity constraints, and the deliberative generation of trust.

Moral philosophers and psychologists agree that individuals wish to consider themselves morally upright. According to Habermas and other deliberative theorists, the desire to be moral manifests itself in the requirement for moral impartiality. An impartial, moral point of view accepts only those norms that could be justifiable to all those affected by it.[47] Whereas the legitimacy of such norms can only be grounded through direct deliberation, the impetus to deliberate comes from the moral awareness that deliberation is needed. Thus, an impartial moral consciousness precedes direct deliberation through the imaginative sense of moral empathy found within internal-reflective deliberation.[48] Although in chapter 2 we noted the dangers of moral empathy without direct deliberation, we also acknowledged that problems of scale might require its usage, albeit with direct deliberative affirmation or correction. Here, we must also note how moral empathy can motivate deliberation itself, even when its flawed content requires deliberative correction.

Unfortunately, when moral impartiality is grounded in empathy, individuals sometimes misconstrue the perspectives of others, thereby hindering the desire to understand them. Consider the following problem. Most White Americans consider biological racism to be morally wrong. However, most Whites tend to have little direct contact with Blacks, have little direct information about racial discrimination, and thus tend to deny or discount its prevalence. Moreover, Whites get most of their information about Blacks from the media, which subtly associate Blacks with social pathologies like welfare, poverty, and crime. The result of combining the moral rejection of racism, the denial that racism persists, and the pathological media portrait of Blacks is a decline in White empathy toward Blacks. Instead, many Whites adopt attitudes of racial ambivalence and animosity, intermediate racial attitudes that lie between biological racism and harmonious interracial reciprocity.

Racial ambivalence reflects a moderate fear of Black political power and a moderate reluctance to admit the persistence of racial discrimination, countered by a willingness to acknowledge the existence of racism when confronted with direct empirical evidence. Racial animosity reflects more intense denials of racial discrimination and fears of Black political power. Moderate racial ambivalence can be tipped into intense animosity through information dynamics, like the media's coverage of Black crime, or political dynamics, like campaign ads that seek to trigger racial animosity.[49] As Entman and Rojecki conclude, "animosity tends to be associated with Whites' rejection of open-minded deliberation on racial inequality as a high priority public policy problem."[50] In other words, racial animosity hinders deliberative reciprocity on racially contentious issues, despite the moral-psychological rejection of biological racism.

A second deliberative motivation provided by deliberative theorists pertains to the cultural self-understandings of a modern world-view. A modern cultural world-view elevates the universalistic and impartial moral point of view above other conceptions of morality that restrict moral justification only to a select few, say a hierarchical caste or a specific cultural, ethnic, or religious group. According to deliberative theorists, the normative self-understanding of modern cultures prompts individuals to reach beyond their specific group and attempt to include the other within the process of moral dialogue. Thus, actors within modern cultures come to justify their norms across group boundaries via cultural motivations grounded in socialization patterns, institutions, and social practices.[51]

This set of motivations might prompt plural deliberation across group boundaries; yet its strength depends upon the specific self-understanding of a given modern culture. For instance, Rogers Smith notes that American political culture has floated between more liberal-universalistic and more particularistic, ascriptive self-understandings, the latter of which clearly coheres with the positional dynamic of group conflict. He cautions Americans against thinking that the former self-understanding would inevitably emerge victorious. Instead, specific social and political conditions have allowed the liberal-universalistic self-understanding to triumph at certain times and the particularistic, ascriptive, positional self-understanding to triumph at others.[52] In a more detailed, historical analysis, Philip Klinkner and Rogers Smith argue that steps to include Blacks as full citizens in the United States have only succeeded when three conditions were met: the United States was involved in a large war that required significant African-American support, the ideological character of the enemy required Americans to emphasize their egalitarian traditions, and domestic protest movements pressured American leaders to live up to their egalitarian ideals.[53] These analyses reveal that the motivating power of modern cultures remains empirically indeterminate: motivations toward moral universality depend upon contingent social and political conditions. Consequently, this motivational basis for plural deliberation might itself require support through independent social, political, or institutional factors.

Indeterminacy also undermines the deliberative motivations within publicity constraints. As I noted in chapter 2, the capacity for public actors to win political debates in the public sphere is constrained by the nature of the public addressed. Ideally, such a public should be active and extended. An active public is one that energetically judges the contributions of public actors, rather than passively viewing or listening to such contributions. An extended public is one that is unrestricted and includes a variety of different groups with divergent perspectives and world-views. Where public actors face an active and extended public, their contributions are unlikely to gain support if they cannot appeal beyond their own particular group. Thus, an active and extended public will ideally motivate public actors to proffer justifications and criticisms that are acceptable to anyone within that public.[54] In chapter 4, I will examine how the ideal of an extended public exists in tension with the ideal of an active public: as a public becomes more extended, its increased size and reliance on mass media may reduce it to a passive audience. For now, I wish to circumvent that issue in order to assess the motivational indeterminacy within publicity constraints even where the ideal of an active and extended public is realized.

First, we must note that publicity constraints work through the emergence of public norms that an extended public uses to rule out certain contributions proffered by various political actors. In the United States, at least two public norms are prominent within public deliberation: those proscribing self-interested claims and those requiring racial equality. Jon Elster elaborates on this theme, arguing that even if self- or group-interested policy proposals are justified insincerely through appeals to common interests, these justifications will still constrain the range of self- or group-interested policy positions and render them testable after adoption. In this way, publicity constraints against self-interested policies impose the "civilizing effects of hypocrisy" upon political actors.[55] In addition, Tali Mendelberg demonstrates that over the course of the twentieth century, and especially since the civil rights movement, a norm of racial equality has come to govern American political discourse.[56] The upshot of these two norms is that public actors are constrained in the types of communicative contributions they can publicly profess.

In the context of plural deliberation, however, these norms can have mixed effects. On the one hand, the norm of racial equality prohibits the explicitly racist political appeals so common prior to the civil rights movement. On the other hand, the norm of racial equality can reduce itself to a shallow requirement to use "colorblind talk,"[57] whereby actors who have positional prejudices against certain groups mask their biases under formally neutral language. For instance, politicians can make implicit racist appeals by focusing on issues like crime or welfare that stereotypically apply to Black Americans. Mark Warren argues that the mere threat of exposure can force public actors to act in more responsible and trustworthy ways,[58] but this threat cannot counteract implicit racial appeals; these openly circulate within public discourse.

Alternatively, colorblind talk, combined with racial animosity or ambivalence and prohibitions against self-interest, can lead to the unreflective rejection of justifications for affirmative action. When Blacks speak out in favor of affirmative action, they may appear to be self-interested violators of racial equality, as Whites may deny the empirical persistence of racism. This is not to say that affirmative action is necessarily justified; it only suggests that publicity constraints and public norms can perversely distort deliberation over affirmative action. Although criticisms of affirmative action clearly have their place within plural deliberation, ideally these criticisms should incorporate accurate understanding across White and Black perspectives and should reflectively engage justifications for preferential policies.

At this point, Elster could respond that critics of affirmative action would be even more subject to the civilizing effects of hypocrisy because they claim to act for the public interest. However, testing various critiques of affirmative action would require accurate information, which is precisely what the information dynamic of conflict hinders. Ordinary citizens may confront disincentives to gaining information from more inclusive sources and instead refer only to misleading, group-specific sources. Conversely, elite actors may experience strong motivations, based on the resource or political dynamics, to provide misleading information or to promulgate positional stereotypes about members of other groups. This danger is especially relevant to group-specific publics. Nancy Fraser argues that such "subaltern publics" help disadvantaged groups to communicate more effectively and fairly within the broader public sphere. However, a critic might fear that these may degenerate into segmented, group-specific media markets susceptible to strategic manipulation by ethnic elites. Fraser is aware of this problem and conceptually distinguishes inclusive subaltern publics from exclusive subaltern enclaves,[59] but she does not explain how actors within subaltern publics are motivated to remain inclusive amidst the information and positional dynamics of conflict, which not only lessen the efficacy of publicity constraints, but also hinder a fourth deliberative motivation, the deliberative generation of trust. According to Mark Warren, deliberation can facilitate altruistic trust through four mechanisms: it can challenge positional stereotypes through alternative narratives that do not demonize the other; it can enable actors to justify actions that otherwise may appear as betrayals of trust; it can enlarge and transform perspectives, enabling participants to discover common interests and identities; and it can force speakers to recognize each other reciprocally.[60] Taken separately, the information and positional dynamics can obstruct all of these positive characteristics of deliberation. Inaccurate group-specific information sources can propagate rather than counter positional stereotypes, can exacerbate rather than allay perceptions of betrayed trust, and can emphasize conflicting rather than shared interests and identities. In turn, well-established positional stereotypes can prevent individuals from recognizing the communicative competence of members of other groups.

Nevertheless, Warren's account contains three redeeming characteristics that emerge if we slightly alter his formulations. First, his discussion of enlarged and transformed perspectives accedes that "the incentives for those transformational processes stem from the pressures for collective action within institutions that mitigate non-discursive influences such as coercion and money."[61] This realization reveals the important role of institutions in providing incentive structures that can foster deliberation across group boundaries. Warren notes only that these institutions should be insulated from "coercion and money," two factors that undermine deliberative autonomy. However, I would emphasize that such institutions might also include specific incentives that encourage plural deliberation across group boundaries.

Second, in discussing reciprocal recognition, Warren points out that even "in the limiting case of war, this dynamic is one reason why diplomats place such importance on getting the belligerents to talk."[62] Although Warren is right to emphasize the value of getting belligerents to talk, he incorrectly suggests that such talk constitutes deliberation, rather than the less demanding communication involved in bargaining. Indeed, most war negotiations do not seek full deliberative understanding and criticism but merely to generate information needed to find common interests. As such, what Warren describes is not the recognition of communicative competence associated with deliberative reciprocity but the recognition of strategic competence indicative of aggregative reciprocity. He conflates aggregative and deliberative reciprocity; distinguishing these dimensions suggests that aggregative reciprocity, even under conditions of war, can be a useful precursor to full deliberation. I shall return to this point at the end of this chapter and again in chapter 4.

Finally, Warren's general argument suggests that the deliberative generation of trust is a reinforcing motivation. Deliberation might not always be able to self-start, but once started it can beget more deliberation by providing improved, more accurate information and by providing real examples of reciprocal relationships. As discussed in chapter 2, plural deliberation seeks to induce reflection upon perspectives and world-views through open-ended, critical questioning, even when full understanding and deductive criticism remain unachieved. In this way, the critical process of plural deliberation tries to enable further deliberation, which might ground more concrete understandings, criticisms, agreements, and points of convergence. Within such an ongoing process, reinforcing motivations can play a crucial role.

I suggest that the deliberative generation of trust, along with the other deliberative motivations, functions most effectively as a reinforcing motivation. In ongoing deliberation, deliberatively generated trust, publicity constraints, modern cultural understandings, and moral psychology can motivate greater deliberation. Such reinforced deliberation can gradually mitigate the information dynamic of conflict, thereby subjecting positional stereotypes to deliberative critique. Because deliberative reciprocity cannot be generated by strategic incentives alone, reinforcing deliberative motivations will remain crucial to the success of plural deliberation.

However, strategic incentives, such as security threats, political calculations, and resource competition, can still bring a self-reinforcing deliberative process to a halt. For this reason, plural deliberation requires institutional designs that can mitigate strategic dynamics of conflict and provide positive incentives for deliberation across group boundaries. As I stated earlier, the term dynamics of group *conflict* is somewhat misleading. Indeed, these strategic dynamics might actually help some individuals or groups engage in plural deliberation, depending on the social and institutional incentives. The dynamics of conflict need not affect all actors in a plural polity equally, and strategic dynamics need not affect them uniformly. Some strategic dynamics will hinder deliberative reciprocity across group boundaries, whereas others may actually aid it. Before addressing institutional designs and public policies aimed at mitigating the dynamics of conflict, I first wish to present a short case study that will provide a more fine-grained understanding of how they affect plural deliberation.

PLURAL DELIBERATION AMIDST THE DYNAMICS
OF GROUP CONFLICT: AN ILLUSTRATION

The reception of African-American civil rights claims within the Jewish-American public sphere from 1915 to 1935 is a clear example of how the strategic dynamics of group conflict affect the capacity of actors to deliberate across group boundaries. This Jewish-American public sphere was anchored in Jewish labor and cultural organizations and Yiddish and English-language newspapers, primarily in northern cities. Although this public consisted of divergent ideological perspectives, from socialist to conservative, its leadership clearly perceived itself as catering to a Jewish audience. For example, the Yiddish press was accessible only to a Jewish clientele, whereas the English press perceived its role as carrying specifically Jewish information overlooked by the mainstream press. Yet despite a group-specific orientation, this public displayed deliberative reciprocity aimed at understanding Black perspectives and interests.

First, unlike many group-specific media sources, such as Hutu hate-radio in Rwanda or Sinhalese newspapers in Sri Lanka, Jewish newspapers and organizations of this era did not simply concern themselves with mobilizing their own group to press strategically for their own interests. Instead, actors within this public reached out beyond their narrow group perspectives in order to engage African-American perspectives. Jewish newspapers displayed an ongoing interest both in the obstacles faced by African Americans and in their intellectual, artistic, and political achievements. Jewish newspapers reported on meetings of African-American political organizations. Leading African-American intellectual and political leaders, such as the scholar-activist W. E. B. DuBois and the labor leader A. Phillip Randolph, often addressed Jewish organizations. In this way, these civil society organizations arguably supported a group-specific, universalistic subaltern public, as opposed to an exclusive enclave.[63]

Second, this deliberative orientation was critical, challenging the prevalent frameworks of American race relations. Jewish spokespersons criticized the harsh, unjust treatment of African Americans and the positional belief of White racial superiority. More strikingly, Jewish newspapers would often criticize anti-Black racism among Jews themselves. This self-critical stance was maintained amidst evidence of Black anti-Semitism, with the Jewish press attempting to prevent a Jewish backlash against such sentiments.[64]

Third, communication within this public aimed at recognizing African Americans as viable and competent communicative partners, although the extent of such recognition is questionable. On the one hand, Jewish organizations invited participation from African-American speakers, and Jewish newspapers clearly recognized African Americans as deserving of full civil and political rights. Yet on the other hand, some Jewish figures may have conflated understanding the African-American perspective with projections of their own perspective. This is exemplified by the tendency to portray the African American as America's equivalent to the persecuted European Jew. Indeed, although moral empathy may have prompted Jews, many of whom had recently fled persecution in Europe, to open themselves to African-American concerns, it ironically may have clouded their ability to understand them clearly. For example, Jewish philanthropists advised Blacks to adopt the Jewish practice of creating separate, group-specific institutions like hospitals, neglecting to recognize how African Americans might interpret this advice in light of legal segregation.[65]

Still, in comparison with the mainstream press and public culture of the time, the level of recognition accorded to African Americans was striking. It is worth examining how the Jewish public sphere adopted deliberative reciprocity across group boundaries and how certain obstacles constrained it. The dynamics of group conflict shed some light on this issue. Group-specific media sources may have helped many Jewish Americans overcome the information dynamic. However, this still begs the question of why these group-specific media sources generated a public receptive to African-American issues, rather than an enclave. The key, I think, lies in the positional and security dynamics faced by Jewish Americans at this time, dynamics that affected Jews differently in the North and the South.

Many northern Jews of this era did not feel fully "White." The perception of permanent foreignness and the presence of broader anti-Semitism hindered them from partaking in the positional dynamic that existed between Whites and Blacks. Yet in important ways, this public sphere did interpret Jewish identity in a positional manner that fostered positive relations with Blacks. The Jewish public sphere interpreted Jewish identity as negotiating a fine line between assimilation into and rejection of the broader American culture. Having fled persecution in Europe, most Jews wished to find a home in America and could not reject its culture entirely. Nevertheless, they were also afraid to lose their distinct identity. Thus, they had to construct a culture within a culture. But the interpretation of Jewish culture within this public sphere was strikingly positional: Jewish culture was perceived as morally superior to mainstream American culture. Indeed, the Jewish press often attributed Jewish racism to the inculcation of un-Jewish, mainstream ideas. By championing African-American causes, the Jewish public sphere could proclaim the Jews as America's "chosen people," those who understood and internalized American ideals of equality and justice more fully than other Americans.[66]

This positional interpretation of Jewish identity in turn helped to shape the northern Jewish perception of the security dynamic. Clearly, the resource dynamic stimulated tensions between Jewish merchants and African-American workers, and this sometimes led to security dynamics and violence between these groups.[67] But while northern Jews were aware of this, they perceived a stronger security threat from non-Jewish Whites. The 1915 Atlanta lynching of Leo Frank, a Jewish businessman charged with raping a White woman, impressed upon northern Jewish newspaper editors the common security threat that a biased, White criminal justice system posed to both Jews and Blacks. In this way, criticizing the treatment of Blacks by civil authorities could help Jews protect themselves from similar abuse.[68]

However, the positional and security dynamics had significantly different effects on southern Jews. Their geographic proximity to the Frank trial and lynching may have intensified their perception of the security threat. Leonard Dinnerstein notes that when northern Jewish organizations attempted to aid in Frank's legal defense, non-Jewish Southerners reacted with virulent anti-Semitism. This reaction led many southern Jews to attempt to assimilate more deeply into the White, southern mainstream.[69] A similar dynamic arose during the Scottsboro trial, when nine African-American boys were prosecuted for allegedly raping two White women. While many northern Jewish individuals and organizations strongly supported the boys, many southern Jews remained wary. Indeed, when Rabbi Benjamin Goldstein of Montgomery publicly voiced his support for the boys, his congregation forced him to resign.[70] Dinnerstein concludes that, although most southern Jews may have privately supported African-American causes, the security dynamic forced them to remain publicly silent on these issues and to go along with the mainstream.[71] As a result, publicity constraints, deformed by unfavorable security dynamics, hindered rather than motivated plural deliberation between Blacks and Jews in the South.

A positional dynamic may also have hindered deliberation between Jews and Blacks. Several scholars suggest that southern Jewish identity became incorporated into the broader southern White identity.[72] Diverse factors may have contributed to this assimilation. It is highly plausible that the security dynamic hindered the assertion of a distinct Jewish identity. On a more benign level, White southerners might have simply perceived Jews as a distinct religious subgroup, with a social status similar to that of Presbyterians or Methodists within predominantly Baptist White communities. Alternatively, the Old Testament foundations of southern, White, Christian fundamentalism might have generated a level of "philo-Semitism," which may have helped to incorporate southern Jews into the White mainstream.[73] As a result, a distinct southern Jewish identity was less able to support the morally superior positional dynamic that bolstered Jewish identification with African-American concerns in the North. Instead, like the Mississippi Chinese discussed in chapter 1, southern Jewish identity may have been incorporated into the broader White identity, thereby reinforcing the dichotomous White versus Black positional dynamic.

The end result was that the positional and security dynamics discouraged southern Jews from publicly supporting African-American civil rights, whereas different security and positional dynamics had the opposite effect on their northern coreligionists. It is important to emphasize that there need not have been anything intrinsic to Jewish identity that fostered these divergent regional approaches to African-American issues. Nor should we assume any essential transcendent connection between these groups. Instead, I believe that different strategic dynamics in the North and the South shaped the capacity of Jews to adopt deliberative reciprocity toward African Americans.

We should emphasize that strategic dynamics led to divergences not only between southern and northern Jews of this era but also among other Jewish subgroups. For instance, Michael Rogin uses the positional dynamic to argue that many Jews within the entertainment sector sought to gain acceptance into the White identity precisely by denigrating African Americans.[74] Alternatively, James Glaser notes that older Jews tend to perceive themselves as an out-group in relation to mainstream White society and thus are more likely to empathize with and support African-American civil rights issues. Younger Jews, however, tend to feel more assimilated into White society. As a result, they have a weaker sense of out-group identity and extend less support to African-American concerns.[75] In a similar vein, Karen Brodkin argues that the position of Jews throughout the country changed following the Second World War. The war against Nazi Germany had undermined the public acceptability of anti-Semitism, and a wave of philo-Semitism spread across an American society eager to distance itself from a former enemy. This, along with Jewish economic mobility and laws segregating Blacks but not Jews, allowed the Jews to cease being an off-White race and instead to become "White folks."[76] These examples suggest that the strategic dynamics affecting Jewish-Black deliberation can vary according to region, economic sector, generation, and historical era. Thus, the development and the motivating power of a collective identity that crosses the positional dynamic of group conflict is a contingent factor that may wax or wane, depending on social and political factors.

MITIGATING OR TRANSFORMING THE DYNAMICS OF CONFLICT

Earlier, I argued that plural deliberation presupposes deliberative reciprocity's orientation toward understanding across group boundaries. I also argued that four deliberative motivations, commonly thought to support deliberative reciprocity, cannot always overcome the five dynamics of group conflict. However, my analysis of the Jewish public sphere suggests that specific strategic dynamics might not only constrain but might also enable different actors to extend deliberative reciprocity across group boundaries. It also suggests that deliberative motivations may sometimes undermine communication across group boundaries. Consistent with Iris Marion Young's concerns, inaccurate moral empathy led some actors in the Jewish public sphere to overlook Black concerns about creating separate Black institutions. In addition, the security dynamic deformed publicity constraints, thereby hindering southern Jews from adopting the deliberative reciprocity toward Blacks that characterized their northern coreligionists. While the problem of inaccurate empathy may be corrected through plural deliberation, deformed publicity constraints might not be. This leads me to proffer four suggestions for fostering plural deliberation across group boundaries by attending to strategic dynamics among groups.

    First, attention to the strategic dynamics of conflict can help to identify which actors, groups, or social movements are best situated to extend deliberative reciprocity across group boundaries. For example, the information dynamic does not equally affect all actors in a plural polity. Thomas Christiano notes that some actors, generally middle- or upper-class white-collar workers, face fewer obstacles than others in gaining information.[77] In a plural polity, these actors may be better able to gain viable information about the interests and perspectives of groups other than their own. They could also more easily gain information on common interests across group boundaries. This reasoning is illustrated by the way activists in the American civil rights movement targeted elite "conscience constituencies," who enjoyed greater access to information.[78]

Circumventing the information, political, and economic dynamics within plural polities is central to designs for postconflict reconciliation, which emphasize the role of "middle level actors," such as respected intellectuals or religious leaders. These actors are less constrained than the masses by the information dynamic, and they are also less constrained than politicians and businesspeople by the political and resource dynamics.[79] Thus, they may more easily gain and disseminate information regarding the means and utility of mitigating group conflict, in order to facilitate deliberative understanding and criticism across perspectives. Still, the capacity of middle-level actors to foster reconciliation depends upon whether they perceive themselves as transcending positional group identities. If such actors perceive their identities as firmly entrenched within the positional dynamic, they may be more likely to use their capacity to acquire and promulgate information to foster group animosity. For example, some Indian Hindu intellectuals fostered anti-Muslim sentiments by providing misleading historical information about disputed religious sites, such as the Babri Masjid in Ayodhya.[80] Thus, we should also examine which actors are most likely to overcome the positional dynamic.

As the case of the Jewish public sphere suggests, not all group identities are equally affected by the positional dynamic of conflict. Especially as we recognize the internal diversity of constructed collective identities as discussed in chapter 1, we can discover which identities may cut across positional group dynamics in order to undermine conflict. Because gender clearly crosses group boundaries, and because female identity often suffers from negative positional stereotypes, women can sometimes play a mediating role in ethnically defined group conflict. Research shows that women are disproportionately represented within North American "antiracist" organizations. Furthermore, many White female antiracists tend to experience double stigmatization, by being either Jewish or lesbian. Because female, Jewish, and lesbian identities occupy a positional status that does not fully cohere with the Black-White positional dynamic, these actors may develop greater moral empathy toward racial minorities.[81] As the case of the Jewish public sphere highlights, intergenerational identities can also cut across positional group boundaries. The Yoruba were able to mediate Muslim–Christian tensions over Sharia law in Nigeria in the late 1970s because their regional, ethnic identity crossed this religious division. Note, however, that their ability to mediate conflicts would diminish regarding purely regional or ethnic tensions.[82]

Yet as tensions among different American minority groups demonstrate, simply being nonWhite is insufficient for generating deliberative reciprocity among minority groups. We must carefully examine the specific attitudes and interests expressed among different collective identities. We should realize that full deliberative reciprocity, and especially the receptivity to criticism, might develop slowly, even among groups that share common interests. Thus, a second suggestion is to encourage aggregative reciprocity among groups with similar interests. Recall that aggregative reciprocity requires only the strategic recognition of freedom and equality, the proportional exchange of resources or favors, and an orientation toward the minimal agreement associated with bargaining or coalition formation. Of course, communication will be necessary within bargaining and coalition formation, but this will involve only minimal exchanges of information and not the robust process of understanding and criticism required by plural deliberation. Nevertheless, by identifying common interests among groups, aggregative reciprocity can gradually generate the trust needed to initiate plural deliberation. In this way, aggregative reciprocity should be seen as a necessary, if insufficient, precursor to deliberative reciprocity. To reformulate Warren's position on deliberative motivations, bargaining and coalition formation can provide the aggregative generation of trust needed to initiate plural deliberation.

But as Edward Chang and Jeanette Diaz-Veizades point out, coalition formation and plural deliberation thrive only when participants go beyond simply communicating and instead actively pursue policy issues of common interest.[83] Coalitions of disadvantaged groups can legitimately address policy issues that affect their private interests, but they should also pursue policies that might enhance plural deliberation in the long run. Thus, the third suggestion for fostering plural deliberation is to pursue policy goals that can neutralize dynamics of conflict, thereby indirectly enhancing the capacity to extend deliberative reciprocity across group boundaries. As Warren notes, deliberation is difficult whenever "participants are faced simultaneously with multiple threats, the limiting case of which is war." The key is to limit risks, thus allowing "participants to talk, listen, negotiate, compromise, generate new interests, and seek common interests."[84]

With respect to the resource dynamic, Simone Chambers and Jeffrey Kopstein provide evidence that membership in xenophobic or hate associations tends to be drawn from working-class individuals facing unemployment. The authors' explanation marries resource and positional dynamics: these workers confront not only diminished material resources (which they perceive as caused by immigrants) but diminished social standing (which they seek to rectify by asserting their superior ethnic status).[85] Thus, coalitions that try to improve the economic lot of such workers can mitigate the resource and positional dynamics of conflict that hinder plural deliberation.

Alternatively, coalitions might seek to reduce the security dynamic by reforming police practices. Concerns about police brutality are common among disadvantaged minority communities. Coalitions among such groups can potentially cooperate in order to press for greater community-based policing techniques, where the police cooperate with community leaders in order to prevent and punish criminal activity. Although New York City's marked decline in violent crime has garnered much press attention, numerous studies suggest that that city's aggressive policing tactics are not the only way to reduce violent crime. Instead, equally effective community policing strategies, epitomized by those practiced in Boston, can incorporate community leaders in disadvantaged minority neighborhoods as part of the solution.[86] The value of such an approach is that it limits two types of security dynamics: the fear of anarchy generated by ineffective policing, and the fear that the police are biased against some groups. If Boston, a city hardly known for cooperative race relations, can manage to reduce crime through cooperative means, then its model of community policing can remain a realistic policy goal that can indirectly enhance the prospects for plural deliberation.

Of course policing reforms and economic redistribution, while potentially neutralizing strategic dynamics of conflict, do not directly harness strategic action to foster plural deliberation. This task falls to the fourth suggestion: institutional analysis and reform. Typically, civil society and the public sphere are identified as the home for deliberation. This makes sense in light of the strategic dynamics of conflict, as civil society, when defined as a nonstate, noneconomic sphere of voluntary and informational organizations,[87] may insulate actors from the political and resource dynamics of group conflict. This argument is cogent but insufficient, because civil society actors can also reinforce positional stereotypes and generate false information.[88] In chapter 4, I will examine the public sphere in light of the elements of plural deliberation, the dynamics of group conflict, and the problem of identity construction. My goals are to clarify how we can judge public sphere actors and to identify public policies that enhance plural deliberation and mitigate dynamics of conflict within the public sphere. But ceding John Dryzek's point that the "public sphere is not a formal institution and so cannot be designed,"[89] I conclude that public sphere actors that foster dynamics of group conflict cannot be reformed away.

Institutional reform aimed at encouraging intergroup communication should focus not only on civil society but also on the democratic state, specifically electoral design. Although normative theorists of pluralism have begun to examine electoral systems, they have generally done so only with respect to enhancing the descriptive representation of disadvantaged ethnic or racial groups. However, Donald Horowitz notes that certain electoral systems can counter the political dynamic of conflict by providing strategic incentives for candidates to appeal to voters across group boundaries.[90] Such strategic incentives clearly affect the prospects for plural deliberation by presenting political candidates with new publicity constraints: if a candidate is more likely to win by espousing positions that appeal across group boundaries, that candidate must communicate in an inclusive manner and eschew ethnically exclusive appeals.[91] An assessment of electoral systems in light of plural deliberation, the dynamics of group conflict, and the problem of identity construction will occupy my efforts in chapter 5. Of course, electoral systems cannot provide sufficient incentives to motivate plural deliberation. But along with institutional reforms in the public sphere, policies aimed at mitigating the dynamics of group conflict, actors favorably positioned within the dynamics of group conflict, and the aggregative generation of trust, favorable electoral systems can be part of an overall political and social environment that is conducive to plural deliberation.

4

Plural Deliberation and the Public Sphere

CIVIL SOCIETY AND THE PUBLIC SPHERE

My investigation into deliberative democracy and the plural polity has thus far introduced three broad themes. First, I have argued that intergenerational collective identities are constructed entities, subject to internal diversity, shifting boundaries, and multiple modes of construction. Thus, members of constructed collective identities should engage in democratic deliberation in order to reach contextually sensitive responses to the specific problems of different groups and subgroups. I have also distinguished among three different types of institutions: formal, decision-making; informal, deliberative; and quasi-formal, deliberative institutions. Second, I introduced plural deliberation, a model of fair deliberation that requires a broad scope of communicative contributions, the achievement of understanding prior to criticism, methods of connecting deliberation to collective decisions, and fairness conditions that include aggregative and deliberative dimensions. This model enables us to judge the fairness of democratic institutions, processes, and participants, to justify withdrawals from deliberation in order to adopt agonist stances, and to reform institutions and processes. Finally, I have examined four deliberative motivations and five strategic dynamics of conflict that can encourage or hinder plural deliberation across group boundaries, depending on the social or institutional incentives.

At this point, I wish to use these three themes to analyze how the public sphere can serve as a site for democratic deliberation in a plural polity. Jürgen Habermas defines the public sphere as "a network for communicating information and points of view."[1] He emphasizes that this communicative network is not a specific institution or organization but the general flow of ideas, proposals, and arguments throughout a modern polity. This communicative network tends to be rooted in civil society, defined as those social organizations that are neither part of the constitutional state nor part of the economy.[2] Typically, civil society actors include nonstate associations, social movements, and the mass media, although capitalist media ownership blurs the distinction between civil society and the economy. Nevertheless, the public sphere is housed in informal, purely deliberative institutions. Civil society institutions are informal because they are not part of the constitutional state; they are deliberative because they do not reach collective decisions that legally bind the entire polity but primarily create and disseminate ideas. The formal, decision-making institutions of the state generate public policies; the informal, deliberative institutions of civil society generate public opinions.

Although the state and the public sphere differ in their institutional types and their products, most deliberative theorists agree that they do mutually affect each other. Minimally, the state enables the existence of a public sphere by guaranteeing certain rights to the population, such as freedom of speech, press, religion, conscience, and association. Civil society and the public sphere influence the democratic state through public opinion: as citizens are affected by the ideas circulated within the public sphere, the democratic state must respond to them or face diminished legitimacy.

For a variety of reasons, deliberative theorists influenced by Habermas tend to favor the public sphere as a site for robust democratic deliberation. John Dryzek, for example, believes that public sphere deliberation circumvents problems of "deliberative economy." Whereas many deliberative theories must, for the sake of empirical viability, limit the number of deliberating participants, public sphere deliberation allows the number to be "indeterminate," enabling deliberation to be practiced by "the many or the few."[3] The public sphere can thus serve as a forum for participatory politics, in contrast to the constitutional state, which remains a realm of representation. Dryzek also believes that public sphere deliberation is less constrained by strategic incentives than are electoral campaigns, and thus can more effectively include marginalized voices. So unlike electoral deliberation, public sphere deliberation "need not be muffled in the interests of strategic advantage. In addition, goals and interests need not be compromised or subordinated to the pursuit of office or access, and there is less reason to repress the contributions to debate of embarrassing troublemakers."[4] Seyla Benhabib finds public sphere deliberation particularly suited to the dilemmas raised in plural polities. "It is in the public sphere, situated within civil society, that multicultural struggles have their place." This is because civil society deliberation can best realize *"egalitarian reciprocity, voluntary self-ascription, and freedom of exit and association,"* the key norms required in a pluralistic society.[5]

Although I agree that the public sphere is a fruitful and indispensable site for deliberative democracy in a plural polity, I fear that deliberative theorists are sometimes too insouciant regarding the dangers posed by certain public sphere actors. Dryzek prudentially excludes terrorists as unacceptable public sphere actors because they seek to destroy rather than influence the democratic state.[6] However, this concession focuses only on what I call the security dynamic of group conflict;

it neglects how public sphere actors can obstruct plural deliberation by aggravating the information dynamic of conflict. Similarly, attention to the information dynamic should temper Benhabib's expectation that the public sphere can best realize reciprocity across group boundaries because social movements, associations, and mass media can propagate misleading or prejudicial information. Moreover, certain associations, including some ethnic or racial ones, can inhibit voluntary self-ascription and freedom of exit through their control over economic resources, thereby aggravating the resource dynamic of conflict. Consequently, deliberative theorists must recognize how the informal, deliberative institutions of the public sphere can foster plural deliberation across group boundaries but also obstruct it and encourage group conflict.

In this chapter, I will attend to the real benefits of deliberation within civil society and the public sphere, while also clarifying its limitations and dangers, emphasizing that public sphere deliberation is not always participatory and in fact requires various forms of informal representation.[7] However, I will argue that such representation is advantageous because the informal, deliberative institutions of the public sphere facilitate flexible representation responsive to shifting identity boundaries, unlike the formal institutions of the state. In addition, I will illuminate the ways in which social movements are influenced by strategic considerations, which sometimes enhance and sometimes constrain their capacity to deliberate across group boundaries. I will even show how social movements sometimes must engage in aggregative bargaining with state officials and ordinary citizens. Finally, I will examine how the mass media can beneficially broaden the public addressed by political actors, thereby imposing more universalistic publicity constraints, but I will also show how mediated publics require greater levels of representation, potentially undermine deliberative equality and autonomy, and aggravate the information dynamic of conflict, thereby hindering deliberative reciprocity across group boundaries.

I will use the three themes of identity construction, plural deliberation, and the dynamics of group conflict to analyze the prospects of plural deliberation within the public sphere. Specifically, I will examine how well the informal, deliberative institutions of civil society enable the public sphere to negotiate problems of internal diversity, shifting boundaries, and multiple modes of identity construction among members of diverse and constructed collective identities. I will also examine how the strategic dynamics of conflict affect public sphere actors, such as associations, social movements, and the mass media. Finally, I will illustrate how the elements of plural deliberation can be used to reform the public sphere and judge its actors. It is important to recognize that attempts at reform are limited by the fact that the public sphere is "not a formal institution and so cannot be designed."[8] These limits are especially apparent in the case of social movements, whereas the mass media and associations can be subject to real albeit limited reforms through public policies. Nevertheless, the difficulties in reforming the public sphere suggest that realizing deliberative democracy in the plural polity requires looking beyond it. Thus, deliberative democratic reform in the plural polity will require addressing two types of institutions within the democratic state: quasi-formal, deliberative institutions, like advisory panels, and formal, decision-making institutions, like electoral systems.

ASSOCIATIONS

Mark Warren provides perhaps the most sophisticated analysis of the relationship between associations and democratic politics. He develops a complex typology of associations, according to three factors: their ease of exit, the means of social integration toward which they are oriented, and the constitutive goods they provide for their members.[9] In turn, associations can have three types of democratic effects: developmental (whereby members develop substantive capacities through participation in associations), institutional (whereby associations enhance the legitimacy of democratic institutions), and public sphere (whereby associations communicate messages to the broader public beyond the associations themselves).[10] Different associations will have different democratic effects, depending upon their mix of factors. Indeed, the very associations that can best produce developmental effects are often least adept at engendering public sphere effects. Consequently, a democracy is more likely to flourish to the extent that its citizens participate within a variety of associations. I will use Warren's framework to address the specific advantages and disadvantages of associations based on intergenerational collective identity, and I will adapt some of his criteria to cohere with the conditions of plural deliberation laid out in chapter 2.

To recapitulate, the factors shaping associations are their ease of exit, the means of social integration toward which they are oriented, and their constitutive goods. Associations can have a high, medium, or low ease of exit. The term *voluntary association,* which implicitly contrasts with the more compulsory membership within the state, is misleading, because all associations bear at least some costs of entry and exit. Social and recreational clubs typically have very high ease of exit: one might at most have to pay a membership fee or regularly attend meetings to remain a member. Residential associations may have much more restrictive characteristics: one must own property in the association's area to become a member, and might have to sell that property to exit the association. All things being equal, associations with low ease of exit will experience strong pressures among their members for internal democracy and deliberation: because it is costly to exit, members will want significant voice over how the association is run. Conversely, associations with high ease of exit will experience fewer pressures for internal democracy; disgruntled members can simply vote with their feet and leave.[11]

Following Habermas and Talcott Parsons, Warren argues that associations tend to be oriented toward one of three means of social integration: political power, like that controlled by the state; economic relations, structured by exchanges within markets; and social resources, such as shared values, norms, customs, traditions, or forms of communication.[12] Warren also distinguishes associations according to whether they are "vested" in the means of social integration presently dominant within society. For example, an association representing successful firms may be vested in existing economic structures because its members clearly benefit from them, whereas an advocacy group fighting to regulate those firms is clearly nonvested because it seeks to alter (even if only marginally) the existing economic relations. Similarly, well-placed political organizations that enjoy good connections to political representatives are vested, whereas marginal political organizations shunned by most politicians are nonvested.[13]

Finally, associations differ according to the constitutive goods that they provide their members. Warren identifies six significant constitutive goods: individual material goods (material entities that can be enjoyed by individuals); inclusive material goods (material, public goods that can be enjoyed by all within society, such as clean air and water); inclusive social goods (symbolic, public goods that can be enjoyed by all within society, such as language, culture, or knowledge); exclusive, personal identity goods (an individual identity, typically formed through family or intimate associations); exclusive, collective identity goods (a collective identity that is not shared by all within society, for example the intergenerational collective identities surveyed in chapter 1); and status goods (individual goods that are enjoyable primarily because they are scarce, such as expensive cars and property or prestigious degrees and awards).[14]

Associations differ according to how they combine these factors. Some associations may, for example, have high ease of exit, be vested in political means of social integration, and provide individual material goods; other associations may have low ease of exit, be nonvested in economic means of social integration, and provide exclusive, collective identity goods. Warren hypothesizes that associations will differ in their democratic effects based on their combination of factors. Let me outline the three democratic effects and clarify which associations will bear which effects.

Developmental effects reflect how participation in associations imbues individuals with specific substantive political capacities, which can be depicted according to plural deliberation's criteria of deliberative equality, deliberative autonomy, and deliberative reciprocity. Deliberative equality, it should be remembered, requires equal consideration of different positions regardless of their present numerical support, as deliberation must enable citizens to alter their preferences through communication. Although certain procedural rules, like equal speaking allotments among positions, can help to realize deliberative equality, certain substantive capacities are also needed if individual participants are to be equally effective in presenting their cases. Most simply, an association can enhance deliberative equality by providing basic information and skills, especially if it is oriented toward political issues.[15] Racial or ethnic political associations can inform their members of political issues important to the group; immigrant associations can help their members acquire English-language skills and navigate immigration and citizenship laws.

In a more complex way, associations can inculcate their members with a general sense of political efficacy and specific political skills, such as public speaking and negotiation, if the association is internally democratic. Internal democracy is most likely in associations that have low ease of exit, where the inability to leave may prompt members to demand a political voice, and that are oriented toward social means of integration, as issues related to values, norms, and traditions are complex but still accessible to laypersons. However, some ethnic or racial economic associations, such as credit associations among immigrant groups, can foster internal deliberation and political skills, despite their high exit. This arises because their economic orientation and their provision of exclusive ethnic identity goods provide strong incentives for member loyalty, which in turn provides the same incentive for voice as does low exit.[16] But although such associations can enhance deliberative equality, they remain prone to the resource dynamic of conflict, whereby individuals tie their economic interests to those of their group.

Associations can enhance the achievement of deliberative autonomy as well. Substantively, deliberative autonomy requires individuals to develop critical, reflective preferences, as opposed to adaptive preferences, which are shaped by diminished expectations or repressive world-views. It requires that preferences develop through deliberative processes suitably free of misinformation, deception, manipulation, or coercion. Associations enhance procedural deliberative autonomy when their internal democratic functions allow members to uncover coercion by imbuing them with the "sophistication to know when one is being pressured, threatened, or manipulated."[17] Associational participation can also achieve substantive deliberative autonomy against adaptive preferences by helping their members to develop the critical skills to reflect upon their preferences.[18]

Like the political skills associated with substantive deliberative equality, the critical skills of substantive deliberative autonomy are best generated by associations with low exit. Low exit can force members to criticize an association rather than just skulking away, but critical skills also depend upon the goods provided by the association. Warren expects more internal criticism in associations that seek to secure inclusive material or social goods, like environmental associations: members of a local conservation group are likely to speak up if their leaders are willing to strike a bad deal with a real estate developer. Conversely, Warren expects less internal criticism in associations that deal with exclusive collective identities.[19] This may stem from the fact that collective identity is difficult to challenge because one's individual identity is closely bound up with it, although this conjecture assumes an interpretive significance to collective identity. Nevertheless, this hypothesis suggests that deliberation in a plural polity will require that citizens participate not solely in group-specific associations, which may be the least adept at generating critical skills.

It is more difficult, I think, to identify those associations that are likely to enhance deliberative reciprocity, the disposition to recognize others as communicatively competent, to engage in the proportional exchange of justifications and criticisms, and seek agreement or convergence on understandings and decisions. For deliberative reciprocity to develop across group boundaries, it is crucial for an association to include members of different groups, but if there is little trust across group boundaries, an association may splinter into warring factions. For this reason, Warren expects that associations with little potential for internal conflict are best suited to generating reciprocity across group boundaries. Such associations will tend to allow high levels of exit, to pursue inclusive social or material goods, and to focus on social issues. For example, sports or recreational clubs might include members from a variety of collective identities under conditions almost devoid of internal conflict. The hoped-for result will be increased levels of intergroup trust and a greater willingness to overcome positional stereotypes and recognize each other as communicatively competent. Politically oriented associations are less likely to achieve such goals because political issues may induce too much conflict, as predicted by the political dynamic of group conflict.[20]

Unfortunately, the reciprocity generated by such low-intensity, apolitical associations might remain at the superficial level of customary reciprocity, where individuals cordially greet and banter with each other without rising to a more political level. Black and White members of a sports club might exchange justifications and criticisms of a baseball manager's decision to have the best hitter lay down a sacrifice bunt, but how will this help them engage in rigorous deliberation over a group-related political issue like welfare policy? Perhaps a more political form of deliberative reciprocity might develop over time, as members interact with each other. Given the occasionally political character of sports, deliberative reciprocity across group lines in a social setting can obliquely lend a more political character to their discussions. Black and White members of a Notre Dame football fan club might jointly cheer the Black head coach, Tyrone Willingham, whose hiring was partially prompted by Black political activism and whose success has prompted greater scrutiny concerning the dearth of Black head coaches in Division I-A college football. As I speculated in chapter 3, deliberative reciprocity on a social level might foster the deliberative generation of trust, which may reinforce deliberative reciprocity on a more political level.

Certainly, deliberative reciprocity across group boundaries on a social level is better than what we might find within group-specific associations. While internally democratic, group-specific associations may foster substantive deliberative equality and autonomy among their members, they are less likely to generate deliberative reciprocity toward outgroups. Indeed, when the maintenance of an exclusive collective identity is the primary purpose of the association, Warren fears the rise of "zero-sum boundaries and distinctions,"[21] just as one might expect through the resource and positional dynamics of group conflict. That being said, the potential benefits of multiple-group associations and the potential costs of single-group associations should not blind us to the benefits of the latter. Nor should we overlook how the freedom of association can protect even virulently chauvinistic groups.

Single-group associations will remain a vital part of the institutional basis for a pluralistic public sphere. But as I will argue at the end of this chapter, some policies might enhance the viability and contributions of multigroup associations, even those that pursue concrete political issues.

Let us now turn to institutional effects. Under this rubric, Warren seeks to elucidate how associations (in my terms, informal, deliberative institutions) can underwrite the legitimacy of the democratic state (and its formal, decision-making institutions). Warren proffers three forms of legitimacy enhanced by associational activity: substantive-outcome legitimacy, process legitimacy, and devolutionary legitimacy.[22] Associations enhance substantive-outcome legitimacy by shaping public opinion that then guides substantive state decisions, in a manner similar to the resonance between public opinion and state policy advocated by John Dryzek.[23] Associations foster process legitimacy by representing their members within the political process, expressing commonalities or differences between their members and the broader public. Finally, associations generate devolutionary legitimacy by assuming certain governmental functions, thereby relocating the locus of legitimacy from the state to the association.

Notably, the associations that Warren expects to generate state legitimacy most effectively are those pursuing inclusive social or material goods, which are common goods shared by all citizens. Conversely, the associations least able to foster legitimacy are those securing exclusive collective identity goods, which, by definition, are not shared by all.[24] I share Warren's concerns over the ability of exclusive collective identity associations to enhance democratic legitimacy, but I wish to disaggregate his conclusion. It is clear that citizens accord less respect to associations perceived as pursuing narrow group interests, as I have discussed in chapters 2 and 3. But in fairness, group-specific associations might be the only representatives their members have, given the underrepresentation of minorities within the formal decision-making institutions of the democratic state. Moreover, when they shape outcomes and enter processes through the public sphere effects discussed below, they may acquire greater legitimacy. The key distinction, I think, is the type of legitimacy examined. Whereas group-specific associations should be granted a greater role in shaping substantive outcomes and in representing their members within the political process, they provoke greater concern about the devolution of state power.

In chapter 1, we saw how devolving welfare distribution to pan-Asian associations, which encompass multiple Asian ethnic groups, furthered the instrumental construction of an Asian identity. Although a pan-Asian identity is not illegitimate per se, welfare distribution through this identity category has overlooked problems of internal diversity. As a result, ethnic Chinese and Japanese Americans tended to dominate these associations, although their ethnicity, language, and class position distinguished them from many of their clients. Beyond this, distributing welfare through identity groups may encourage the opportunistic, instrumental-agency mode of identity construction and the resource dynamic of conflict when individuals come to identify their particular interests with those of a specific group. This dynamic can become more dangerous when an association's control over vital welfare resources constrains its members from easily exiting it. Thus, significant concerns adhere to the devolution of state power to racial, ethnic, or cultural associations, despite the benefits of devolving power to other types of associations.

Whereas devolving state power to group-specific associations raises troubling concerns, these associations can more legitimately influence substantive outcomes and participate in informal political processes when they employ public sphere effects. When associations send messages to the broader public sphere, which of course will mainly include individuals who are not members of the association, they are constrained by the publicity effects discussed in chapters 2 and 3. Because the broader public is not part of the association, the association must find common grounds upon which to justify any policies or positions it wishes to advance. For group-specific associations, this means simultaneously representing their differences (how their perspectives or conditions differ from those of the broader public) and their commonalities (how any disadvantages they suffer conflict with commonly shared norms or values).[25] As I shall argue below, the ability to represent differences and commonalities simultaneously helps to explain the deliberative success of the Black American civil rights movement.

Which associations are likely to take their concerns to the broader public, rather than trying to lobby government through more secretive channels? The first relevant factor is high ease of exit: by making it easy for members to leave, the association can more easily formulate clearly defined political preferences or interests without the fear of significant internal dispute. Consequently, the low-exit associations likely to enhance the developmental effects of substantive deliberative equality and autonomy are least likely to have public sphere effects. Different associations will make different contributions to democracy. The second factor is whether the group is vested in the political means of social integration. When an association has clearly defined political preferences or interests and already enjoys access to political officials, it is more likely to avoid the public sphere and pursue its ends through lobbying.[26] On the other hand, when an association has clearly defined political preferences or interests but does not enjoy privileged access to political officials, it is more likely to "go public," through the mass media or social movements, the topics of the next two sections.

SOCIAL MOVEMENTS

Unlike associations, social movements are noninstitutional actors and thus are less likely to lobby state officials through closed-door communication.[27] Indeed, social movements are almost by definition public sphere actors; their hallmark activities (protest marches and civil disobedience) are effective precisely because they occur in public. This necessarily public character and the perception that social movements enable ordinary citizens to participate directly in politics endear them to deliberative democrats. However, the deliberative approbation of social movements should be qualified in light of four factors: their dependence on broader institutional support, the fact that their specifically deliberative contributions rely on articulate representatives and can render them transitory, their positioning relative to other actors or groups, and the fact that they engage in strategic action and even aggregative bargaining.

Most social movements must rely on preexisting associations in order to acquire members, leaders, communication networks, and the sense of associational solidarity that encourages participation in controversial, time-consuming, and often risky protest activity.[28] Social movements also rely on the mass media to communicate their message to the nonparticipating public and to potential participants.[29] Elections, electoral calculations, and even political parties can provide a favorable political opportunity structure for social movement activity.[30] The mass media and electoral politics can crucially assist social movements in their specifically deliberative functions.

The specifically deliberative functions of social movements pertain to their "cognitive praxis," their ability to convey meanings or messages within the public sphere.[31] According to the framework of plural deliberation, a social movement's most valuable cognitive praxis is the ability to generate understanding and criticism across perspectives and world-views. Movement representatives must communicate their own perspectives while accurately understanding the perspectives of others. In addition, they must be articulate, accurate, and precise, in order to avoid causing others, especially the mass media, to misunderstand the issues they seek to communicate. They must also develop and use rhetorical tropes that are likely to persuade members of other groups. Apart from the role of movement leaders, the deliberative function of social movements is often transitory: if they are successful in persuading others that their perspectives, justifications, and criticisms are valid, they are likely to dissipate as others come to internalize the message. Against the perception that social movements are simply co-opted by the state or society, a deliberative approach suggests that social movements' success in convincing others can also serve as the ground for their demise.[32]

We must also attend to the positioning of the social movement with respect to other social actors. Social movements address multiple actors, which can be divided into three crucial types: the democratic state, receptive publics, and adversaries. The democratic state can affect the deliberative success or failure of a social movement through positive responses (passing desired laws or physically protecting protestors) or negative responses (passing unfavorable laws or coercing protestors or social movement associations). In particular, democratic states are typically more responsive to social movements that disrupt social order, but only in an explicitly nonviolent manner and only to seek reform-oriented goals. Democratic states are less responsive and are often repressive toward movements that use or advocate violence to realize revolutionary goals. This distinction stems from the fact that democratic regimes accept free speech and nonviolent procedural change but reject nonstate violence.[33] Receptive publics are those that are open to the message and sympathetic to the plight of social movements, whereas adversaries are the oppositional "other" to be fought by social movements.[34] Social movements are apt to enjoy deliberative success only if they can position themselves within a virtuous triangle, where the state and receptive publics come to favor them over their adversaries. They will more likely experience deliberative failure when they confront a vicious triangle, when their adversaries gain sway over the state, to their detriment and that of their receptive public.

The positioning of social movements within the state, receptive publics, and adversaries helps illuminate how even those that engage in deliberative, cognitive praxis are not simply deliberative or communicative actors but use strategic action and even aggregative bargaining. They engage in communicative action and plural deliberation primarily with receptive publics, although they may also occasionally deliberate with receptive state officials. They clearly employ strategic action in their encounters with adversaries.[35] Finally, although social movements must typically act in public and outside of formal institutions, they can nevertheless participate in noninstitutionalized, aggregative bargaining with the state and with their adversaries. This is not to demean the deliberative role of social movements, which can serve as important vehicles for plural deliberation aimed at understanding and criticism across perspectives and world-views. The point is simply to reveal social movements as complex phenomena that use both communicative and strategic action to engage in deliberative and aggregative politics. The Black American civil rights movement exemplifies such complexity and how it affects the deliberative success or failure of social movements more generally.

The early civil rights movement clearly embodied plural deliberation across the black and white perspectives that divided Americans. Its success flowed largely from the ability of its most prominent representative, Martin Luther King, Jr., to communicate to the receptive, northern White public through the rhetorical tropes of democratic political equality and Christian forgiveness. The focus on democratic political equality communicated to northern Whites that the American values they held dear simply did not apply to Blacks in the south. King enabled northern Whites to view the American polity from a Black perspective. From a White perspective, America was the world's preeminent democracy; from a Black perspective, it was a caste-ridden society ruled by coercion without consent. Moreover, King's use of Christian forgiveness allowed northern Whites to support Black criticism of American evils without condemning themselves or America to eternal political damnation.[36] By acting as the Black representative to northern White Americans, King fostered understanding across perspective and generated criticism without condemnation. In this way, he practiced plural deliberation in a manner largely consistent with communicative action.

Yet the success of the civil rights movement in deliberating with the northern White public clearly depended upon what Doug McAdam calls "strategic dramaturgy." By intentionally choosing to demonstrate in cities with virulently racist and violent police officials, civil rights leaders strategically provoked their southern White adversaries into violent confrontations. As a result, the receptive northern public and the federal government were presented with images of southern Whites violently suppressing nonviolent, well-dressed, devoutly Christian, and seemingly lawful Blacks.[37] This strategy resulted from the failure of a demonstration in Albany, Georgia, in 1961, where the police chief avoided violent repression while denying protestors their demands. King and other leaders realized that they had to choose sites where violent confrontations were more likely, in order to present to northern Whites an image of good Blacks versus evil southern Whites. Thus, they intentionally chose Birmingham as their next site and made sure to march prior to the scheduled departure of Bull Connor, that city's racist, violent, and lame-duck police commissioner. Similarly, they intentionally chose Selma, whose Sheriff, Jim Clark, was also prone to violent repression. In each case, the civil rights leaders' strategic choices paid off: Black demonstrations led to violent White reprisals, which in turn favorably swayed White public opinion in the North.[38]

The strategic engagement of White public officials not only bore deliberative fruit with the receptive, northern White public, it also resulted in gains through noninstitutionalized aggregative bargaining with the federal government. The violently repressed marches in Birmingham and Selma helped to secure the respective passage of the 1964 Civil Rights Act and the 1965 Voting Rights Act, by shaming the federal government into action. Although such shaming could manifest plural deliberation, with the images from Birmingham and Selma serving as deliberative criticism of federal inaction, the aggregative effects cannot be overlooked. The early civil rights movement provided a threat to order through nonviolent but disruptive collective action. An even clearer case of how Black protest could serve as a threat to social order and thus as an aggregative bargaining chip predates the civil rights movement. Civil rights leaders scheduled a march on Washington for July 1, 1941, to protest racial discrimination in the defense industry. The federal government preempted the march by partially acquiescing to their demands when President Roosevelt signed Executive Order 8802 on June 25, 1941. This change in federal policy reflected the growing electoral strength of northern Blacks, the security threat of a mass demonstration when war appeared imminent, and the government's fear that foreign powers would use the march as a propaganda tool.[39] Thus, the march never took place, but its threat served as a useful bargaining chip against the state.

Plural deliberation can help to justify and clarify the success of the early civil rights movement. Clearly, its success was aided by the virtuous triangle involving (1) the civil rights movement; (2) a receptive, communicatively engaged northern White public and federal government officials; and (3) strategically engaged southern adversaries. Though most deliberative models underemphasize these strategic and aggregative dynamics,[40] plural deliberation can justify such behavior through its acceptance of both communicative and strategic action. Moreover, its inclusion of aggregative fairness conditions, particularly aggregative reciprocity, can pro-vide normative justification for the bargaining dynamics within the civil rights movement. Because Blacks had been effectively shut out of the bargaining processes and institutions through which other ethnic groups had pressed for their legitimate interests within the democratic state, their use of noninstitutionalized bargaining was warranted.

Deliberative theorists are usually quick to cite the early, integrationist, civil rights movement as a model for the role of social movements within a deliberative democracy;[41] however, few assess the role of the Black Power movement of the late 1960s and early 1970s. This avoidance is not surprising. Black Power repre-sentatives tended not to reach out to White audiences as did King and other inte-grationist civil rights leaders. And indeed, many leaders and participants in the Black Power movement clearly violated some or all of the elements of plural delib-eration. For instance, Black Power proponents intentionally prevented Whites from understanding the Black perspective: Black Power student activists assumed that White students would remain unable to understand Black perspectives; Black Power musicians assumed that Whites could not understand soul music; and Black Power supporters even strategically hid or altered Black argot, in order to exclude potential White interlocutors. Perhaps most important, Black Power representa-tives strongly eschewed deliberative reciprocity with Whites by openly demean-ing them or advocating violence against them.[42] On a more charitable interpretation, Black Power representatives were incredibly imprecise in their statements, allow-ing the media to focus on their radical language while overlooking the substance of their economic and social grievances. On university campuses, their shrill tones often obscured the legitimate concerns they raised about the educational content and administrative structure of higher education.[43]

As a result, deliberative democrats might dismiss Black Power as a purely ago-nistic movement that valued ethnic separatism over integration, or they might view the movement simply as a noninstitutionalized form of aggregative bargaining. Student activists bargained with university officials to create Black student centers and Black Studies programs; labor activists bargained with White unions to en-hance Black representation; and community activists bargained with White busi-nesses and school boards to establish "community control" over schools and stores in Black neighborhoods.[44] Most spectacularly, Black Power mobilization arguably helped to spark the 1960s urban riots, which led to federal action favorable to Blacks in the form of urban funding. Not surprisingly, although the urban rioting did lead to beneficial federal action, it did not bring a receptive White public over to the Black perspective. Whereas White public opinion following the early, non-violent demonstrations placed civil rights high on the list of national priorities, it focused on law and order after the urban riots.[45] Thus, one could interpret Black Power as serving only an aggregative bargaining function between Black activists and state officials, not a deliberative function between a Black movement and the White public.

While there is much to this interpretation, plural deliberation can provide a more nuanced approach to the Black Power movement, justifying certain aspects of its eschewal of deliberative reciprocity and its adoption of noninstitutionalized bargaining. For instance, plural deliberation requires us to assess the rejection of deliberative reciprocity in light of the deficits in deliberative autonomy and deliberative reciprocity that Black Power activists perceived in their relations with White interlocutors. Black Power activists felt that many, if not most, Whites were not genuinely interested in understanding the Black perspective. And even if they were, the extremely unequal power relations between the White-dominated culture industry and Blacks would have undermined the deliberative autonomy of many exchanges across these perspectives. We must also recognize that Black Power activists sought to shield black culture from White understanding based on the fear that White-owned entertainment and media conglomerates would exploit Black culture simply to further their own economic goals. On a more insidious level, they feared that the disproportionate presence of Blacks as police officers in TV shows served as a subtle form of social control: lawful Black TV cops as a counterpoint to unruly Black urban populations.[46] Plural deliberation clearly cannot justify all aspects of Black Power, such as issuing violent (if idle) threats or enforcing internal conformity by tagging some Blacks as Uncle Toms. However, the rejection of deliberative reciprocity itself can find some justification.

Plural deliberation can also make some sense of Black Power's use of noninstitutionalized bargaining. Given deficits in deliberative autonomy and deliberative reciprocity, perhaps the fairest short-term relationship between Blacks and Whites would have been aggregative reciprocity within bargaining processes. Indeed, Black separation as a precursor to fairer bargaining was a common sentiment shared both by moderate, "interest-group pluralists," who sought community control over Black neighborhood businesses, and by more radical, territorial nationalists, who sought a Black state in the south. We should remember that Charles V. Hamilton and Stokely Carmichael's *Black Power,* the founding document of the movement, explicitly advocated fair coalitions with Whites as one of its goals.[47] Although understanding and criticism across perspectives and world-views was not the ultimate goal of Black Power, its advocacy of intergroup coalitions clearly could find some justification as a necessary though insufficient precursor to plural deliberation.

Though Black Power did not generate deliberative understanding across Black and White perspectives, it arguably did achieve significant understanding across various nonWhite perspectives. Advocates for community control over Harlem schools, for instance, supported teaching not only Black history but also Chinese history, given the presence of Chinese students in the area. Similarly, the Black Panther party communicated with Latino, Asian, Native American, and even poor White radical parties in their machinations to overthrow capitalism.[48] Such extensions of deliberative reciprocity, directed primarily toward nonWhite groups, was not lost on other minority activists: "Red Power" became a rallying cry for the

American Indian movement, "Chicano Power" gained vogue among Latinos in the Southwest, and "Yellow Power" briefly surfaced as a motto in the Asian-American movement.[49]

For each of these movements, Black Power was a strong and inclusive rhetorical trope that crossed various nonWhite perspectives. From a Black perspective, it signified a radical political response to the economic and social obstacles that persisted throughout the country, despite the demise of de jure segregation in the South. This perspective clearly resonated with Latinos, Asians, and urban-dwelling American Indians, who no longer faced legally enshrined discrimination but continued to confront economic and social inequality. The specific goals sought by the Black Power movement also resonated with members of nonWhite radical groups, as did the method of noninstitutionalized, aggregative bargaining with state and educational officials. Organizations within the Asian-American movement, for instance, sought Asian-American studies programs in universities, community control over Asian neighborhoods, and even a form of territorial nationalism akin to that sought by Black nationalists in the South.[50] More directly, Red Power groups, with their strategies of occupying federal land and offices, provided a radical flank that encouraged federal officials to accept claims for tribal self-government by more moderate tribal lobbyists.[51]

Like Black Power, plural deliberation cannot endorse all aspects of these minority "power" movements, which sometimes emulated the most unsavory aspects of Black Power: advocating violence, enforcing internal conformity, and fabricating nationalist myths to cement collective identities. However, these radical movements did include deliberatively justifiable goals and actions. Perhaps most important, Black Power's focus on rehabilitating Black self-perception resonated strongly with members of other nonWhite groups, who felt excluded and demeaned by White-dominated mainstream culture. And whereas power relations and insincere attempts at understanding may have justified agonism toward Whites and aggressive bargaining with the state, the common experience of exclusion and powerlessness may have fostered deliberative understanding across nonWhite perspectives. Indeed, one might even suggest that the Black Power movement enjoyed deliberative success with other nonWhite groups through a complementary set of triangular relations. Although a vicious triangle hindered deliberation among (1) Black Power activists, (2) northern and southern White adversaries, and (3) the state, a virtuous triangle may have existed among (1) Black Power activists, (2) the strategically engaged adversaries in the northern and southern White publics and the White-dominated state, and (3) communicatively engaged, receptive minority publics. To this extent, Black Power's position may have been analogous to the integrationist civil rights movement, albeit involving different actors.

Black Power arguably achieved some degree of plural deliberation across non-White perspectives; however, some later manifestations of it have failed to do so. This failure is best represented by the 1990 Red Apple boycott of two Korean-owned produce stores in Flatbush, Brooklyn. Stemming from the alleged assault of a female Haitian customer (Ghislaine Felissaint) by a male Korean merchant, this boycott was initially led by Haitian activists, who were then supplanted by leaders from the Black Power December 12th Movement. A lack of understanding across perspective was manifest from both sides. First-generation Korean merchants generally had little understanding of the history and continuing legacy of Black oppression in the United States, leading many of them to blame Blacks for their economic plight. On the other hand, some Black boycott leaders, working under the Black Power community control principle, falsely contended that Korean merchants had benefited from preferential treatment by the federal government and White-owned banks. This belief persisted, despite the fact that personal savings or assistance from friends constituted nearly all of the start-up capital for these merchants.[52]

Boycott leaders also demonstrated a lack of political reciprocity, in both its deliberative and aggregative dimensions. The initial Haitian boycott leaders were willing to negotiate with the merchants in order to achieve legal redress for Felissaint, increase neighborhood economic empowerment, and force Korean merchants to treat Black customers with respect. But when the Haitian leadership lost control of the boycott, the December 12th Movement refused to negotiate and instead demanded that the merchant issue a public apology, that he be prosecuted to the full extent of the law, and that the two stores be closed.[53] Thus, the December 12th Movement eschewed even aggregative reciprocity in the form of noninstitutionalized bargaining with the merchants.

The Black Power boycott eventually failed, and a Korean countermobilization successfully prodded the Black mayor, David Dinkins, to end it. Although information and political dynamics may have led the mainstream media to favor the Koreans over the Black boycotters, at least part of the problem lay with the boycott movement's representatives. The December 12th leaders were not racist; however, they were unable to police their lay participants, some of whom uttered anti-Asian remarks on the picket line in front of the targeted stores. The representatives themselves were not always articulate in emphasizing that the boycott was not racist, a failing lamented by sympathetic Black and Korean critics. On the other hand, the Korean countermobilization—the "peace rally for racial harmony"— maintained strict control over speeches and placards, filtering out any content that could be construed as racially provocative.[54]

Although the Black boycotters and the Korean merchants failed to achieve much understanding across perspective, it is remarkable that critics on both sides exhibited as much deliberative reciprocity and understanding as they did. For instance, Haitian critics of the boycott sought to negotiate a settlement without shutting down the stores, but they received death threats for doing so. Similarly, Korean-American critics of the countermobilization tended to be highly educated, second-generation professionals, who had a greater understanding of Black oppression in America and had internalized the American public norm of racial equality.[55] This suggests that movement critics, not movement leaders, more closely approximated plural deliberation's requirement of understanding prior to criticism.

But could plural deliberation justify the boycott or the countermobilization as forms of agonistic protest or aggregative bargaining? In my estimation, this could not be the case. Plural deliberation allows for the agonistic rejection of deliberative reciprocity when one party experiences deficits in fairness conditions relative to another party. In the case of the original Black Power movement, activists clearly suffered deficits in deliberative autonomy; the White-dominated media had much greater power over the use of Black culture, and Black bargaining power within the White-dominated government was severely constrained. In the case of the Red Apple boycott, the Black movement leaders and the Korean merchants were in relatively symmetrical power positions. Korean merchants had greater financial power, but Black residents and customers clearly enjoyed greater political power, through their access to elected Black representatives and through collective action. Thus, plural deliberation cannot be invoked to sanction the December 12th Movement's agonistic stance toward the Korean merchants. And whereas high levels of mistrust may have undermined any likelihood of deliberative reciprocity between the parties, the aggregative reciprocity exhibited by the Haitian activists would clearly have been the most justifiable response to this situation. But though the Red Apple boycott cannot be justified according to the elements of plural deliberation, the information dynamics of group conflict can help to explain why deliberative and even aggregative reciprocity were so difficult to generate between the two sides. I will examine such dynamics in the next section, after first exploring broader problems concerning the mass media's role in a plural polity.

THE MASS MEDIA

Deliberative democrats remain ambivalent about the mass media. On the one hand, it is derided for destroying the deliberative capacities of the public sphere by reducing politics to sound bites, prioritizing profits over accurate and critical information, and crowding out associations from the public sphere.[56] On the other hand, there is an awareness that a public sphere in a modern, complex democracy could not exist without mass media.[57] As I mentioned earlier, associations and social movements both rely heavily on the mass media in order to communicate with nonparticipants and participants alike, a point illustrated by the civil rights movement. King and the other civil rights leaders rcognized the importance of the mass media, particularly television, in conveying their strategic dramaturgy to the northern White public. Like most disadvantaged social movements, they lacked the conventional resources to communicate their message. To compensate, they provoked spectacular events that would draw television news reporters seeking compelling new images, like the epic battles between White police officers and Black protesters. In this way, the mass media extended the scope of the public addressed by the civil rights movement, allowing television images to reach northern and western American households far from the southeast. Perhaps more important, television coverage of the civil rights protests was also picked up by Soviet propagandists eager to exploit this hypocrisy within American democracy.[58] In this way, the mass media extended the scope of the public that judged public sphere actors: northern Whites and the world at large could exercise moral judgment upon the civil rights protesters, their southern White adversaries, and the federal government.

The mass media places more encompassing and universalistic publicity constraints upon political actors, whose contributions must appeal to a wider, more diverse set of respondents. However, this extended public, connected only by the mass media, will likely grow less active and more passive. The result is a potential degradation of the public's deliberative autonomy, relative to those actors who actively communicate in the media,[59] undermining the effectiveness and fairness of publicity constraints. Recall that in chapter 3, I suggested that two publicity constraints strongly influence public deliberation in the United States: proscriptions against self-interested policy advocacy and the norm of racial equality. But recall also that the latter publicity constraint can be circumvented through implicit racial appeals, which use code words like "crime" or "welfare" that are stereotypically associated with Black Americans. Challenging implicit racial appeals requires an active public, not a passive audience. But when a public sphere is anchored primarily in the mass media, the active repudiation of implicit racial appeals cannot arise from the public at large but from one of its informal representatives within the media.

Three types of informal representatives are most likely to play an active role in mass media communication: elected officials, policy experts, and professional communicators. Elected officials exercise significant power in setting the media's deliberative agenda, as media reporters tend to follow their actions and pronouncements; policy experts provide detailed analyses of issues in which they have specialized knowledge; and "professional communicators" translate policy experts' specialized analyses into language accessible to the broader public.[60] As a result, the media's informal representatives control the agenda and monopolize the contributions to public debate, thereby exercising greater power over the lay public and undermining deliberative autonomy.

On the other hand, the lay public might well retain enough deliberative autonomy to appropriate the contributions of media representatives in order to develop their own reflective preferences, interests, or opinions. Benjamin Page contends that the lay public, despite its lack of policy expertise, has the capacity to process the contributions of policy experts that get filtered into the mainstream media during intense public attention to specialized topics.[61] Similarly, William Gamson shows in painstaking detail how ordinary citizens take media information, combine it with insights from their own lives, and develop autonomous public opinions concerning not only domestic issues but also complex international affairs, like the Arab–Israeli conflict.[62] As a result, people are not simply duped by the media but can appropriate media information, combine it with their own beliefs and experiences, and develop deliberatively autonomous public opinions.

Citizens suffer from deficits in deliberative autonomy in setting the agenda and contributing viewpoints in media deliberation, but they retain the deliberative autonomy to develop their own opinions from the viewpoints represented in the media. However, the capacity to form deliberatively autonomous opinions requires that citizens be exposed to opposing positions. As I noted in chapter 2, citizens are less likely to be swayed by political elites if there are counterelites to provide opposing viewpoints. Consequently, deficits in deliberative autonomy may stem less from the capacities of the citizenry than from the fact that the mainstream media simply do not include the full panoply of perspectives on public issues. As a result, the crucial fairness condition violated in media deliberation is deliberative equality: all possible viewpoints are not equally represented in the media.

With respect to mediated deliberation regarding race, deficits in deliberative equality are manifest in the three types of informal media representatives: policy experts, professional deliberators, and elected officials. Black policy experts rarely appear in the mass media, and when they do, they overwhelmingly discuss issues that are explicitly or implicitly associated with Blacks, like discrimination, homelessness, welfare, crime, gangs, or Martin Luther King, Jr. When nonBlack issues are discussed, the overwhelming majority of policy experts are White.[63] The increasing number of Black professional communicators, moreover, does not enhance the representation of Black perspectives in the media because journalistic norms require them to convey news stories in an objective, race-neutral manner. For instance, Black reporters covering crime issues do not communicate Black public opinion, which shares Whites' concerns with crime but supports strongly different views on its "causes and cures."[64]

Black elected officials, on the other hand, can and often do communicate a specifically Black perspective on news issues. The problem is that there are disproportionately few Black elected officials, and the media tend to portray them negatively. In an analysis of Chicago local news, researchers found that White elected officials were ten times more likely than Black officials to be shown speaking on public interest issues. Black officials were more commonly seen speaking about specifically Black issues, furthering the perception that Blacks violate publicity constraints by excessively focusing on group interests over common interests. Turning to national news coverage, Black politicians are more likely to be the focus of a scandal and are more likely to criticize government policy than are White politicians. In each case, nonracial factors can lead to these findings. For example, the national news media primarily cover public officials either because they are in a high profile office or because they are involved in a scandal. Given the paucity of Blacks in high elected office, they are more likely to be covered due to scandals. Similarly, Black officials are likely to be more dissatisfied with public policy, given the history and legacy of racial discrimination. The cumulative effect is a portrait of Black elected officials as scandal-prone complainers concerned only with Black interests.[65]

We thus face two interrelated problems regarding publics connected only through the mass media. First, implicit racial appeals can circumvent the publicity constraint of racial equality. Challenging implicit racial appeals requires an active public, but publics connected by mass media tend to be relatively passive and dominated by informal representatives. Second, although citizens have the capacity to incorporate media information in order to generate deliberatively autonomous opinions, actually doing so depends on realizing deliberative equality among the perspectives informally represented by professional communicators, policy experts, and public officials. Unfortunately, Black representatives in these three roles tend to be constrained in their ability to communicate a Black perspective, either through their invisibility, professional norms, or negative media portraits.

Both problems are vividly portrayed in the controversy surrounding the infamous "Willie Horton" advertisement supporting the elder George Bush's 1988 presidential campaign. In his treatment of this case, James Bohman suggests that a passive audience transformed itself into an active public in order to impose a public veto on this implicitly racist ad.[66] However, this public veto arose not from the general public itself but from two, more specific sources: the Black counterelite and the Black counterpublic. As Tali Mendelberg carefully points out, it was Jesse Jackson, the defeated candidate for the Democratic presidential nomination, who alerted the mass media to the implicit racism of the Horton ad. Stemming either from their deference to a sitting president or their desire to appear objective and nonpartisan, the mainstream media were unwilling to suggest that the ad was racist. Instead, they simply followed the Bush campaign's explicit claim that it merely raised questions about law and order. Jackson inserted this issue into the mainstream media's agenda, but the Democratic nominee, Michael Dukakis, did not; he was still seeking the votes of moderately conservative Whites.[67] So ultimately discrediting the Willie Horton ad stemmed not simply from the actions of the general public but from the specific actions of a member of a counterelite, an informal representative of the Black community.

Yet Jackson's leadership on this issue must itself be put into context. Jackson, like many Black public officials, generally received negative coverage in the mainstream media, indicative of the second type of problem: the lack of deliberative equality for Black representatives in the public sphere. During the 1988 campaign, the media focused on his ties to and public embrace of Louis Farrakhan, the anti-Semitic leader of the Nation of Islam. This focus persisted, despite the fact that the embrace occurred during Jackson's 1984 campaign and that Jackson distanced himself from Farrakhan during the 1988 campaign.[68] Indeed, Jackson's ability to lead the criticism of the Willie Horton ad depended not on his status in the mainstream media but on the support and advocacy of the Black media. The mainstream press followed the Bush campaign in framing the Willie Horton ad as a crime policy issue; the Black press immediately perceived its racist overtones.[69] Consequently, a Black, subaltern counterpublic, anchored in the Black press, took a strongly divergent stand from the general public anchored in the mainstream press.

Indeed, as Mendelberg carefully demonstrates, the White public was initially quite receptive to the Horton ad, rejecting it much later than the Black counterpublic and only when prompted by Jackson, a member of the Black counterelite.[70]

In general, counterpublics and counterelites can correct problems within the mainstream media and more effectively represent minority perspectives because they may be more capable of gaining hidden information and catering to smaller, overlooked media markets. Thus, they enhance deliberative equality by increasing the number of perspectives in the public sphere. Three examples can illustrate this. Susan Herbst demonstrates how in the mid-twentieth century the Black newspaper, the *Defender,* monitored racial violence, employment discrimination, and unequal service provision, issues ignored by the mainstream press.[71] Elizabeth Maguire points out that Black booksellers and the Black academic public supported Black authors when mainstream presses ignored them as unmarketable to a White audience.[72] Finally, Yen Le Espiritu documents how the mainstream and Asian-American press diverged in their coverage of a 1989 school shooting in Stockton, California. Whereas the former framed the event in terms of the need for gun control, the latter called it a racial issue, given that the school was seventy percent Asian, as were all of the dead and most of the wounded. Responding to pressure from informal representatives of the Asian community, police uncovered the perpetrator's history of racial resentment and ultimately concurred with the interpretation of the shooting as a racially motivated hate crime.[73]

Minority counterpublics also face problems in realizing deliberative equality with respect to their own internal diversity and shifting boundaries. Michael Dawson argues that the unified Black counterpublic disintegrated once segregation ended because this issue united Blacks and submerged latent fissures related to gender, class, and ideology.[74] And as discussed in chapter 1, Philip Kasinitz identifies ethnicity as another fissure in the Black public, given differences in how African-American and Caribbean media sources assessed Caribbean support for Ed Koch's 1985 mayoral campaign. The African-American media uniformly dismissed "Caribbeans for Koch," whereas the Caribbean media expressed a variety of affirmative and negative perspectives on this issue. But when deteriorating relations between Whites and Blacks led African-American and Caribbean publics to converge in their support for David Dinkins in 1989, this did not signal the end of the ethnic fissure but revealed its responsiveness to different political and social dynamics.[75] Intraracial, ethnic fissures also undermined deliberative equality within the Asian-American public. According to William Wei, Japanese Americans tended to dominate the Los Angeles paper *Guidra,* foreign-born Chinese tended to control New York's *Bridge,* and articles covering Japanese and Chinese American issues initially prevailed in UCLA's *Amerasia.* Such problems plagued these presses, even though they aimed to overcome parochial ethnic divisions in order to represent a unified, pan-Asian perspective.[76]

Whereas Dawson laments the divisions within the Black public sphere, Kasinitz and Wei suggest that deliberative equality may be enhanced as the proliferation of mediated counterpublics matches that of newly emerging collective identities. Although pan-Black and pan-Asian media sources are likely to exclude some perspectives, because of the internal diversity within these and other racial groups, the possibility exists that alternative counterpublics can emerge to represent the excluded perspectives. This reflects one of the greatest benefits of the public sphere: its flexible representation of new and divergent collective identities. If some media sources tend to be dominated by some groups, new media sources can represent publics that themselves run counter to the relatively dominant counterpublics.

Thus far, I have focused on how and to what extent counterpublics can enhance deliberative equality. However, they can also enhance deliberative autonomy in two ways. First, they can equalize or neutralize power relations between dominant and subordinate groups, thereby enabling members of subordinate groups to develop critical, reflective preferences. For example, the *Defender* was able to discuss racial grievances openly because its customer base was entirely Black, making it immune to White economic reprisals.[77] Second, counterpublics can enhance deliberative autonomy internally. The smaller size of counterpublics grants nonelites greater opportunities to respond actively to their informal media representatives. This capacity is illustrated in the case of *Guidra,* the Japanese-dominated newspaper, whose editors altered their politically radical editorials in response to criticism from their more moderate readers.[78]

These gains in deliberative equality and deliberative autonomy, however, can come at a potential price in terms of deliberative reciprocity. Counterpublics typically cater to a specific group, and potentially intensify the information dynamic of group conflict. However, this dynamic is enhanced not only by group-specific media but also by the mainstream media. In order to illustrate how both types of media contribute to information dynamics, let us revisit the 1990 Red Apple boycott, along with two other cases: the 1991 Los Angeles shooting of a Black teenager by a Korean merchant and the 1991 Crown Heights riots involving Lubavitcher Hasidic Jews and Caribbean immigrants in Brooklyn.

With respect to group-specific information, all three cases reveal common information dynamics. In the Crown Heights case, a car in a Lubavitcher motorcade fatally injured a Guyanese child. This sparked a riot, partly due to rumors among Caribbean bystanders that a Lubavitcher ambulance failed to attend to the injured child.[79] In the Los Angeles case, a Black teenager, Latisha Harlins, was shot by a Korean merchant, Soon Ja Du, following a physical altercation. Black resentment toward Korean merchants in the aftermath of this killing was aggravated by rumors that Korean merchants benefited from preferential policies by private banks and the federal government. These rumors falsely conflated Korean immigrants with Southeast Asian refugees, who did benefit from such policies. The corrosive effect of these rumors built up through articles and editorials in the African-American paper, the *Los Angeles Sentinel,* which depicted Korean merchants as taking over the Black community.[80] This portrait overlooked the fact that Korean merchants, particularly liquor store owners, had bought their businesses from African-American owners, who made significant profits prior to exiting this risky sector for more stable business opportunities.[81] In the Red Apple boycott, the alleged beating of a Haitian woman by a Korean greengrocer quickly led to mass mobilization, once false rumors emerged among the Haitian bystanders that the woman had been beaten into a coma. In turn, the Korean-language newspapers were more than willing to portray the boycott as a form of racism aimed at all Koreans, ignoring the fact that boycott leaders targeted only two specific stores and explicitly rejected any anti-Korean animus.[82]

But whereas group-specific information encouraged conflict, in all three cases the mainstream media also contributed to the information dynamic. Carol Conaway's analysis of New York newspaper coverage of the Crown Heights case reveals that the *New York Times* persistently framed this as a Black-White racial conflict, whereas the *New York Post* eventually shifted frames from Black-White racial conflict to Black anti-Semitism. Moreover, both papers rarely identified the three specific ethnic groups involved: African Americans, Caribbean Americans, and Lubavitcher Jews. This failure overlooked the tendencies among the interviewees to identify themselves and each other in specifically ethnic terms, thereby overlooking their specific grievances and their perceptions of each other. Conaway attributes these findings to the lack of well-informed reporters able to distinguish the specific ethnicities involved in the conflict, the unwillingness of the *Times* to report anti-Semitism for fear of appearing inflammatory, and the tendency of White journalists to overlook ethnic differences among African-descended individuals.[83]

In the case of the Red Apple boycott, substantial evidence suggests that New York newspapers, from the elite *New York Times* to tabloids like the *New York Post* and the *Daily News,* all portrayed the Black and Haitian protesters as irrationally scapegoating innocent and industrious Korean merchants. In the Los Angeles case, conversely, the *Los Angeles Times* portrayed the Korean community as callous and rude toward Black customers. Moreover, Los Angeles television stations played only the sections of a security tape showing the merchant shooting the teenager, omitting prior footage revealing that the two were engaged in a physical fight. This selective coverage fostered the image that the teen was an innocent victim of a money-grubbing Korean merchant. Claire Kim attributes the mainstream coverage of the Red Apple boycott to the internalization of positional stereotypes regarding lazy African Americans and industrious, almost super- (or sub-) human Asians. However, analyses comparing the New York and Los Angeles cases challenge this interpretation and instead suggest that the divergent coverage stemmed from political dynamics: African Americans were well established members of Los Angeles's ruling political coalitions, and African-American politicians promoted criticism of Korean merchants through media appearances.[84]

The presence of the information dynamic of conflict within group specific and mainstream media sources raises important problems for public sphere deliberation in a plural polity. However, strict regulation of group-specific and mainstream media in the name of fostering deliberative reciprocity would clearly contradict the communicative freedoms that remain central to a deliberative public sphere. Still, this does not mean that certain policies encouraging deliberative reciprocity within the public sphere should remain beyond the pale. This is a delicate matter that must determine whether the cure is worse than the disease. Assessing the prospects and dangers of trying to restructure the public sphere is the task of the next section.

RESTRUCTURING THE PUBLIC SPHERE?

I began this chapter by suggesting that my earlier themes of identity construction, the model of plural deliberation, and the dynamics of group conflict can provide helpful tools for assessing the deliberative role of civil society and the public sphere in a plural polity. Although I concur with many deliberative theorists that the public sphere remains a vital forum for deliberation among members of diverse collective identities, I contended that attention to my three themes would help clarify the dangers encountered by the public sphere in a plural polity. Attention to both the advantages and disadvantages of deliberation within the public sphere would, I asserted, aid our judgments of specific public sphere actors while also guiding possible reforms of the public sphere.

One of the most attractive features of the public sphere in a plural polity is its ability to provide flexible representation of internally diverse and shifting collective identities. The case of the Caribbean public sphere in New York nicely exemplifies this capacity. This public allowed Caribbean immigrants to separate themselves from the broader Black public sphere in order to debate openly whether the Caribbeans-for-Koch movement made political sense, an issue that was immediately dismissed by the Black public. However, as political and racial situations changed, the Caribbean public sphere came to align itself more closely with the Black public. This example suggests that the public sphere can allow for the flexible growth and decline in the representation of groups and identities that would otherwise lack representation within the democratic state because of their small numbers or lack of a territorial base.

But although the public sphere facilitates flexible representation, it is not immune to various dynamics of group conflict. For instance, group-based associations can enhance the substantive achievement of deliberative equality and autonomy among their members while also hindering deliberative reciprocity across group boundaries. Similarly, devolving state powers to group-specific associations can encourage the instrumental construction of identity and the resource dynamic of conflict. Social movements can successfully embody plural deliberation across group boundaries but also face difficult strategic dilemmas that can enable or constrain their deliberative success. Finally, the mass media can facilitate plural deliberation, but mediated deliberation potentially suffers deficits in deliberative equality and deliberative autonomy. Moreover, the presence of information dynamics within both the mainstream and group-specific mass media can lead social movements to intensify group conflict rather than plural deliberation. In response to these problems, plural deliberation provides criteria for judging the associations, media sources, and social movements that populate the public sphere. Such judgments will remain indispensable to deliberative democracy in a plural polity. However, plural deliberation, the dynamics of group conflict, and the idea of identity construction also provide criteria for reforming the public sphere and finding alternative sites for deliberation across group boundaries.

Given the vulnerability of the public sphere to dynamics of group conflict and the difficulty in redesigning informal, deliberative institutions, we might look to state institutions as alternative sites for plural deliberation. Of course, situating deliberation within the state is hardly without problems. Indeed, one of its most serious problems is the mirror image of one of the greatest benefits of the public sphere: state representation tends to be less flexible than public sphere representation, as representatives within the state must be formally authorized to speak for their constituents. In chapter 5, I will examine how electoral systems can enable flexibility within the process of authorizing representatives to speak for members of plural and constructed collective identities. Here, I wish to examine how the state can house relatively flexible representative deliberation through advisory panels, which are quasi-formal, deliberative institutions that advise state agencies but do not have full decision-making authority. Entertaining this alternative requires us to rethink how we identify an authentic deliberative setting.

There are at least two ways of identifying an authentic deliberative setting. Jean Cohen and Andrew Arato adopt an institutional approach, which argues that authentic deliberation emerges from civil society associations and social movements that are distinct from the economy or the state.[85] Alternatively, Mark Warren identifies deliberative settings not according to types of institutions but according to types of relations. For Warren, the critical trait of a deliberative setting is the existence of associational relations "based on normative influence."[86] Such associational relations can be found both within civil society organizations and economic firms or state institutions and agencies. Recall that Black booksellers were part of the institutional framework that helped support Black authors within the Black public sphere. According to Cohen and Arato's framework, booksellers should be classified as economic firms, not civil society actors. Conversely, Warren's framework can identify the role of booksellers within the public sphere in light of the associational relations that animate their practices. For instance, the business practices of the Black booksellers in question were clearly influenced by normative commitments supporting the circulation and influence of Black literary voices. Similarly, although the *Defender* was a business that sought to sell newspapers, its actions were influenced by its normative commitment to representing the perspectives of the Black community within and outside of Chicago. The profit imperative of these businesses remains unavoidable, but the role of normative, associational commitments should not be overlooked.

Associational relations within the state may also support public deliberation. A key function of the public sphere, Habermas argues, is to link the private sphere with the state. Specifically, the public sphere functions to detect problems suffered by ordinary citizens in their private lives, to develop possible solutions, and to transmit these solutions to the state.[87] Publics constituted by state agencies, I suggest, can also perform such functions. Because administrative agencies intersect with the private lives of citizens in order to administer policies, they often require the voluntary cooperation of those citizens in order to function effectively.[88] For the most part, researchers have focused on how environmental and planning agencies use deliberative settings to determine how best to carry out projects with community support. In this section, I will examine a case involving racial and ethnic groups.

In 1977, the federal Office of Management and Budget (OMB) issued Directive 15, recommending that all federal agencies adopt five racial/ethnic categories to measure federal compliance with civil rights legislation. The Census Bureau, in order to determine the effectiveness of these categories, created minority advisory committees populated by Black, Hispanic, Asian, and American Indian representatives. These advisory committees came up with the 1980 census classification of four racial categories (White, Black, Asian/Pacific Islander, and American Indian), one ethnic category (Hispanic, which could apply to members of any race), and the ethnic subcategories under the Asian/Pacific Islander (API) heading. Prior to the 1990 census, these advisory committees made significant additions to the ethnic subcategories under the API heading in order to improve response rates.[89]

In 1993, the Census Bureau and the OMB sought to assess these categories as used both in the census and in other federal agencies. This review, according to Melissa Nobles, "was significantly more open to public input and expert evaluation than the 1977 meetings had been."[90] The OMB sought public comment through an interagency committee made up of representatives of thirty federal agencies. This committee held congressional hearings, during which it considered adding four additional racial categories: multiracial, middle eastern/Arab, Native Hawaiian, and Hispanic.[91] Associations representing members of each of these groups participated equally in the hearings.

Three of the proposed changes were placed on the agenda by representatives of the minority associations: representatives from multiracial associations argued that exclusive racial categories failed to recognize their mixed status; Arab-American representatives argued that their present inclusion under the White category overlooked the forms of discrimination they suffered through negative media portraits and informal social prejudices; and Native Hawaiian representatives sought to exit the API category because they were an indigenous population not descended from immigrants. Only the proposed Hispanic race category was not initiated by a minority organization but emerged from the Census Bureau, which worried about Hispanics' high use of the "other race" category.[92]

In addition to setting the agenda, minority representatives did exert some influence on the final outcome, albeit amidst bureaucratic resistance. For instance, the Census Bureau sought to create four new racial categories. However, Arab and Hispanic representatives explicitly rejected this form of classification because they understood their collective identities as ethnic or cultural, not racial.[93] For census officials, creating discrete racial categories would simplify the tabulation of responses and cohere with the American conception of discrete racial groups. Indeed, even the multiracial category, while reflecting the reality of interracial procreation, nevertheless still presupposed the idea of miscegenation between individuals from two discrete races.[94] However, Arab and Hispanic representatives were able to defeat the measure, because they accurately predicted that the categories would prove unreliable.[95] In addition, a discrete multiracial category was rejected in favor of allowing individuals to choose multiple racial categories. The only proposal accepted in its original form was the new Hawaiian racial category, a change that Hawaiian representatives themselves had initially sought.

These hearings can be usefully analyzed using the conditions of plural deliberation. Recall that this is a quasi-formal, deliberative institution. Thus, the OMB and the Census Bureau remained free to accept or reject the findings of the hearings, but group representatives could not directly generate collective decisions over the census categories. As a result, the Hispanic and Arab representatives could not block unfavorable categories, which were eliminated only when the census realized that they would generate inaccurate tabulations.[96] On the other hand, this lack of decision-making power allowed this setting to fulfill deliberative rather than aggregative equality. The different minority associations were represented relatively equally, not in proportion to their greatly divergent demographic populations. Moreover, the lack of decision-making power may have also enhanced deliberative autonomy within these hearings. Though census officials and Congressional representatives enjoyed much greater capacities to determine the final outcome, Hispanic and Arab representatives had every incentive to remain assertive; they had nothing to lose and everything to gain by vocally expressing their preferences, a key procedural goal of deliberative autonomy. It is, however, more difficult to assess deliberative reciprocity, except to the degree that participants had little choice but to hear each other's viewpoints.

Although quasi-formal deliberative institutions may provide an alternative site for plural deliberation, this leaves open the question of whether public policies can improve the functioning of the public sphere itself. As we discussed earlier, the primary actors in the public sphere are social movements, associations, and the media. Using public policies to shape social movements seems both ineffective and dangerous: it would be ineffective because social movements, unlike associations and the mass media, are not institutional actors; it would be dangerous because social movements allow nonvested groups, those lacking ties to political officials, to bypass formal political processes and take their claims to the public. State-sponsored social movements might thus crowd out spontaneous social movements, leaving marginalized groups even fewer means of political influence. Some social movements representing intergenerational groups can foster conflict or chauvinism rather than plural deliberation. It seems counterproductive for the state to sponsor inclusive social movements. For better or worse, social movements should remain a truly spontaneous factor within the public sphere.

However, public policies can affect associations and the media in order to realize the criteria of plural deliberation and to neutralize the dynamics of conflict. This, of course, is a matter of some controversy. Yael Tamir and Nancy Rosenblum reject state involvement in associations as illegitimate, counterproductive, and inherently partisan.[97] However, Mark Warren accurately responds that the state is almost always already involved. The key question in most instances is "not *whether* the state should be involved, but rather *how* it should be involved."[98] At the very least, the state enables associations to exist by guaranteeing rights to expression and association. John Dryzek responds that states should do no more than this; incorporating civil society organizations into the state could ultimately deprive them of their vitality, as has occurred in Mexico. Civil society organizations should only be incorporated if their goals are congruent with state goals and if their incorporation does not deplete civil society.[99] Dryzek, however, is primarily concerned with the vitality of civil society; he is decidedly less troubled by the dangers associated with the dynamics of group conflict. As I have tried to demonstrate in this chapter, these dynamics remain a problem within a pluralistic public sphere, and consequently public policy should seek not only to maintain a vital civil society but to mitigate these dynamics and to realize plural deliberation.

Warren, I believe, steers us in the right direction. He outlines five ways that state policies can intervene into associations: direct regulation; equalization of bargaining power among associations, such as between labor unions and firms; income supports to reduce individuals' economic dependence on associations; economic incentives, like tax exemptions, to encourage certain types of associations; and public-private partnerships, such as the use of private resources for public benefit. For Warren, the advisability of state intervention depends upon two factors: an association's ease of exit and the means of social organization toward which it is oriented. State intervention is less justifiable when associations are easy to exit but more justifiable when they impose high exit costs, as an individual's autonomy is not constrained if he can easily leave an association. In turn, the state more justifiably intervenes when an association controls either economic or political resources than when it merely provides less tangible social goods. If an association can distribute valuable economic goods, or if the state devolves to it certain official powers, then the state intervenes more appropriately.[100] From this, Warren concludes that the state more justifiably intervenes into a church-run university than into the church itself.

With respect to realizing plural deliberation and neutralizing dynamics of group conflict, these distinctions are crucial. As the case of pan-Asian welfare associations demonstrates, intergenerational associations that distribute resources clearly implicate instrumental modes of identity construction and the resource dynamic of group conflict. For when an individual's resource base is closely related to membership in an ethnic or religious organization, that individual has a strong incentive to identify with that group, even absent any strong interpretive significance. And when a group association perceives that its resource interests conflict with those of another group, deliberative reciprocity between those groups will likely suffer. Thus, the state should avoid distributing resources through ethnic or religious organizations; this provides incentives for organizations to conflate collective identity and resource interests. In addition, the state is more justified in regulating intergenerational organizations that do not allow their members to exit easily. So if an association prevents girls from getting an education or leaving their homes, the state can intervene to guarantee education and free transit.

These examples are both negative cases, where the state works against an association. Alternatively, the state could try to encourage associations that further the criteria of plural deliberation and counter the dynamics of group conflict. For instance, the state could support multigroup associations that explicitly challenge positional stereotypes or promote intergroup deliberation. Two examples related to the problem of group conflict are the Black-Korean Alliance (BKA) and the Latino-Black Roundtable (LBR), both established by the Los Angeles city government's Human Rights Commission.[101] Made up of leaders from religious, business, and advocacy associations, these institutions conducted workshops wherein participants explicitly sought understanding across perspectives in order to mitigate conflict. In turn, each institution was able to generate some significant, conflict-reducing measures. The LBR discussed concerns shared by both groups, such as police brutality, and issues that divided the groups, such as city and county legislative redistricting. The BKA reached a consensus on a code of ethics according to which Korean merchants should interact with customers. Although each institution was able to generate some deliberative understanding across perspectives, each ultimately disbanded after a gradual decline in membership and participation. Moreover, the BKA's progress ran up against the 1991 Latisha Harlins shooting and the 1992 riots.[102]

In each case, four factors undermined these deliberative institutions. First, both institutions suffered from a lack of human and financial resources. Although the Los Angeles city government was willing to establish these organizations, it subsequently provided little ongoing funding. Second, their membership was not sufficiently representative of the communities involved. Although these associations included Black, Latino, and Korean participants, they tended to be wealthier and more educated than their general communities. In the case of the Latino-Black Roundtable, the Latino representatives were primarily Mexican-American, although a large proportion of the population was Salvadoran. And perhaps most problematically, members participated as individuals, not as representatives of specific associations or communities. As a result, they lacked input from the residents they were supposed to represent.[103]

Third, these organizations were too vague in their calling. In each case, they were established for the rather indistinct purposes of generating understanding across perspective and reducing conflict. They did not pursue any specific policy goal or institutional reform. Although such concrete aims can provide grounds for conflict among groups, well-chosen goals affirmed by the parties involved can help prevent the elimination by attrition that both organizations suffered. Plural deliberation's incorporation of strategic and aggregative dimensions can provide greater justification for incorporating interest-based, coalitional functions, along with the more purely deliberative functions of such organizations.

Finally, the Black-Korean Alliance reveals how external factors, like the Latisha Harlins killing or the 1992 riots, can undermine even intentionally structured deliberative processes. Here, we must recall that information dynamics of group conflict propagated by the mainstream and group-specific media can undermine the understanding across perspective so painstakingly sought by multigroup associations like the BKA and the LBR. Future multigroup associations might include among their goals public policies or other measures aimed at restructuring the mass media in order to mitigate the information dynamics of conflict and to create deliberative conditions. Realizing these conditions within restructured media, of course, means that we must restructure common conceptual understandings of the mass media. To use Warren's framework, we must pursue policies to promote associational relations over profit-oriented relations among media professionals.

Warren's focus on associational relations can help direct reforms aimed at improving the journalistic ethos of media professionals. The goal of such an ethos must be to enhance the deliberative autonomy of the citizens served by the media.[104] Norms for accurate reporting and balanced viewpoints are well established within the journalistic community, and these can enhance deliberative autonomy to some degree. And because some analysts of the information dynamic of conflict suggest that group-specific media sources lack these norms, propagating them may not only enhance deliberative autonomy but also mitigate group conflict.[105] However, Entman and Rojecki argue that these norms are insufficient to realize deliberative autonomy within the mainstream media because media professionals adhering to them can inadvertently propagate positional stereotypes. As a result, they argue that media professionals must strive to provide additional context when reporting on racially divisive issues. When accurately reporting on a crime involving a Black suspect, journalists should include relevant contextual information, such as the fact that Black and White crime rates are similar when controlled for employment status. Journalists enhance the deliberative autonomy of citizens not simply through the communication of accurate facts and balanced opinions; they must attempt to create a self-critical and contextual understanding of racially divisive situations and issues within the minds of their readers, listeners, or viewers. With respect to race, "audience understanding," beyond minimal accuracy, must become the animating impulse behind journalistic ethics.[106]

Entman and Rojecki realistically concede that a journalistic ethos oriented toward audience understanding requires external prodding. Thus, they suggest a national program of media monitoring of racial issues. Akin to the well-financed monitoring of violence in the media, race-related media monitoring would seek to mitigate the information dynamic of conflict by countering tendencies to propagate positional stereotypes in the mainstream media. Such monitoring could itself spark more widespread deliberation on the role of the media in exacerbating positional and information dynamics of conflict. Media monitoring, and the public deliberation surrounding it, can potentially generate the self-reinforcing, deliberative generation of trust that can help motivate plural deliberation. Whites, for instance, can gain a greater appreciation for the subtle and often unintentional misrepresentations of Blacks that are common in the mass media. Blacks, on the other hand, can come to realize that White apprehensions about Black crime need not be grounded in malevolent racism but in the misinformation that the media provide.[107] Although we cannot expect a quick elimination of the information and positional dynamics of conflict, media monitoring and its accompanying deliberation can foster the circular, deliberative generation of trust that in turn grounds deliberative reciprocity across racial lines.

Apart from this, policy reforms can also target restructuring the mass media. More specifically, plural coalitions can aim at policies to enhance the diversity of media sources within the public sphere. Clearly, freedom of the press must allow for independent, profit-oriented media to grow and multiply. However, the dominance of private, market-oriented media can be balanced by enhancing the role of politically independent, publicly owned media, on the model of the CBC or the BBC. Because such information sources need not follow the profit motive, they should be less prone to the sensationalism of capitalist media. However, we must recognize that public media will still be affected by broader cultural factors that perpetuate positional stereotypes. For this reason, diversifying the sources of information should also include policies and regulatory rules that support media ownership by racial and ethnic minorities, a goal granted constitutional validation by the United State Supreme Court in the *Metro Broadcasting* case. In doing so, the state recognizes that media licenses are not simply financial resources but points of access to a deliberative, pluralistic public sphere. Focusing on the deliberative character of a racially and ethnically diverse media, however, will require that licenses ideally be distributed according to deliberative, not aggregative, equality. In other words, the Federal Communications Commission should try to distribute media licenses equally among groups, not in proportion to their relative demographic sizes.

Of course, we must recognize that diversifying the ethnic or racial control of media sources can enhance deliberative equality without concurrently enhancing deliberative reciprocity. Increasing the number of groups able to communicate through the media does not guarantee that they will represent the perspectives of other groups accurately. Deliberative reciprocity within minority-owned media sources is likely to develop only by cultivating an improved journalistic ethos and by monitoring all media sources in the manner described above. Restructuring the media, like restructuring the public sphere, will require multiple reforms that deal with diverse problems. Achieving deliberative democracy in the plural polity will not be easy, but deliberative theory should elucidate the contours that political action must take to achieve this goal. I contend that the model of plural deliberation, the dynamics of group conflict, and the account of identity construction more precisely map these contours.

Yet if my theoretical claims are correct, achieving deliberative democracy in the plural polity will also require that reform-oriented political action move beyond the public sphere. The complex legitimacy of plural deliberation requires not only fair processes of deliberative understanding and criticism; it also requires that the informal, deliberative institutions of the public sphere be adequately connected to the formal, decision-making institutions of the state. And while various means are necessary to secure this connection, including interactions within quasi-formal advisory panels and the resonance between public opinion and public policy, elections will remain indispensable links between democratic public spheres and democratic states. Thus, in chapter 5 I will use the framework of plural deliberation, the political dynamic of group conflict, and the problem of identity construction to investigate how electoral systems can help to realize deliberative democracy in the plural polity.

5
Plural Deliberation, Representation, and Electoral Design

ELECTORAL SYSTEMS AND PLURAL DELIBERATION

If nothing else, the 2000 American presidential election brought popular attention to the role of electoral systems in translating votes into seats. Whereas the Democratic candidate, Al Gore, won the largest share of popular votes, Republican George W. Bush gained the majority of seats in the Electoral College. Apart from its many complex constitutional and political controversies, this race illuminated the simple fact that votes do not directly become seats. Rather, electoral systems transform votes into seats, in more or less proportional ways. But despite their complexity and importance to representative democracy, electoral systems have historically received little attention from political philosophers. With the notable exception of John Stuart Mill, most major political philosophers have not engaged in detailed analyses of electoral systems, let alone their relationship to deliberative democracy in a plural polity. More recently, however, three groups of political theorists have examined these institutions, using rigorous, normative arguments.

The first group of theorists focuses exclusively on how electoral systems aggregate citizens' votes. For these theorists, the normative analysis of an electoral system should focus exclusively on its ability to aggregate existing voter preferences accurately. Typical of this approach is Michael Dummett's claim that assessing the fairness of electoral systems reduces to two principles.

(1) Given the preferences of the electors in a constituency between the candidates, (A) which of those candidates will best represent that constituency, and (B) what system will as often as possible bring about the election of such candidates?

(2) Given the preferences of the electors in the nation at large between the political parties, (A) what should be the distribution of seats within Parliament of

those parties, and (B) what electoral system will as often as possible bring about such a distribution?[1]

In a similar vein, Burt Monroe claims to address the normative expectations regarding electoral systems through his "fully proportional representation" model. This model examines both first preferences and all lower preferences, whether they are based on personal interests or opinions of the common good.[2] With their focus on existing voter preferences, even if they include lower preferences, this group of aggregative analysts fails to incorporate the insights of deliberative democratic theory into their investigations.

A second group of scholars is somewhat more attuned to the concerns of deliberative democratic theory. Charles Beitz, for instance, comparatively assesses the single-member district plurality (SMDP) system used in the United States and the proportional representation (PR) system used in several European countries. He concludes that neither system is normatively superior to the other; both systems adequately fulfill citizens' three regulative interests in recognition (as authors of laws), equitable treatment (as subjects of laws), and deliberative responsibility (as reasonable and thoughtful assessors of laws).[3] Whereas proportional representation appears fairer, because it does provide more voters with the chance to vote for a winning candidate, this advantage is normatively unimportant because it does not reflect any of the three regulative citizen interests. Instead, SMDP is equally adept at recognizing citizens as equal authors of the laws, equally adept at treating citizens equitably, and equally able to promote public deliberation over a wide array of candidates, albeit within political party primaries rather than in general elections.[4] Thomas Christiano, on the other hand, favors PR over SMDP because the former allows more voters to support a winning candidate and enhances public deliberation by focusing general electoral campaigns upon a few, ideologically coherent parties rather than on thousands of individual candidates.[5] These theorists examine the relationship between electoral systems and deliberative democracy, but their analyses exclude several pertinent electoral systems, their portraits of deliberation are not terribly robust,[6] and their examinations of deliberation among a plurality of intergenerational groups are inadequate.[7]

However, a third group is particularly concerned with the relationship between electoral systems and deliberation among diverse intergenerational groups. Scholars such as Susan Bickford, Jane Mansbridge, and especially Melissa Williams have provided subtle and powerful arguments in favor of adopting different electoral systems that can better elect members of disadvantaged groups into representative assemblies. These scholars seek enhanced minority representation precisely in order to generate fair and inclusive deliberation across group boundaries.[8] But because they focus their attention on legislative rather than electoral deliberation, they primarily assess electoral systems in light of their capacity to aggregate the preferences of women or racial minorities more fairly, enabling these disadvantaged groups to elect descriptively similar representatives. They do not assess how different electoral systems can alter deliberation during election campaigns, nor do they examine how electoral systems can aggravate or mitigate dynamics of group conflict.

Interestingly enough, the role of electoral systems in shaping campaign deliberation has been most clearly perceived by empirical social scientists studying democracy in conflict-prone plural polities. For example, in his analysis of electoral systems for a democratic South Africa, Donald Horowitz concludes that the "test of a good electoral system is not to be found merely in the ratio of seats to votes or in the number of parties that emerge. The test lies instead in the posture adopted by parties with respect to other parties and with respect to other voters. Concretely, does the electoral system dispose the parties to ethnic and racial inclusion or exclusion?"[9] Similarly, Andrew Reynolds and Timothy Sisk, in discussing elections and conflict management in Africa, depict elections not only as translating votes into seats but also as a form of "social communication," whereby parties and candidates are forced to articulate their visions of society. In this way, electoral systems serve the more "normative function" of structuring "the boundaries of 'acceptable' political discourse."[10]

Although these scholars are primarily concerned with how electoral systems mitigate the political dynamic of conflict, their analyses illuminate how electoral systems differ in the publicity constraints they impose upon candidates and parties. If an electoral system effectively requires candidates and parties to win votes from diverse groups in order to gain election, it forces these candidates and parties to expose themselves to a wider and more diverse public. The result is that candidates and parties must campaign in a more inclusive manner; they cannot seek victory on the basis of one group's votes alone. Moreover, if an electoral system increases the number of candidates or parties that run in an election, it can subject them to the critical scrutiny of counterelites, like other candidates. As a result, candidates can be exposed to a more expansive public, and if they try to circumvent this broader publicity constraint through implicit racist claims, challengers can expose these appeals, as Jesse Jackson did during the 1988 presidential campaign.

For this reason, a normative analysis of electoral systems for a plural polity must assess not only how they translate votes into seats or how well they aid the election of minority representatives; it must also examine how they influence the campaigns that shape voter preferences in the first place. Do certain electoral systems foster campaigns that include a wide variety of racial, ethnic, or cultural perspectives? Do they encourage candidates to engage voters across diverse perspectives and worldviews? Do they reward ethnically exclusive candidates or political parties at the expense of more inclusive candidates or parties? The importance of these questions suggests that preference aggregation is a necessary but insufficient criterion for normatively evaluating electoral systems in a plural polity. Instead, adequate normative assessment demands plural deliberation's three conditions—political equality, political autonomy, and political reciprocity—in their aggregative and deliberative dimensions.[11] Let me sketch how these criteria would apply to electoral systems.

Most clearly applicable to electoral systems is the criterion of aggregative equality, which requires one person ⇔ one vote/equal votes ⇔ equal value.[12] This criterion applies directly to the problem of wasted votes, those cast either for losing candidates or in excess of what a winning candidate needed for election. No electoral system can eliminate all wasted votes; democratic procedures always create some losers. Nevertheless, electoral systems differ greatly in the number of votes that go wasted, especially in elections for legislative assemblies.[13] Differences in wasted votes generate differences in the proportionality between a party's votes and seats. Wasted votes also contribute to the problem of minority vote dilution, where members of disadvantaged racial or ethnic minorities, such as Black Americans or Muslim Indians, are unable to gain election due to their geographic dispersion and the persistence of discriminatory voting by numerically dominant groups.

Aggregative autonomy assesses the extent to which an electoral system provides citizens with feasible choices among alternative candidates or alternative political constituencies. With respect to alternative candidates, aggregative autonomy judges negatively those systems that allow only a single political party, encourage uncontested elections, or excessively hinder the introduction of new candidates or parties. It applies primarily to parliamentary parties or candidates, those that end up gaining representation within the legislature, as opposed to elective parties or candidates, those that only contest elections but rarely, if ever, gain representation.[14] Ralph Nader, for example, can be considered an elective candidate because he contested the 2000 presidential election and contributed to campaign deliberation but had little chance to win office. With respect to alternative constituencies, aggregative autonomy is reduced by those electoral systems that group citizens into a constituency prior to their political activity. Voters enjoy greater autonomy to the extent that they can exercise more choice over how they will define themselves politically, as opposed to being defined as a constituency a priori by judicial or other governmental bodies, for example when race-conscious electoral districts are drawn.[15]

Aggregative reciprocity reflects the willingness of candidates and representatives to engage in fair bargaining with those supported by other groups. Electoral systems can affect aggregative reciprocity on two levels. On the legislative level, they can affect the bargaining power of group representatives by enhancing or diminishing their legislative representation. Parties with more seats can more effectively bargain with other parties. Here, legislative votes become the good to be exchanged. On the electoral level, electoral systems can provide incentives or disincentives for candidates from different groups to make campaign alliances with each other. Parties can agree not to field candidates in districts sought by their electoral allies, so long as this favor is reciprocated. Here, expected voter support becomes the bargaining resource. Aggregative reciprocity on the legislative level roughly corresponds with the intergroup, seat-pooling strategy associated with Arend Lijphart's consociational model of democracy in plural polities. Here, electoral systems are assessed in terms of their capacity to enable representatives of different groups to strike fair bargains following an election. On the electoral level, conversely, it corresponds with the intergroup, vote-pooling strategy advocated by Donald Horowitz. Here, candidates or parties from different ethnic or racial groups seek to make alliances prior to an election.[16]

Even though aggregative criteria are commonplace in the assessment of electoral systems, deliberative criteria are rarely applied, despite the fact that they are crucial for assessing electoral campaigns. Recall that *deliberative equality* requires that all relevant viewpoints must enjoy equal opportunities to make their case within a public, deliberative forum, regardless of their numerical support. Within electoral competition, this condition is most prominent in formal debates, which commonly grant equal speaking time for all viable candidates, regardless of their popularity. Although pragmatic concerns might justify excluding fringe candidates, viable candidates are still granted equal speaking time, even if one clearly enjoys more popular support than the others. Similarly, deliberative equality reflects the sensibility behind some countries' requirement that candidates receive equal amounts of media time, regardless of their previous or predicted numerical support.[17]

Electoral systems subtly enhance deliberative equality through their encouragement of elective, as opposed to parliamentary, parties. Whereas aggregative autonomy assesses the inclusion of diverse parliamentary candidates or parties, deliberative equality assesses the inclusion of elective candidates or parties. The potential importance of elective candidates and parties becomes clearer by recalling the Willie Horton ad discussed in chapter 4. In this case, Jesse Jackson, the defeated Democratic presidential primary candidate, exposed the implicit racial message behind that ad. In certain electoral systems, a candidate like Jackson, who had little chance of winning the general election, would not have been excluded by the primary. Instead, he could have contested the general election, without harming his most favored alternative candidate, Democratic primary winner Michael Dukakis. Although Jackson was able to remain politically active during the 1988 campaign, his activity was constrained because he did not contest the general election. Thus, electoral systems that encourage elective parties or candidates to continue to campaign in the general election can facilitate criticism of parliamentary candidates and parties, while introducing new ideas and positions within campaign deliberation.

Perhaps most important, electoral systems can differ significantly in their capacity to foster *deliberative reciprocity* across group boundaries. Because deliberative reciprocity reflects the dispositions held by participants within deliberation, it requires distinct deliberative motivations grounded in moral psychology, cultural self-understandings, publicity constraints, and the deliberative generation of trust. However, certain electoral systems can provide strategic incentives for candidates to extend deliberative reciprocity across group boundaries by transforming the political dynamic of group conflict. Under certain circumstances, some electoral systems can reward candidates who appeal to voters across group boundaries, while punishing those who make ethnically exclusive appeals. In effect, these electoral systems subject candidates to wider publicity constraints, requiring them to appeal to a broader and more diverse public. The result is a strategic incentive to adopt deliberative reciprocity.

Such deliberative reciprocity might not be sincere; however, insincerity also affects the deliberative motivation within publicity constraints. Recall Jon Elster's argument regarding the civilizing effect of hypocrisy. If candidates are forced to appear as if they care about the interests of multiple groups, this can constrain their ability surreptitiously to introduce policies that really benefit only one group. Electoral incentives intensify such publicity constraints; candidates can be directly and actively punished by voters, who retain the power of the ballot. This contrasts with the weaker publicity constraints of the public sphere, where the public lacks any formal power over speakers. Moreover, when an electoral system combines the strategic generation of deliberative reciprocity with the inclusion of more diverse elective candidates and parties, those candidates who would introduce implicit racist appeals remain doubly vulnerable to voters and to elective challengers. So although strategic, electoral incentives cannot motivate deliberative reciprocity to its fullest extent, they can do so indirectly, by imposing effective publicity constraints on candidates.

Deliberative autonomy proves to be the most difficult criterion to apply in comparing electoral systems. Recall that deliberative autonomy aims at having citizens develop critical, reflective preferences regarding candidates by negating coercive, economic, or cultural power within plural deliberation. Election monitors can neutralize coercive power, and equitable campaign funding and media access might neutralize economic power among candidates; however, both of these measures can equally improve all electoral systems and thus cannot be used to differentiate among them. Neutralizing cultural power, even if alternative forms of communication are included, remains tricky in any deliberative forum, not just in electoral campaigns. Finally, the problem of applying deliberative autonomy intensifies when we examine deliberation between citizens and representatives or candidates.

Plural deliberation can proceed along three axes: among citizens, among representatives or candidates, and between representatives or candidates and citizens. Horizontal deliberation among citizens or among candidates or representatives can be assessed using all of plural deliberation's fairness criteria because all participants along these axes are relatively equal in standing. In general, there should be no classes of citizens or representatives privy to information inaccessible to others. However, vertical deliberation between citizens and political elites, like representatives or candidates, typically violates deliberative autonomy. Candidates, and especially representatives, have access to legislative and policy information beyond the reach of most citizens. Even relatively well-informed citizens tend to defer to their representatives.[18] This leads to a curious asymmetry regarding deliberation along this axis. Candidates and representatives enjoy great opportunities to educate or manipulate citizens, but they are not allowed to argue critically with their constituents, who may even become irate when they try to do so.

William Bianco claims that this behavior confirms rational choice theory's postulate that political communication is not binding but merely "cheap talk," as all speakers could be lying. Gerry Mackie, however, argues that cheap talk models err by failing to recognize that communication would break down if all people really were liars. Drawing on analytical philosophy and personal experience, Mackie argues that political communication typically assumes that interlocutors do tell the truth. But once a single lie is revealed, the liar is communicatively ostracized.[19] How do we reconcile these conflicting claims? Plural deliberation can provide an answer. As Jürgen Habermas points out, deliberation can only proceed under conditions akin to what I have called deliberative autonomy. Within our social and political life, the practice of deliberation only works to the extent that we enjoy the autonomy to decide freely whether a speaker's reasons are convincing. This autonomy distinguishes being persuaded through reasons from being talked into something through misinformation, deception, manipulation, or coercion.[20] Whereas the more symmetrical relations among citizens or political elites are more likely to approximate deliberative autonomy, the highly asymmetrical relationship between a representative and a citizen typically violates it thoroughly.

Citizens dismiss as cheap talk representatives' attempts to persuade them because they cannot reliably determine whether they are being rationally convinced or being talked into something. These violations persist even when representatives meet with highly educated constituents, including those with doctoral degrees or considerable policy information, because most citizens are not privy to the parliamentary procedures or strategic bargaining of a modern legislature. Thus, even if a representative can be criticized for supporting a policy that falls far short of the ideal, she can still argue that this inferior policy was the best option in this legislature at this time. Most citizens, even highly educated ones, lack the information to assess such justifications, unless they are Congress scholars or lobbyists.

But if citizens do not deliberate critically with representatives and candidates, they do judge the consistency of their actions and the content of their positions in relation to competitors.[21] So although deliberative autonomy may be violated in interactions between citizens and candidates or representatives, it is important to realize deliberative autonomy among candidates in election campaigns, so that citizens can judge their competing positions. Furthermore, deliberative autonomy and deliberative equality among candidates can enable more candidates to enter campaign deliberation and potentially expose each other's inconsistencies. Finally, electoral incentives for deliberative reciprocity can raise the costs to candidates who appeal to a narrow public, especially if competing candidates have incentives to expose hypocrisy or implicit racial appeals. Deliberative criteria clearly are important for assessing electoral systems. However, we cannot overlook the fact that electoral systems cannot be distinguished according to deliberative autonomy along the citizen–representative axis. Instead, assessing electoral systems along this axis requires recourse to aggregative autonomy, which reflects the capacity of citizens to choose among different candidates or constituencies. This point will complicate our assessment of deliberative theories of representation.

ELECTORAL SYSTEMS AND THE PROBLEM OF DELIBERATIVE REPRESENTATION

Unlike participatory theories of democracy, deliberative theories do not necessarily disparage representation and representative institutions. Given the aim of securing collective decisions through reflective preferences, and given the size and complexity of modern polities, deliberative theories see representation as a legitimate way to allow a smaller group of representatives to engage in more informed, reflective, and critical deliberation. The key for deliberative theories is to strike a balance between two concerns: the requirement that representatives be sufficiently free to transform their policy preferences during legislative deliberation, and the requirement that they remain connected to their constituents through deliberation along the representative–citizen axis. Thus, deliberative representatives must embody trustee and delegate aspects of representation, although there is considerable disagreement on how to balance the two.

Amy Gutmann and Dennis Thompson argue that representatives must enjoy trustee independence from constituents' policy preferences during the legislative session so that they can alter their initial policy preferences while deliberating. Such alterations are justified because legislative deliberation can achieve two things: it can reveal that representatives' initial policy preferences would not actually fulfill their constituents' interests, and it can expose representatives to the interests of citizens outside their own constituencies. On the other hand, the representative is more like a delegate to the extent that he must regularly deliberate with his constituents, especially to justify legislative decisions that deviate from their preferences.[22] Iris Marion Young's model of deliberative representation requires a more complete blending of the trustee and delegate aspects. Representatives acting as trustees during legislative deliberation are nevertheless bound by delegate constraints in two ways: they recollect the deliberations of their constituents during the previous election and they anticipate future deliberations with constituents, either in the upcoming election or in representative–citizen assemblies between elections.[23]

What hamstrings both models are the expectations placed upon representative–citizen deliberation. Representatives are asked to justify their independent legislative actions to citizens, to persuade these citizens that such actions were wise. The problem is that citizens are unlikely to accept such justifications or attempts to persuade, given the deficits in deliberative autonomy caused by representatives' near monopoly on parliamentary information. Although citizens may be willing to grant certain representatives significant leeway to make independent trustee decisions during the legislative session, they remain unwilling to engage in persuasive or justificatory deliberation with those representatives.[24] At most, citizen–representative communication allows for mutual information exchanges: representatives inform citizens of their legislative activity and citizens inform representatives of their concerns. What is exchanged is information, not justifications or criticisms. As a result,

such communication reflects the pooling of information associated with aggregation, not the critical testing of claims associated with plural deliberation.

Aware that violations of deliberative autonomy pervade citizen–representative
deliberation, we might consider Thomas Christiano's alternative depiction of the
trustee-delegate relationship in deliberative representation. Representatives are del-
egates bound by citizen mandates regarding broad political aims (interests, opinions, perspectives, or world-views), but they are trustees over the technical means
(policy preferences) to secure such aims. Thus, elections allow candidates to offer
contesting sets of aims and allow citizens to choose among those aims. Legislative
sessions then allow representatives to determine the means to achieve them.[25] At
first blush, Christiano's alternative has considerable merit. The policy preferences
of most citizens are often vague or entirely absent; they more consistently express
concerns about ends, whether these reflect their personal interests or opinions about
the overall condition of the polity.[26] But before endorsing Christiano's account, we
must address two points.

First, the contestation of aims requires critical, deliberative exchanges only
among candidates or parties. To the extent that candidates or parties appeal to citizens, they engage in aggregative information pooling, not in critical deliberation.
Citizens acquire this information and then deliberate among themselves before
exercising aggregative autonomy in choosing the aims offered by a candidate or
party. Second, this model requires candidates or parties to provide a clear platform
of broad aims from which voters can then choose. Christiano favors representation
by party over representation by individuals because such clear platforms are more
typical of disciplined, ideologically coherent parties. And because disciplined, ideological parties are more common in the party list, proportional representation system (list PR), he favors this over the Anglo-American, single-member district
plurality system (SMDP).

Both Bernard Manin and Anne Phillips take issue with the last point for two
reasons. First, policy questions have become more complex, rendering it more
difficult to anticipate which issues will be most salient over the years between elections. Second, society's relevant cleavages have become more complicated, with
ethnicity and gender now competing with the class cleavages reflected by most
political parties. Such policy and identity flux precludes tight adherence to party
platforms; consequently, voters cannot prospectively direct their representatives'
actions but can only retrospectively judge the actions taken, which leads to greater
representative independence.[27] Such increased trusteeship, Phillips concludes, increases the importance of descriptive representation: citizens can be expected to
trust trustees who bear a greater resemblance to themselves. In this way, descriptive
representation may provide a new, more flexible model of accountability under
conditions of trustee representation and retrospective voting.[28]

However, Manin and Phillips base their claims on relatively little comparative
empirical research. Indeed, Richard Katz provides considerable evidence that parties in PR systems remain more disciplined and ideologically coherent than par-

ties in SMDP systems.[29] Manin and Phillips overlook the possibility that racial or ethnic parties may develop in order to reflect the ethnic fissures overlooked by class-based parties. As a result, the type of party representation that Christiano seeks might remain relatively more viable in party list PR systems when compared to SMDP, even if we cede the points made by Manin and Phillips. On the other hand, Christiano does overstate the capacity for party list PR to create ideologically coherent, disciplined parties, as these are affected not only by the electoral system but also by a society's political culture and a state's legislative-executive structure. Ideological, disciplined parties are aided by parliamentary systems that fuse the legislature and the executive, whereas weak, American-style parties are facilitated by presidential systems that separate these two branches of government.

That being said, we are still left with the first part of Christiano's model. Critical deliberation primarily occurs along the two horizontal axes involving candidates or citizens. Along the vertical axis involving citizens and candidates, we can primarily expect aggregative information pooling: citizens use the information provided by candidates or parties to exercise aggregative autonomy in choosing representatives. These representatives may be individuals or parties, or even a combination of the two, such that citizens use party labels to simplify their choice of individual candidates. Following electoral deliberation, citizens may choose descriptive representation in the form of individual candidates or group-based political parties, should the latter exist. However, descriptive representation should be justified through critical deliberation among citizens and among candidates, wherein claims of trust between descriptively similar representatives and citizens are critically tested.

The importance of descriptive representation in generating trust is well grounded. For instance, descriptive similarities can ground citizens' willingness to grant representatives the legislative leeway associated with trustee representation.[30] More precisely, descriptive similarities can lead citizens to trust that they share interests and opinions with their representatives. Focusing on interests, Melissa Williams notes that Reconstruction-era Black citizens were concerned that White representatives would not be subject to the same race-based laws that confronted them. She also points out that contemporary, facially neutral laws, such as drug penalties, capital punishment, or hate-crimes laws, can have divergent effects on Blacks and Whites.[31] In this way, Black constituents may justifiably assume that Black representatives will share their interests. With respect to shared opinions, David Lublin documents how Black members of the House of Representatives better represent Black public opinion, which is far to the left of most White public opinion, even that of White Democrats. Thus, Black representatives provide substantive representation of Black opinions through their consistently left-leaning legislative activity.[32]

Lublin identifies a close relationship between Black public opinion and Black representatives' legislative activity, but he finds a more complex picture when examining Latinos. Whereas Puerto Rican public opinion falls on the left of the Democratic party spectrum, Mexican public opinion falls within its median, and

Cuban public opinion falls on the right of the political spectrum, well within the ideological boundaries of the Republican party. Latino representatives tend to reflect the public opinion of their own ethnic group only when that group constitutes the district majority. When elected from a district that is Latino-majority but composed of multiple Latino ethnic groups, a Latino representative will track the opinion of his district rather than his own ethnic group. Thus, the legislative activity of Representative Bob Menendez, a Cuban American, matches the public opinion of his mixed Latino district rather than that of his own Cuban ethnic group.[33] In this way, descriptive representation confronts internal diversity within Latino opinion.

The internal diversity of Latino opinion can be matched by internal diversity regarding interests. As was discussed in chapter 1, Latino immigrants in New York confront legal vulnerabilities not faced by Puerto Rican representatives, who are citizens by birth. Thus, the discrepancy in interests that Williams finds between White representatives and Black constituents can be replicated when Latino representatives differ in nationality from their constituents. Under certain circumstances, this problem may also emerge when African-American representatives represent West Indian or African immigrant constituents, especially in local settings not addressed by Lublin's analysis of Congressional representation.

As I argued in chapter 1, I do not think that Iris Marion Young's idea of perspective solves the problem of descriptive representation amidst internal diversity. While Young admits that intergenerational groups can differ in their interests and opinions, she argues that they share a social perspective through their position in society. Thus, Latinos should share a social perspective that grounds their differing interests or opinions. However, because multiple and distinct social perspectives may inhabit a single collective identity, Young ultimately is forced to admit that social perspective does not resolve the problem of internal diversity.[34] According to my analysis in chapter 1, intergenerational collective identities can include multiple and distinct social perspectives, through differences generated by different modes of identity construction. Instrumental-structural sources, like informal perceptions and laws, may lump all Blacks together, but interpretive sources may distinguish West Indians, African immigrants, multiracial individuals, and African Americans. Moreover, different instrumental-structural sources may differentiate groups: informal perceptions may assimilate all Latinos, whereas citizenship laws may differentiate immigrants from citizens.

Despite these concerns, I do not wish to dismiss the importance of social perspective or descriptive representation within a plural, deliberative democracy. Rather, I wish to emphasize that the choice of representatives depends upon critical deliberation that tests the validity of claims to shared interests, opinions, and even perspectives. As I argued in chapter 2, the claimed political relevance of a perspective must be subject to critical deliberation. But note that such critical deliberation should occur primarily along the horizontal axes among citizens and among candidates. Candidates, of course, will have an interest in portraying themselves as sharing interests, opinions, and perspectives with as many citizens in their district as possible. But because deliberative autonomy is so often violated in deliberation between citizens and candidates or representatives, we cannot expect fair and critical deliberation along this axis. Representatives and candidates are likely to send signals or information to citizens that they share their interests, opinions, perspectives, or world-views, but such communication bears less resemblance to critical deliberation than to the information pooling associated with aggregative democracy. Critical deliberation aimed at generating reflection regarding interests, opinions, perspectives, and world-views is likely only among citizens or among candidates.

Candidates must critically test each other regarding whether a certain perspective is politically more relevant than another. So, for instance, an African-American candidate might debate a West Indian candidate over whether district voters require representation as Black Americans or as West Indian immigrants. Alternatively, candidates may debate whether a shared perspective trumps shared interests or opinions. Citizens, in turn, must critically test the political relevance of different perspectives among themselves, while also deliberating on the relative weight to place upon shared perspectives, world-views, interests, or opinions. Once such critical deliberation occurs, citizens can then use the information provided by representatives to exercise aggregative autonomy in choosing which representative best reflects the characteristic they want represented.

Yet the ability of citizens to exercise aggregative autonomy over representatives requires that they have an adequate array of alternative candidates from which to choose. And in a plural polity, this means having candidates who can reflect not only different interests and opinions but also different perspectives and world-views. In a plural polity citizens must also exercise aggregative autonomy over their constituencies. Citizens must not only decide which candidate best reflects their interests, opinions, perspectives, or world-views; they must also decide which other citizens sufficiently share these characteristics to constitute a common constituency. In order to clarify how an electoral system may or may not enable citizens to exercise aggregative autonomy over constituencies, we must distinguish between the objective and subjective senses of "constituency."

An *objective constituency* reflects the legal grouping of citizens into geographic, occupational, or group-based electoral rolls. For example, in territorially based electoral systems, objective constituency is reflected in a geographic electoral district. *Subjective constituency* reflects the autonomous choice of citizens to come together as a community that shares interests, opinions, a social perspective, or a world-view. Iris Marion Young describes the subjective sense of constituency when she claims that constituencies are formed only in anticipation of the act of selecting a representative, when citizens come together in a public sphere to deliberate regarding what they wish to have represented.[35] Charles Beitz clarifies how electoral systems can either enable or constrain the aggregative choice of subjective constituency. He argues that in single member district plurality (SMDP) systems "constituencies are established by politicians and judges who apportion the population among districts." This contrasts with proportional representation (PR) systems, where "constituencies define themselves through the voting process."[36] Beitz's general intuition is correct, but he overlooks how most PR systems do require drawing some district lines.

The assessment of electoral systems and their forms of objective constituency in a plural polity should not only include aggregative autonomy over representatives and constituency; it should also depend upon the enhancement of deliberative reciprocity across group boundaries. Enhancing aggregative autonomy and deliberative reciprocity will require attention to three structural characteristics of an electoral system: its objective constituencies or geographic districts, its electoral formula for selecting representatives, and its ballot structure. Together, these features interact to shape an electoral system's thresholds of representation and exclusion, which vitally influence its capacity to enable aggregative autonomy over constituency and deliberative reciprocity across group boundaries. Let me briefly explain these structural characteristics.

Objective constituencies or geographic electoral districts differ in their *district magnitude* (DM), or the number of representatives elected from a single district. Single member districts, like those in the United States, have a DM of one; multimember districts can vary greatly in their DM, which will always be more than one. All things being equal, multimember districts enhance aggregative autonomy over representatives because there is a greater number of candidates from which to choose. Electoral districts can also differ in whether they include a homogeneous or heterogeneous set of groups within their borders. In a plural polity, heterogeneous districts are a necessary but insufficient condition for aggregative autonomy over constituency and for deliberative reciprocity across group boundaries. Campaign deliberation can only cross group boundaries if there are members of different groups within the district.

Electoral formulas differ in how they allow a candidate to be elected. Under a *plurality* formula, a candidate wins simply by getting the most votes, even if this number falls short of a numerical majority. When there are more than two candidates, it is possible for the plurality winner to garner less than the majority of votes, as occurred in the 2000 presidential race when George W. Bush won Florida even though he had less than half of the votes cast there. Under a *majority* formula, a candidate wins only when securing over 50 percent of all votes cast. Should no candidate win a majority, a candidate is chosen either through a run-off election among the top two candidates or by transferring ballots, as will be discussed below. Under a *proportional* formula, candidates in multimember districts are elected when they secure a certain minimal proportion of the vote. The specific proportion needed for election can vary greatly under different proportional systems, but generally the proportion decreases as the district magnitude increases.

Three types of ballots are pertinent to the systems discussed below. With a *categorical* ballot, citizens cast one vote per party or candidate; with a *cumulative* ballot, they cast multiple votes and can lump their votes onto a single candidate or distribute them among multiple candidates; with an *ordinal* ballot, voters rank their preferences among candidates. Ordinal ballots typically are combined with an electoral formula that includes a transfer mechanism. Thus, if your first-preference candidate finishes last, the electoral system then tallies your second preferences. Ordinal ballots with a transfer mechanism can be used with majority or proportional electoral formulas. All things being equal, ordinal ballots tend to improve deliberative reciprocity by favoring candidates who can gain lower preference votes from different groups. I will discuss this in much greater detail below.

District magnitude (DM), the electoral formula, and the ballot structure together shape the percentage of votes that are usually required to elect a representative. This percentage can be expressed through two thresholds: the *threshold of inclusion* (also known as the threshold of representation) and the *threshold of exclusion*. The threshold of inclusion reflects the minimal number of votes needed to elect a candidate under the best of circumstances. In effect, it answers a candidate's question, "What is the smallest number of votes I need to have a chance to get elected?" The threshold of exclusion reflects the minimum number of votes needed to gain election under the worst of circumstances, typically meaning only one other candidate with cohesive voter support. In effect, it answers the candidate's question, "What is the smallest number of votes I need to guarantee getting elected, no matter how many other candidates there are?" The threshold of exclusion is higher than the threshold of inclusion. And according to Arend Lijphart, the threshold of exclusion is much easier to calculate than the threshold of inclusion because the latter varies greatly with the number of candidates or parties contesting the election, whereas the former varies only with the structural characteristics of the electoral system.[37]

Consider the threshold of inclusion for an American SMDP district. If there are three candidates, then one could potentially get elected with just over one-third of the vote if the other two candidates equally split the rest of the vote. But if there are five candidates, then one could potentially get elected with just over one-fifth of the vote, again as long as the other four equally split the rest of the vote. The threshold of exclusion, on the other hand, remains at 50 percent; if a candidate wins just one vote more than this, that candidate is guaranteed to win.[38] Thresholds of exclusion in proportional and semiproportional systems are lower than those in plurality or majority systems; in addition, they decline as the district magnitude increases. Consequently, advocates of enhanced minority descriptive or substantive representation tend to favor proportional and semiproportional representation systems with at least moderately sized district magnitudes.[39] This is because aggregative autonomy over constituency is greatly enhanced as a group's population nears the district's threshold of exclusion. When this occurs, a group can easily elect a representative beholden to it if its members feel they desire representation along group lines; but if that group's members desire a different form of representation, say according to class rather than race, individuals within the group can coalesce into a different subjective constituency.

I have suggested that ordinal ballots tend to enhance deliberative reciprocity; this, of course, presupposes that candidates seek election and reelection as a goal. Clearly, the election motive is not exhaustive: representatives may seek to enact beneficial laws, whereas candidates may contest elections simply to promote their positions within public deliberation.[40] Yet, because a representative cannot enact policy without getting elected,[41] and a candidate cannot gauge support for his position without getting votes, the desire to be elected, or simply to gain votes, remains a strong incentive behind the actions of representatives or candidates. For this reason, electoral incentives will remain an important, if not exclusive, motivation behind representatives and candidates, and, as a result, electoral systems will differ in the incentives they provide candidates to extend deliberative reciprocity across group boundaries.

I realize that electoral extensions of deliberative reciprocity will not overcome the deficits in deliberative autonomy that characterize communication between citizens and representatives or candidates. Thus, the incentives that electoral systems provide to extend deliberative reciprocity across group boundaries will not generate fully critical deliberation along this axis. We cannot expect candidates to criticize citizens' preferences, interests, opinions, perspectives, or world-views: perhaps more precisely, we cannot expect citizens to accept such criticism. Instead, we should expect incentives toward deliberative reciprocity to encourage candidates to portray themselves as inclusive with respect to diverse interests, opinions, perspectives, and world-views. Candidates will signal to citizens that they will reach out to perspectives or world-views that they themselves might not fully share. If our hopes are fulfilled, electoral incentives toward deliberative reciprocity should discourage the exclusivist political dynamic of group conflict and encourage an inclusive form of campaigning. For example, White candidates should be encouraged not to heighten racial fears but to reach out to Black voters. Although such incentives will not obviate the potential benefits of descriptive representation, they can still play an important role in generating substantive representation of interests and opinions without descriptive representation, and in encouraging inclusive campaign deliberation.

In sum, we can assess electoral systems according to most of plural deliberation's criteria. Aggregative equality can assess problems of wasted votes, proportionality, and minority vote dilution; aggregative autonomy can assess the capacity of citizens to choose their subjective constituencies and parliamentary candidates or parties; aggregative reciprocity can assess the capacity of candidates to make electoral alliances and of representatives to make legislative alliances. Deliberative equality can assess the inclusion of a wide array of elective candidates or parties, those that contest elections but have little chance of winning election. Finally, deliberative reciprocity can assess the incentives that an electoral system provides for candidates to reach out and communicate inclusive signals across group boundaries. Deliberative autonomy is almost always violated in communication between citizens and candidates or representatives. And although it can be enhanced through campaign finance and media reforms, these reforms are possible in all electoral systems. As a result, deliberative autonomy among candidates or between citizens and candidates cannot justify favoring one electoral system over another.

In the next two sections, I will use the framework of plural deliberation to provide a comparative assessment of several electoral systems. I have chosen to focus only on those systems that have garnered significant attention and use in plural democratic polities. As a result, I do not discuss two systems (the Borda count and approval voting) that have drawn the attention of several electoral scholars but have not gained widespread use or attention in plural polities. In assessing the systems I do examine, I will focus not only on their aggregative qualities but also on their deliberative characteristics, including, where available, information about campaign characteristics. This will prepare the ground for more contextually sensitive recommendations for adopting or reforming electoral systems in order to enhance plural deliberation in the United States.

PLURALITY SYSTEMS AND RESERVED SEATS

Single Member District Plurality (SMDP)

Single member district plurality (SMDP) systems are used in the American House of Representatives and Senate, the House of Commons in Britain and Canada, and the Indian Lok Sahha. The country is divided into geographic constituencies from which one representative is elected. In these systems, only a plurality is required for election, so that the candidate winning the most votes is elected even if she fails to gain a full majority of votes. Finally, SMDP elections use a categorical ballot, so that voters vote for only one candidate. These structural characteristics (a district magnitude of one, a plurality electoral formula, and a categorical ballot) shape the thresholds of the SMDP system. As was discussed above, the threshold of inclusion is inversely related to the number of candidates, and can be represented as (100%/# of candidates) + 1. So if ten candidates fairly evenly split the electorate, a candidate can win with just over 10 percent of the vote. The threshold of exclusion, however, remains at 50 percent + 1, regardless of the number of candidates; if one candidate among many is able to garner just over half of the votes cast, that candidate is guaranteed victory.

The high threshold of exclusion and the potentially low threshold of inclusion lead SMDP to produce a large number of wasted votes. Focus first on the threshold of exclusion. If a candidate is guaranteed to win with just over 50 percent of the votes, then just under 50 percent of the votes cast for the losing candidate are wasted. The number of wasted votes becomes much higher given the variable threshold of representation. If ten candidates fairly evenly split the vote, allowing one candidate to win with just over 10 percent of the vote, then just under 90 percent of the votes are wasted. More pertinent to the politics of a plural polity is the consequence of wasted votes on minority groups. As I mentioned earlier, wasted votes can generate the problem of minority vote dilution, when a racial or ethnic minority is unable to elect a representative of its choice because of its geographic dispersion and cohesive, polarized voting by the majority. Consequently, the problem of wasted votes leads SMDP to fare poorly according to the criterion of aggregative equality.

Notably, not all democratic theorists perceive the problem of wasted votes as normatively important. Although he recognizes that proportional representation systems waste fewer votes than single member district plurality systems (SMDP), Charles Beitz dismisses this difference as insignificant, even when confronting the problem of minority representation. Proportional representation will grant minorities only minority status within the legislature; this does not guarantee that their interests will gain equitable treatment in that assembly. On the other hand, Beitz does justify the creation of minority–majority racial districts in an SMDP system, precisely because doing so will enhance the equitable treatment of the interests of racial minorities. Beitz resolves this apparent contradiction by admitting that granting representation to minority racial groups will not guarantee the proportional satisfaction of their interests but should at least protect them from majority tyranny.[42]

This conclusion depends on the contextual claim that White representatives often ignore or deliberately harm the interests of American racial minorities. Unfortunately, this contextual claim is insufficiently contextual. Given the problems of internal diversity, shifting boundaries, and multiple modes of identity construction discussed in chapter 1, the creation of majority–minority districts raises difficult normative questions. Do minority–majority districts assume that identity boundaries are stable and structurally imposed? Do they submerge internal minorities within the targeted minority identity, such as different Black, Latino, or Asian ethnic groups? Beitz rightly recognizes that American racial minorities have suffered and continue to suffer from majority tyranny, but his straightforward advocacy of minority–majority districting overlooks the problems of identity construction.

Indeed, the problem of minority–majority districting generates a perhaps more blatant violation of aggregative autonomy. When legislators or judges group citizens who share a racial identity into a common geographic district, they potentially deprive citizens of the opportunity to choose their own subjective constituency. This can be a serious problem when targeted racial groups contain internal minorities that may have interpretive, ethnic identities that conflict with their instrumental-structural, racial identity. This problem affects not only minority–majority districts but also majority-White districts; racial minorities or members of distinct ideological or religious world-views can also lose their capacity to choose their own subjective constituency. Although recent American Supreme Court decisions have exhibited a "racial bias" by only exposing the deprivations of aggregative autonomy created by minority–majority districts,[43] all SMDP districts tend to violate this criterion.

SMDP systems also tend to violate aggregative autonomy through their tendency to discourage a robust range of parliamentary candidates and parties. As Maurice Duverger's famous (or infamous) law suggests, proportional representation systems tend to favor multiparty systems, while SMDP tends to foster two-party systems. Duverger explained this law through recourse to its "mechanical effect," whereby vote aggregation systems differentially reward parties with parliamentary seats, and its "psychological effect," whereby leaders of disadvantaged parties become discouraged and cease to contest elections. Because SMDP disproportionately rewards larger, geographically based parties and candidates, smaller or geographically dispersed parties tend to gain a smaller proportion of parliamentary seats than votes. Lijphart's statistical findings tend to substantiate Duverger's "mechanical effect" on parliamentary parties, those parties likely to gain representation.[44]

Before leaving this issue, we must emphasize that SMDP systems tend to favor parties that constitute a majority or a strong plurality within a geographically concentrated area; conversely, they penalize parties that appeal broadly, across the country, but fail to have intense support in any one area. As a result, it is not uncommon to find multiparty systems within SMDP countries with significant regional cleavages, such as Canada and India. Such dynamics, however, are regionally based, generating something closer to several regional, two-party systems rather than a countrywide, multiparty system. Thus, in Canada we find the French-separatist Bloc Quebecois competing against the Liberal party in Quebec; in India we find the Telugu Desam party competing with the Congress party in Andhra Pradesh; and the DMK and the AIADMK, two Tamil nationalist parties, competing with each other in Tamil Nadu. True multiparty competition is only found in Ontario in Canada and in Kerala and a few northern states in India. Given that India and Canada are often cited as disconfirming Duverger's law,[45] this regional factor is important.

There is a greater problem related to SMDP's regional factor. Because this system rewards parliamentary parties and candidates whose supporters are geographically concentrated, this tends to reduce electoral competition and the aggregative autonomy that citizens can exercise in choosing representatives. Scholars of African politics have argued that SMDP generates ethnic fiefdoms.[46] In the United States, this problem is most acutely felt in minority–majority districts, where Black and Puerto Rican candidates are overwhelmingly Democrats and tend to win by overwhelming margins.[47] Indeed, several of these districts become safe seats, where incumbents face little or no electoral challenge. Although this problem can be acute in minority–majority districts, safe seats and incumbency protection are common problems in the United States and thus reflect the general deficit in aggregative autonomy within the SMDP system. Of course, the two-party system and incumbency protection arise not simply through SMDP but also through the presidential system, cultural understandings of political parties, and laws that hinder the entry of third parties.[48] Nevertheless, SMDP plays a crucial role in suppressing aggregative autonomy over parliamentary candidates or parties.

In the United States, minority representatives elected from SMDP minority–majority districts confront obstacles in their exercise of aggregative reciprocity at the legislative level. This arises because the creation of minority–majority districts in southern states tends to leave the remaining districts with higher proportions of White and conservative voters. So when, for example, creating minority–majority districts enables the election of Black liberal representatives, those representatives may be less able to bargain effectively with White conservative representatives in the legislature. This problem is not replicated by the creation of minority–majority districts in the North, however, where the adjoining districts tend to be populated by more liberal Whites. Furthermore, it can be remedied in the South by simultaneously drawing minority–majority and Democratic-leaning districts. However, pursuing this dual strategy typically requires bizarrely shaped districts of the sort subject to strict judicial scrutiny.[49] Consequently, creating southern, minority–majority districts that pass judicial review places minority representatives in an inhospitable legislative environment that hinders their ability to make the bargains necessary to pass laws upholding the interests or opinions of their minority constituents.

Turning to deliberative criteria, SMDP systems tend to embody not only Duverger's "mechanical effect" in restricting aggregative autonomy over parliamentary parties and candidates; they also tend to uphold Duverger's "psychological effect" in depressing the number of elective candidates and parties.[50] Elective parties and candidates have little chance to win election, and Duverger's psychological effect leads them to give up contesting elections. The result is a decline in deliberative equality because the positions expressed by elective parties are excluded from campaign deliberation. The obstacles to deliberative equality reflected in the decline of elective candidates and parties result significantly from the categorical ballot employed by SMDP systems. As we shall see, preferential ballots can enhance the standing of elective candidates and parties even without a proportional representation system.

The use of a categorical rather than an ordinal ballot also affects the prospects for deliberative reciprocity within SMDP electoral campaigns. The combination of a categorical ballot with a plurality electoral formula means that candidates can appeal exclusively to a fairly narrow plurality of district voters in order to win election. Under conditions of group-polarized voting, this means that a candidate can appeal only to members of the collective identity that constitutes the plurality or majority in that district. Of course, if there is no majority in a district, candidates may have an incentive to selectively extend deliberative reciprocity across group boundaries in order to build a coalition of groups to secure election. This incentive is most prevalent in two types of districts: minority-influence districts, where demographics enable candidates to build coalitions between minority-race voters and White liberals (often Jews); and multiracial, minority–majority districts, where two minority groups (usually Blacks and Latinos) together constitute the district majority.[51] In chapter 3, we saw that plural deliberation is most likely only among those groups that cut across positional dynamics of conflict. Minority influence or multiracial, minority–majority districts may enhance deliberative reciprocity among these types of groups, and this might be the best option for plural deliberation under SMDP.

Despite the many apparent drawbacks of the SMDP system when assessed according to plural deliberation, its supporters often cite a specifically deliberative advantage: a single member's connection to a single district is thought to enhance citizen–representative deliberation. The problem with this response is that, like models of deliberative representation, it overlooks the common violations of deliberative autonomy along this axis. Given that critical, persuasive deliberation is not likely between citizens and their representatives, the most that can be expected is improved aggregative information pooling between them. But even if we shift to this diminished criterion, we find that citizens in SMDP elections for the American House of Representatives do not seem to gather much information regarding specific candidates. According to Morris Fiorina and Paul Peterson, only a third of voters can recall the name of their incumbent, only 10 percent can recall how their incumbent voted on any particular bill, and even fewer can recognize challengers. Consequently, most voters rely on party labels in choosing an individual candidate.[52] This finding supports Thomas Christiano's claim that it is more difficult to obtain information about individual representatives or candidates than about the broad platforms of ideologically cohesive parties in a party list PR system.[53] Consequently, SMDP's putative advantage in the citizen–representative dimension seems overstated.

In sum, the SMDP system, even when combined with minority–majority districts, comes up short when assessed according to the criteria of plural deliberation. It is worth noting, however, that this system may be susceptible to reforms that, while leaving it inferior to other systems, nevertheless bring it closer to the aims of plural deliberation. Deliberative equality could be enhanced if elective parties engage in fusion strategies with parliamentary parties. Fusion, common in New York State, reflects how minor elective parties, like the Liberal party, endorse candidates from the Democratic or Republican parliamentary parties. Because these endorsements can tip a close election, elective parties can keep their ideas alive within campaign deliberation, even when they are unable to elect candidates to a legislature.[54]

An even simpler but possibly more effective reform of the American SMDP system would be to increase the number of districts within the House of Representatives. Given that the number of House seats is frozen at 435 through federal law,[55] and given that parliaments of smaller countries contain larger numbers of representatives, increasing the number of seats is a viable reform that could improve the functioning of the SMDP system. Increasing the number of districts would tend to improve the party proportionality of SMDP systems greatly, thereby enhancing aggregative equality.[56] It would also enable creating more minority–majority districts, enhancing the aggregative equality of minority voters, and might also facilitate the simultaneous creation of Democratic-leaning and minority–majority districts without making them bizarrely shaped. This can enhance the aggregative reciprocity of minority legislators without provoking judicial ire. These factors suggest that, although the SMDP system will not best satisfy the criteria of plural deliberation, it can be improved in moderate yet meaningful ways.

Multimember District Plurality (MMDP)

The multimember district plurality system (MMDP) shares most of SMDP's structural characteristics, except for its district magnitude (DM). MMDP elects multiple representatives rather than one from a single district, using a plurality electoral formula and a categorical ballot. So in a three-seat district, the three candidates with a plurality of the votes are elected. The election can be conducted in two manners. In one version, the three seats are numbered, and candidates must choose which seat they wish to contest; thus, candidates A and B will contest seat 1, candidates C and D will contest seat 2, and candidates E and F will contest seat 3. In the alternative version, all candidates (A–F) will compete for all three seats.[57] In either case, voters cast the same number of categorical votes as there are seats, in this example three, and they cast only one vote per candidate.

By sharing most structural characteristics with SMDP, MMDP has the same thresholds of inclusion and exclusion. However, its one difference from SMDP—multimember districts—leads to a pronounced difference in its effects on the representation of minority groups. In effect, MMDP functions as a series of simultaneous SMDP elections, drawn from a larger geographic district. As a result, if an intergenerational group is the majority and votes cohesively in this larger district, it can outvote the minority group for all of the district's seats. And when MMDP is employed in a single district covering an entire municipality or county, it does not allow for the SMDP remedy for minority-vote dilution, the creation of one or more minority–majority districts.

Not surprisingly, there is a fairly widespread consensus that the multimember district plurality system (MMDP), also known as the "at large" election, is poorly suited to plural polities. Indeed, MMDP was introduced in southern jurisdictions following passage of the 1965 Voting Rights Act precisely in order to reduce the voting power of newly enfranchised southern Blacks.[58] Subsequently, in *Thornburg v. Gingles,* the United States Supreme Court ruled that MMDP electoral systems violated the Voting Rights Act whenever it could be shown that an SMDP system would enable the creation of more minority–majority districts and thus more representatives accountable to minorities than the existing MMDP system.[59] Of course, this technique uses a poorly performing system to assess an even worse system, a problem that has not escaped the notice of legal critics.[60] Nevertheless, the comparison between SMDP and MMDP reveals how greatly the latter violates aggregative equality by wasting the votes of minority voters. Indeed, MMDP even provides incentives for minority voters intentionally to waste their votes. For example, if a single Black candidate is running in a three-seat, racially polarized district, Black voters might vote only for that candidate, for fear that casting their additional two votes for White candidates might help those candidates win election at the expense of the Black candidate.[61]

Such deficits in aggregative equality also work to diminish aggregative autonomy. In the above example, Black voters have an incentive to coalesce around a single Black candidate, thus diminishing their opportunity to choose among various alternatives. And though multimember districts usually enable greater aggregative autonomy over subjective constituency, this applies only for majority voters in MMDP as the plurality electoral formula and the categorical ballot prevent minorities from voting according to multiple interests, opinions, perspectives, or world-views. Aggregative reciprocity also suffers at the legislative level, with minority representatives often shut out of the assembly, and at the electoral level, where there is no incentive for majority candidates to build alliances with minority candidates. The categorical ballot diminishes any incentives for deliberative reciprocity: majority candidates need not appeal to minority voters, and minority candidates have an incentive to encourage minority voters to vote cohesively and exclusively along group lines. In principle, deliberative equality might benefit because multiple seats will allow a greater number of candidacies within a single district. However, the disproportionality of MMDP is likely to impose Duverger's "psychological effect" on candidates who are far from the majority opinion. Thus, we should not expect terribly diverse positions within campaign deliberation: instead, MMDP provides incentives for majority group candidates to appeal exclusively to majority group voters, leading to more candidates than SMDP but with relatively homogeneous, and potentially racially exclusive, positions.

Plural deliberation's standard of complex legitimacy requires that we recognize tradeoffs among its diverse aggregative and deliberative fairness conditions. Because it is unlikely that any electoral system will best satisfy all conditions, we must exercise judgment and moderation in assessing the advantages and disadvantages of different systems. While this may leave room for improving rather than replacing SMDP, this does not seem to be the case with MMDP. There are no significant advantages to balance against the numerous disadvantages of this system. And given that in many instances it was adopted precisely to minimize the electoral strength of racial minorities, we should feel little compulsion to maintain this system in a plural polity. Nevertheless, it remains in force in many municipal and state jurisdictions in the United States.[62] Given that viable alternatives exist to replace MMDP at the state and local level, replacing this system should be at the forefront of public sphere action aimed at institutional reform. The remaining question, of course, is what should replace MMDP. Two options that should raise significant concerns are open roll and closed roll reserved seats.

Reserved Seats

Reserved seats are legislative seats that can only be occupied by members of designated groups. Not a full-fledged electoral system per se, reserved seats nevertheless deserve mention, given their historical and contemporary use and their occasional embrace by normative democratic theorists.[63] Typically, reserved seats are adopted to enable the representation of groups that are so numerically small that they cannot otherwise gain legislative representation. However, they can also be used to guarantee proportional representation of minority groups that would otherwise be numerically underrepresented.

There are two broad types of reserved seats. In *closed roll* systems, members of designated groups are placed on a distinct electoral roll. Only members of these groups can cast votes for candidates from their own group. A similar system was used in New Zealand for the Maori, who can choose to vote either on the designated Maori roll or on the general roll. Alternatively, reserved seats can be filled through an *open roll*. This system was formerly used in Lebanon and remains in use in India for caste representation.[64] It designates certain seats to be filled only by candidates from specific groups, but voters from any group can vote for these candidates. Thus, in the Lebanon case, two Maronite candidates may compete for a reserved Maronite seat, but these candidates must pursue the votes not only of fellow Maronites but also of Shi'ites, Sunnis, and Druze. In the Indian case, an SMDP electoral district adds a second seat, for which only members of designated castes can run. However, these designated caste candidates must compete for the votes of constituents from various castes within the district.[65]

Despite the common effect of guaranteeing the election of a representative from a targeted group, these two systems have diametrically opposed electoral dynamics. Because the objective constituency of a closed roll system is restricted to members of the targeted group, the general problem of minority vote dilution is eliminated: minority-group voters cannot be outvoted by a majority group, and thus they do not waste votes relative to that majority. However, this gain in aggregative equality is diminished to the extent that the minority group is internally diverse. Should an internal majority vote cohesively against the interests, opinions, or perspective of an internal minority, the reduction in aggregative equality through minority vote dilution is simply replicated within the overarching minority collective identity.

A closed roll reserved seat can allow for a certain amount of aggregative autonomy in both senses. It can allow for autonomy over candidates because the closed roll protects the minority group from the threat of being outvoted by the majority. Thus, it obviates the incentive to run only a single minority candidate in MMDP systems or the tendency to create safe seats in SMDP systems. It can also allow for autonomy over constituency if voters can opt out of the reserved roll, as in New Zealand's closed Maori roll.[66] However, aggregative autonomy in this sense is preserved only in a relatively inflexible manner. Citizens must decide prior to an electoral campaign whether they wish to remain within a constituency. Thus, they really exercise aggregative autonomy only over objective constituency, much as a citizen in SMDP could exit an unfavorable district by changing residence. They do not have the opportunity to exercise aggregative autonomy over subjective constituency following campaign deliberation; during the electoral process they cannot coalesce with other like-minded voters into a community of interest, opinion, perspective, or world-view. And again, internal diversity within the targeted group roll can lead to further violations of aggregative autonomy in both senses.

Aggregative reciprocity tends to fare very poorly under closed roll electoral systems. At the legislative level, majority representatives have little or no incentive to bargain with representatives of groups that remain a minority and do not represent any voters of the majority group. This problem historically plagued closed roll representation of the Maori in New Zealand. At the electoral level, aggregative reciprocity is entirely negated, with the inclusion of only one group eliminating any incentive for candidates from different groups to secure electoral alliances with closed roll candidates. Deliberative equality suffers under closed rolls; the positions of targeted group candidates will only be taken up by electoral deliberation within that group. Candidates and citizens in the general election have no incentive whatsoever to take up minority candidate positions within their own campaign deliberations. Deliberative reciprocity also falters under closed roll reserved seats, for candidates by necessity will only reach out to voters from their own group.

Although deliberative reciprocity across group boundaries is a victim of closed roll reserved seats, it is actually enhanced under open roll reserved seats. Because open roll reserved seats typically exist only in districts where the targeted group is a minority, and candidacy is restricted to members of the targeted group while constituents are drawn from all groups, minority candidates are all but required to make electoral appeals across group lines. If a candidate appeals only to the targeted group, he runs the risk that his opponent, also a member of the targeted minority group, will gain election by appealing to the majority of voters outside the minority group. But this deliberative reciprocity comes at a high price: a minority-group candidate favored by most majority-group voters can win an election over another minority-group candidate favored only by most minority-group voters. The ironic result is that representatives elected through open roll reserved seats sometimes overlook the interests of the very groups from which they come.[67] The tokenism of minority-group representatives beholden primarily to majority-group voters is most colorfully illustrated by Indian cases, where the BJP, a Hindu nationalist party dominated by upper-caste Hindus, will often successfully run low-caste candidates in open roll reserved seats. This reveals that violations of aggregative equality through minority vote dilution can apply equally to open-roll reserved seats as to SMDP districts.

Open roll reserved seats employ the same type of objective constituencies and electoral formulas as SMDP, so they tend to match that system's performance in relation to the criteria of aggregative autonomy and deliberative equality. The single seat constrains citizens' aggregative choices over candidates and subjective constituency through Duverger's "mechanical effect"; the "psychological effect" depresses the number of elective candidates and parties that contest elections. Finally, aggregative reciprocity at the legislative and electoral levels does not differ significantly from SMDP; minority-group representatives and candidates are beholden to the same constituencies as are majority-group representatives. Because they are accountable to all voters in their district, their minority identity is merely window dressing, and they can be expected to act legislatively and on the campaign trail in much the same fashion as majority-group representatives and candidates.

PROPORTIONAL, SEMI-PROPORTIONAL, AND MAJORITY SYSTEMS

Party List PR

Party list PR systems have four distinctive structural characteristics. First is the existence of multimember geographic districts from which several representatives are elected. (Recall that the number of representatives elected from a single district is typically called the district magnitude, or DM.) The second characteristic is a proportional electoral formula, which grants seats to political parties in proportion to their share of the popular vote. The most common electoral formulas are the least remainders (LR) formula, the Droop quota, the D'Hondt formula, and the St. Lague formula.[68] Third, party list PR systems use categorical ballots, whereby voters choose only one party, as opposed to an ordinal ballot, whereby they express ordered preferences for multiple parties or candidates, or a cumulative ballot, whereby they can apportion multiple votes to a single candidate or multiple candidates. Finally, parties award seats to individual representatives according to party lists. Closed party lists grant party leaders full control over which representatives receive a party's seats, whereas open party lists grant voters the opportunity to select not only the party but also the specific representative to sit in the legislature. In essence, closed lists compel voters to vote for a party; open lists enable voters to vote for individuals as well.

Alterations within these structural characteristics can shape the character of party list PR systems. Closed party lists, especially when combined with a larger DM, tend to foster representation by ideologically coherent, disciplined parties; open party lists, especially when combined with a smaller DM, tend to foster representation by individuals. This difference shapes issue orientation within electoral campaigns: party representation fosters ideological, issue-oriented campaigns and individual representation fosters personal campaigns.[69] In addition, the thresholds of inclusion and exclusion decrease as the DM increases. The threshold of exclusion usually reflects the equation $100\%/(DM + 1) + 1$.[70] Thus, the threshold of exclusion for a three-member district is $100\%/(3 + 1) + 1$, or $25\% + 1$ vote: if a party gains this amount, it is guaranteed to win at least one seat. The threshold of inclusion is much more difficult to predict because it also varies according to the number of parties contesting the election and to the specific electoral formula in use. For a three-party contest in a three-seat district using the D'Hondt electoral formula, Lijphart calculates a threshold of inclusion of 20 percent. Thus, a party can elect one member if the other two parties equally split the vote (each getting just under 40 percent) or if one party gains just below 60 percent and the other just below 20 percent.[71] For his broader statistical analysis of electoral systems, he calculates a typical threshold of inclusion according to the equation $100\%/2 \times DM$ for party list PR systems.

The low thresholds tend to render party list PR a very proportional electoral system. The proportionality between votes cast and seats awarded to parties is directly and strongly related to increases in the DM.[72] It is less clear that changes in the electoral formula have strong and consistent effects on proportionality.[73] Nevertheless, there is widespread agreement that all PR formulas are more proportional than plurality or majority formulas. The low thresholds and high proportionality of party list PR directly bears on its performance according to two of plural deliberation's criteria of fairness. Party list PR fosters aggregative equality through its high level of proportionality between seats and votes. Because a high proportion of citizens' votes translate into the election of some representatives from the party of their choice, there are fewer wasted votes spent on losing parties or as surpluses for winning parties. In addition, party list PR may enhance both types of aggregative autonomy. Given Duverger's mechanical effect, the decline in wasted votes should generate an increase in the number of parliamentary parties, a claim generally upheld by statistical analyses.[74] Thus, aggregative autonomy over representation will increase because voters will have a greater number of parliamentary parties from which to choose. Moreover, given that closed list PR tends to generate ideologically coherent, disciplined parties, voters should be able to process campaign information more efficiently, enhancing their ability to exercise their aggregative autonomy effectively.[75] Party list PR may also bolster aggregative autonomy over subjective constituency because the low threshold of exclusion, especially in districts with higher DM, can allow individuals to coalesce according to various racial, ethnic, or cultural constituencies. Instead of being forced into an objective constituency by a districting body, as in SMDP minority–majority districts, list PR's large districts can allow minority-group voters to choose their subjective constituency according to their interests, opinions, perspectives, or world-views.[76]

On the other hand, aggregative equality and autonomy benefit minority identity groups under party list PR only if minority-group parties are created or if minority-group members are granted proportional representation on the lists of nonethnic parties. If minority-group parties do not develop or if minority candidates are underrepresented on party lists, minority vote dilution can again arise. This possibility prompts Melissa Williams to question the capacity of party list PR to enhance the representation of marginalized groups. She first notes that advantaged groups will be better able to create and support political parties than will disadvantaged groups. She then argues that party list PR tends to favor class-based ideological parties over those based solely on ascriptive identities. As a result, she supports electoral systems that foster representation by individuals over party list PR, in the belief that individual candidates from disadvantaged groups can more feasibly be elected.[77]

Williams's first concern is more compelling than her second. Donald Horowitz shows that in Guyana, parties based largely on ethnicity, not class, emerged and prospered when that country adopted party list PR.[78] This counters any necessary relationship between party list PR and ideological rather than group-based political parties. The next question is whether all groups will equally be able to form such parties. To the extent that disadvantaged groups have fewer financial or organizational resources, they are less likely to organize parties that reflect their distinctly group-based interests, opinions, perspectives, or world-views. However, I am not sure that individual candidacy and representation will favor disadvantaged groups, given the advantage that personal wealth plays in individual-based candidacies. Moreover, collective action by disadvantaged individuals can offset their political inequality by allowing them to pool resources for collectively shared aims.[79] To the extent that political parties serve as collective action organizations,[80] they may in fact enable disadvantaged groups to participate more equally. For this reason, I remain unconvinced that we should favor individual over party-based representation.

While I do not think that the aggregative autonomy of ethnically defined collective actors need suffer under party list PR, I am more doubtful about the deliberative potential of this electoral system. Christiano suggests that party list PR improves deliberative equality by increasing the number of political parties that contest elections.[81] But whereas it tends to generate more parliamentary parties than other systems do, it need not always create more elective parties. Party list PR systems clearly foster more elective parties than SMDP does, but the difference closes when compared to majority systems like the alternative vote (AV).[82] Thus, in purely deliberative terms, party list PR might not be significantly better than AV at increasing the range of deliberative viewpoints within an electoral campaign. Only if parliamentary parties are more likely to be heard in electoral campaigns does party list PR surpass other systems in deliberative equality.

It is not clear that party list PR does much to motivate deliberative reciprocity across group lines. To the extent that party list PR encourages group-based parties, such parties may orient themselves exclusively to their own groups and not toward other groups. Although party list PR does not discourage parties from appealing across group boundaries, it does not provide any specific incentives to do so. Party list PR's categorical ballot may actually discourage citizens from voting across group lines. Consider the following hypothetical example. Imagine that the United States adopted a party list PR system, and as a result distinct Black, Latino, Asian, and White parties developed, along with a group-neutral party that sought votes across racial lines. Now, recall that a categorical ballot requires citizens to vote for a single party. Should a voter seek descriptive representation, she should vote for the political party that represents her own descriptive identity. If a Black voter seeks descriptive representation, she should vote for the Black party. But if that voter is attracted by the gender policy of the group-neutral party, she may face a difficult dilemma; voting for the neutral party will deprive the Black party of her vote. If this type of dilemma is replicated among the race-based parties, members of different groups will have strong incentives to encourage all other members to remain loyal to their respective parties, weakening support for the neutral party. This incentive holds for party list PR categorical ballots whether lists are open or not; in both cases voters must first vote for a party.[83] Thus, the all-or-nothing character of a categorical ballot may lead party list PR systems to discourage parties that make cross-group appeals, potentially weakening support for deliberative reciprocity across group boundaries and even exacerbating the political dynamic of group conflict.

Lijphart responds by suggesting that ethnic parties, if they wish to gain power, will make legislative coalitions with other ethnic parties.[84] He then argues that ethnic parties have incentives under PR to make preelectoral alliances with other parties across group lines, allowing them to campaign together using cross-group appeals.[85] Neither response fully meets the deliberative critique; they only address the issue of aggregative reciprocity at the legislative and the electoral levels respectively. They do not show incentives for candidates or parties affiliated with one group to appeal directly to voters from another group. Moreover, it is not clear that there are even any specific incentives for aggregative reciprocity at the electoral level. Should parties create electoral alliances, they do so not because of strong incentives within the party list PR system but simply as a precursor to postelection legislative bargaining. This incentive can be equally prevalent within SMDP systems, particularly those with regional cleavages that support a regionally segmented two- or multiparty system. Thus, preelectoral alliances among regionally based ethnic parties are common in India's SMDP system, where the Hindu nationalist BJP often makes electoral alliances with southern regional parties. Incentives toward cross-group deliberative or aggregative reciprocity are not a particular feature of party list PR, but they are inherent in ordinal ballot systems.

The Alternative Vote (AV)

The alternative vote combines a preferential, ordinal ballot with a majority electoral formula, using either single or multiple member districts. The majority electoral formula means that a candidate wins election only by gaining over 50 percent of all votes, as opposed to the mere plurality required in SMDP or the proportion required in party list PR. Thus, the AV generates a unified threshold of inclusion and exclusion of 50 percent: a candidate can only get elected and is in fact guaranteed election by gaining just over 50 percent of the vote. The AV ensures a majority vote, even amidst multiple candidacies, through its ordinal ballot and vote transfer mechanism. The ordinal ballot allows voters to rank candidates in order of preference. After the votes are cast, the first preferences are tallied first. Should a candidate win an absolute majority of the first preference votes, then he is elected. If no candidate wins an absolute majority of first preferences, then the last place candidate is eliminated and the second preference votes from those ballots are tallied and distributed among the remaining candidates. If these second preference votes do not create a winner, then the bottom finisher after the second count is eliminated, and her second and third preference votes are transferred. This process goes on until a candidate passes the 50 percent threshold. The ordinal ballot, the majority electoral formula, and the typically low DM prompt individual, rather than party, representation.[86]

Assessing the proportionality of AV is somewhat complex. It is less proportional than party list PR, and Jack Wright argues that AV in Australia consistently creates a disproportionate relationship between seats won and countrywide votes cast, although this assessment references only first-preference votes.[87] However, Lijphart notes that AV is probably considerably more proportional than SMDP as it decreases incentives to vote strategically. Under SMDP, voters have an incentive to vote for candidates from larger parties in order to avoid wasting votes on smaller party candidates who have little chance of winning. This leads to a decline not only in parliamentary parties but also in elective parties. However, AV fosters a significantly higher number of elective parties: voters can sincerely vote for smaller party candidates who have little chance of winning seats; their votes will not be wasted but can be transferred to larger party candidates who have a chance of winning.[88] But though such incentives to vote sincerely may generate more elective parties, AV's majority electoral formula, like SMDP's plurality formula, favors larger, centrist, parliamentary parties.[89]

The proportionality of AV is further complicated by the influence of DM. Although increases in DM are directly related to proportionality in PR systems, DM is inversely related to proportionality in plurality and majority systems, including the AV. Thus, multiple-member AV systems, like the American at-large MMDP elections discussed earlier, tend to be highly disproportional.[90] Multimember AV districts were used for Australian Senate elections from 1919 to 1946, when three Senate seats would be filled through simultaneous but separate elections. This system tended to produce widely disproportionate countrywide outcomes. For instance, in 1925 the Labour party won 45.03 percent of first-preference votes but failed to win any of the 19 Senate seats contested, whereas in 1943 Labour managed to win all 19 contested Senate seats with only 55.09 percent of first preference votes.[91] This magnification of the winner-take-all dynamic of SMDP would be troubling in a plural polity; minority groups could be shut out of the legislature, as so often occurred in American MMDP elections.

These characteristics significantly affect the assessment of AV through the criteria of plural deliberation. In terms of aggregative equality, AV initially appears to do well, because its ordinal ballot and vote transfer mechanism reduce wasted votes by creating a unified threshold of exclusion/inclusion of 50 percent. This means that just under half of all votes could be wasted on a losing candidate, but the identical threshold of inclusion precludes the possibility that over half of all votes could be wasted on multiple losing candidates, as can occur in a plurality election with multiple candidates. However, this improvement in aggregative equality fades due to a curious property of all ordinal ballots, *non-monotonicity*. In certain circumstances, ranking a candidate higher on a ballot can actually hinder his chances to get elected, because doing so may alter the transfer of lower preferences, thereby changing the order in which candidates are eliminated.[92] Consider the following example.

Table 5.1 First AV Election

Group	Number of Voters	Preferences
A	7	Tom, Dick, Harry, Shirley
B	6	Dick, Tom, Harry, Shirley
C	5	Harry, Dick, Tom, Shirley
D	3	Shirley, Harry, Dick, Tom

Imagine twenty-one voters choosing among four candidates: Tom, Dick, Harry, and Shirley, according to the preference orderings given in Table 5.1. When we count the first preference votes, we find that no candidate has a majority of eleven votes, and thus Shirley is eliminated as the last-place candidate. Consequently, the second preference votes of her supporters are tallied and transferred to Harry, who now has eight votes. Because we still lack a majority, Dick is eliminated, because he is in last place with six votes. His second preference votes now are transferred to Tom, who is now declared the winner with thirteen votes.

Now imagine a second election, in which group D abandons Shirley, making her their last preference and Tom their first, as rendered below in Table 5.2. Intuitively, one would think that Tom, the winner of the first election, would benefit from gaining Group D's first-preference support. However, Tom, in fact, loses. After the first tally, Tom is in the lead with ten votes but still falls short of a majority. Shirley is immediately eliminated, but because there are no ballots with her as the first preference, we must now eliminate Harry, who has only five first-preference votes. Group C's ballots for Harry are transferred to Dick, who now wins the second election. Nonmonotonicity emerges because Tom, who in the second election gained three extra first-preference votes, actually ends up losing, rather than winning by a larger margin. This occurs because in the first election, Dick was eliminated before Harry and his second-preference votes went to Tom, whereas in the second election Harry was eliminated before Dick and his second-preference votes transferred to Dick.[93]

Nonmonotonicity remains an analytical possibility in all ordinal ballot systems, including both the AV and the single-transferable vote (STV), which will be discussed below. This analytical possibility need not eliminate ordinal ballot systems from consideration, however, for two reasons. First, it is not clear how often

Table 5.2 Second AV Election

Group	Number of Voters	Preferences
A	7	Tom, Dick, Harry, Shirley
B	6	Dick, Tom, Harry, Shirley
C	5	Harry, Dick, Tom, Shirley
D	3	Tom, Harry, Dick, Shirley

nonmonotonic results occur. Using data from British SMDP elections, Crispin Allard claims that nonmonotonic results would occur only 0.28% of the time if STV were used. Michael Dummett, a critic of the AV and STV, asserts, without any statistical evidence, a "conservative estimate" of 2%.[94] Gerry Mackie claims that under Northern Ireland's STV, there have been no instances of nonmonotonicity over a span of twenty-two years, although he acknowledges some minor evidence of it in a recent election.[95] I cannot resolve this debate here, but it seems that nonmonotonicity need not be a terribly common occurrence. Indeed, when there are only three candidates, as often occurs in single-member AV elections, the problem of nonmonotonicity evaporates. But apart from this, a second reason for keeping AV under consideration is that nonmonotonicity compromises only aggregative equality, just one of the criteria for assessing democratic institutions in a plural polity. While nonmonotonicity reflects a real deficit in aggregative equality, this system should be assessed according to all of plural deliberation's criteria.

But discounting the problem of nonmonotonicity nevertheless leaves AV vulnerable to other aggregative failings, which in the context of a plural polity may be more damning. Sticking with aggregative equality, we should note that AV might exacerbate minority vote dilution, as it is less proportional than list PR. In districts where a majority votes cohesively against a minority, single-member and multimember AV systems function no differently than SMDP or MMDP respectively. The aggregative autonomy of AV is compromised by its tendency to reduce the number of parliamentary candidates and parties. In addition, citizens' capacity to exercise aggregative autonomy over representation declines because of information processing problems; representation is by an individual rather than by a party. This will especially be the case in multiple member districts, where voters must assess many candidates contesting several seats. AV may restrict autonomy over subjective constituency more than party list PR. Single member district AV, like SMDP, confronts the dilemmas related to ethnic gerrymandering, where districting bodies may constrain subjective constituency by grouping voters according to a priori assumptions about their interests, opinions, perspectives, or worldviews. Ethnic gerrymandering is reduced in multimember AV, but its greater disproportionality increases the threat of minority-group exclusion. As a result, minority-group voters may be limited in their choice of subjective constituency.

Proponents of AV reject this criticism as based on a rigid adherence to descriptive representation. Donald Horowitz, for example, claims that fair representation requires only "incorporating the concerns and interests of a given ethnic or racial group in the calculations of politicians belonging to a variety of groups."[96] In this way, the ethnic disproportionality of AV is balanced by the fact that vote transfers and the majority electoral formula should make elected officials more accountable to voters across group boundaries. Because candidates require a majority vote, they are more likely to seek support across group lines through second-preference votes.[97] In effect, if AV limits aggregative autonomy over constituency or descriptive representation, this cost is more than balanced by incentives for candidates to extend deliberative reciprocity across group lines in search of lower preference votes. However, these incentives depend, in large part, on the demographic balance within a district. Consider the following example.

While it was still an Australian colony, Papua New Guinea used the single member AV system during its 1964, 1968, and 1972 elections, before switching to SMDP at independence. The high level of ethnic diversity in the colony, which included several thousand clans, encouraged ethnic candidates to seek the lower-preference votes of citizens from other clans. This had ambiguous effects on deliberative reciprocity. On the one hand, it prompted most clan candidates to invite members of different and even hostile clans to attend campaign rallies and meetings. This tendency might augur well for understanding across group boundaries. On the other hand, interclan campaigning tended to be very civil; candidates did not want to sling mud at other candidates whose supporters were sought on lower-preference ballots. To this degree, AV's accommodative tendencies may dampen criticism across group boundaries.[98]

Papua New Guinea's shift to SMDP in 1975 radically transformed campaign strategies. The possibility of winning on a mere plurality of votes, without the need to gain a majority through lower-preference support, prompted two developments. First, candidates pursued divisive campaign strategies, aimed at mobilizing a relatively narrow group of clan-based supporters. This strategy was quite rational; in the 1977, 1982, 1987, and 1992 elections, between 80 to 90 percent of all successful candidates won with less than 50% of their district's vote. Second, this tendency has been aggravated by the proliferation of candidates who rationally see the potential to win by securing only a very narrow segment of the vote. So whereas under AV the average number of candidates per district never exceeded 6.1, under SMDP this average reached 15.2. Ethnically divisive campaigning has been accompanied by increased electoral violence, to the point that clan-based candidates do not even campaign in territory occupied by other clans for fear of their lives. From this, Ben Reilly concludes that adopting SMDP has almost totally obliterated the accommodative practices engendered by AV.[99]

Now, this test case does not settle the matter. As Horowitz points out, the accommodative incentives of AV accrue only if group-based candidates cannot secure election on first preferences alone. The extreme ethnic diversity of Papua New Guinea assured such a scenario; no group's population exceeded the threshold of 50 percent. In the American case, AV might enhance deliberative reciprocity in minority-influence districts, where racial minorities can act as a swing vote, or in districts where Blacks and Latinos together constitute the district's majority. Where districts are less diverse, such that a majority group can win a majority on first preferences alone, AV need not prompt any incentives toward deliberative reciprocity. For this reason, other proportional and semiproportional systems are advocated for situations where ethnic minorities face electoral exclusion.

Before turning to those systems, we should assess AV according to the last two pertinent criteria of plural deliberation. Deliberative equality tends to be enhanced by AV's tendency to foster elective candidates and parties that contest but rarely win elections. Because of the vote transfer mechanism, voters can sincerely support a minor elective party or candidate without wasting their votes and inadvertently aiding a less favorable candidate. Consider the scenario of using the AV in the 2000 presidential election in Florida. Presuming that supporters of the Green party candidate, Ralph Nader, would have preferred Democrat Al Gore to Republican George Bush, these voters could have supported Nader without aiding Bush. If we replicate this scenario over multiple elections, we can expect AV to encourage elective parties and candidates. In this way, minority points of view can still be expressed within campaign deliberation, even if they are unlikely to win parliamentary seats.

In terms of aggregative reciprocity, AV may also accrue gains. On the electoral level, the competition for lower-preference votes would likely encourage electoral alliances among candidates or parties. For instance, parliamentary candidates might seek the endorsement of elective candidates for their supporters' second-preference votes. Elective, minority-group candidates could use such alliances to force more parliamentary candidates to incorporate their group interests into their electoral campaigns and their legislative activity. This last effect would, in turn, enhance aggregative reciprocity at the legislative level as well.

The Single Transferable Vote

The single transferable vote combines the ordinal ballot of the AV with multimember districts and a proportional electoral formula. Although any proportional formula could be used, in practice every STV system uses the following Droop quota: $100\%/(DM + 1) + 1$.[100] So if 100 votes are cast for a 3-seat district, then a candidate is elected if she gains 26 votes (100 votes$/[3 + 1] + 1$). One should note that the Droop quota reflects the threshold of exclusion for the STV system. By using it as the electoral formula, it also functions as the threshold of inclusion. Consequently, once they know the district magnitude (DM), candidates know exactly how many of the votes cast they need to be elected. Note also that the threshold of exclusion diminishes as the DM increases.

Like the AV, the STV uses an ordinal ballot and a vote transfer mechanism to avoid the difficulty of some candidates not reaching the combined threshold of exclusion and inclusion. The STV's transfer mechanism is significantly more complicated, however, because of its multimember districts and proportional electoral formula. Let us return to our example of a 3-seat district with 100 votes. If all three seats are not filled after an initial count of first-preference votes, votes can be transferred in two ways. The simpler transfer method occurs when a last-place candidate is eliminated and his second-preference votes are transferred. The more complex transfer occurs when a candidate, once passing the threshold, has her excess ballots used for second-preference transfers. For example, if a candidate gains 39 first-preference votes, 13 of those ballots should be transferred to other candidates. But because it matters greatly which of those 13 ballots gets transferred, the following method is used. First, all 39 ballots are distributed according to the second-preference candidates indicated. Then, a transfer quotient is calculated by dividing the excess number of first-preference ballots (39 − 26 = 13) by the total number of first-preference ballots (39). One then multiplies this quotient (0.33 or ⅓) by the number of second-preference ballots that each candidate receives from the transferred ballot. So if candidate X gains 12 second-preference ballots from the elected candidate, X gains an additional 4 votes, whereas if candidate Y gains 1 second-preference ballot from the elected candidate, Y gets only ⅓ of an additional vote.

Because voters cast preferential votes for individual candidates, the voting process in STV can become very complex. For example, if a district is electing ten representatives, it is likely that at least twenty candidates will contest these seats. The ordinal ballot would allow voters to rank all twenty candidates, a fairly complex demand. Thus, STV systems usually restrict DM to between 3 to 5 seats per district. Lijphart argues that while STV's Droop quota is among the most proportional of electoral formulas, the system's overall proportionality is hindered by its need for a small DM.[101] Moreover, a small DM not only constrains proportionality, it also can raise the possibility of ethnic or racial gerrymandering. Some claim that a DM of at least 5 neutralizes most attempts to gerrymander,[102] but there is still evidence that gerrymandering does occur in STV systems.[103] Finally, because STV not only uses individual-based representation but also allows candidates from the same party to compete with each other, it tends to weaken intraparty discipline. As a result of these factors, STV has different effects on party systems than do party list PR systems. The general tendency is for moderate, 2 to 4 party systems that tend to have candidate-centered electoral campaigns, as opposed to the larger number of parties and more ideological campaigns associated with party list PR.[104]

In terms of aggregative equality, STV minimizes wasted votes by combining properties of party list PR and AV. Like party list PR, STV's proportionality allows a greater number of voters to elect representatives; like AV, the ordinal ballot and transfer mechanism allows many citizens who vote for losing candidates to transfer their ballots to candidates with a chance to win. However, the existence of multiple seats and candidates means that STV is even more prone to problems of nonmonotonicity than is AV. Again, there are real questions about the empirical frequency of nonmonotonic results under STV, as was discussed above. Nevertheless, plural deliberation must accept the logical possibility of nonmonotonic results, while simultaneously recognizing that this failing affects only one of the five criteria for assessing electoral systems in a plural polity.

Notably, Michael Dummett, whom I earlier cited as a critic of all ordinal-voting systems, nevertheless recommends STV as the optimal system for electing members of minority groups.[105] His limited approbation of this system stems from its perceived ability to enhance minorities' aggregative autonomy. However, Dummett's praise is perhaps premature, as STV actually has an ambiguous relationship to aggregative autonomy. On the plus side, STV's relatively low threshold of exclusion, which gets even lower as DM increases, increases aggregative autonomy over subjective constituency by allowing minority voters at the threshold to coalesce into a constituency and elect a representative, following campaign deliberation. Moreover, the ordinal ballot allows voters to identify with multiple subjective constituencies and to rank each one's relative importance to them. This capacity is well documented in the case of STV voting in Cincinnati, where Black laborers used multiple preference votes to express a primary subjective constituency in terms of their Black racial perspective and a secondary subjective constituency in terms of their working-class interests.[106] Finally, the ordinal ballot and vote transfers enhance aggregative autonomy for minority voters. For example, if two Black candidates compete for a Black minority population at the threshold of exclusion in an STV district, they need not worry about splitting the Black vote and defeating each other; the transfer mechanism can allow the trailing candidates' votes to transfer to the leading candidate. This last characteristic of STV is a notable advantage when compared to the cumulative vote (CV).[107]

But on the minus side, aggregative autonomy can suffer under STV. Recall that the ordinal ballot requires a relatively small DM because voters must rank multiple candidates. As I mentioned earlier, a DM of ten might force voters to rank twenty candidates. Given the candidate-centered campaigns common under STV, voters' ability to make an informed choice might be undermined. This can lead to the problem of "donkey voting," wherein voters fill in preferences according to the alphabetical or sequential order of the candidates on the ballot.[108] The result is diminishment of aggregative autonomy over representation. Lowering the DM to avoid this, however, hinders aggregative autonomy in three ways. First, if DM falls below 5, STV districts are potentially prone to racial gerrymandering, whereby districting bodies group citizens prior to any electoral deliberation. This, of course, undermines aggregative autonomy over subjective constituency. Second, a lower DM tends to lower the number of parliamentary parties, diminishing aggregative autonomy over representation. Finally, lowering the DM will raise the threshold of exclusion, as is the case in all proportional electoral systems, and this will lower aggregative autonomy over subjective constituency. STV thus confronts a recurring district magnitude dilemma. In terms of aggregative autonomy, ultimately, STV will surpass plurality systems, reserved seats, and AV, but it will lag behind party list PR.

Where STV surpasses party list PR is in the deliberative criteria. Even with a relatively small DM, between 3 and 5, STV can still enhance deliberative equality; the ordinal ballot and transfer mechanism allows for a larger number of elective candidates to campaign even if they have little chance to gain election. Voters can safely support such long-shot candidates; lower-preference vote transfers avoid wasting votes. Moreover, the deliberative input of elective candidates can influence the legislative action of parliamentary candidates. For example, support for independent, unsuccessful Black candidates first prompted the local Republican party to attend to Black issues under Cincinnati's STV system.[109]

This outcome, of course, also depended on incentives for deliberative reciprocity across group boundaries. Like AV, the ordinal ballot of STV allows voters to split their ballots across group boundaries. So a Black voter could give a first-preference vote to a Black candidate and a second-preference vote to an inclusive White candidate. In contrast to the categorical ballot of party list PR, the Black voter can support an inclusive White candidate without harming the chances of the Black candidate. This creates an incentive for inclusive candidates to pursue second- and lower-preference votes across group lines. For instance, an inclusive White candidate can benefit over an exclusive White candidate. The former will likely gain second-preference from both Whites and Blacks; the latter will likely gain second-preference votes only from Whites. In this way, inclusive candidates have greater potential to draw lower-preference support from across group lines, if during the campaign they introduce and promote issues that appeal to members of multiple collective identities. However, these incentives for deliberative reciprocity work only to the extent that the candidates need second-preference votes.

Party campaign strategies can undermine the need for lower-preference votes. An empirical analysis of campaign strategies in Ireland reveals the practice of bailiwick politics, whereby a district is divided between candidates from the same party. In this way, the district can function as two separate districts, allowing the party to avoid dividing its electoral support and increasing its chances of winning seats on first-preference votes alone.[110] Even in the absence of specific bailiwick politics, STV can fail to prompt competition for lower-preference votes simply because of its proportional electoral formula. When Northern Ireland reintroduced STV in its 1973 elections, parties were able to gain a proportional number of seats on first-preference votes alone, obviating the need to make cross-group appeals for second-preference votes. As a result, extreme loyalist parties captured the majority of the Protestant vote, undermining the viability of the new assembly. Not surprisingly, the government fell shortly thereafter.[111]

From this, Horowitz concludes that the majority electoral formula of AV makes it preferable to the proportional STV. We have already discussed the difficulties with the AV. Here, I wish only to suggest that the disappointing results in Northern Ireland may reflect the extremely difficult situation faced in 1973, one of the most violent periods of the "troubles." The 1921 and 1925 STV elections in Northern Ireland did not undermine communal peace. Indeed, the latter election saw the Nationalist party first enter peaceful, democratic politics. Moreover, STV's proportionality broke the Unionist party's stranglehold over the region's politics, a stranglehold they regained after successfully lobbying the Crown to reestablish SMDP. This allowed them to dominate the northern six counties from 1929 until 1969, prompting the Nationalists to exit electoral politics and eventually to adopt coercive tactics.[112] The proportional STV would prove more viable in settings like Cincinnati, where Blacks constitute only 11 percent of the population, a sufficiently small minority to be totally submerged under AV.[113]

The Cincinnati example also reveals how STV can enhance aggregative reciprocity at both the electoral and legislative level. At the electoral level, the presence of transferable lower-preference votes provides a strong incentive for candidates to make electoral alliances. These electoral alliances often translate into legislative alliances, should both candidates be elected. Because representatives can be supported from multiple subjective constituencies, they have an incentive to strike legislative bargains among different representatives elected by different groups. Consequently, STV provides incentives for group representatives to seek compromise and strike bargains in their legislative activity.[114]

The Cumulative Vote

The cumulative vote is one of several "semiproportional" electoral systems that include the limited vote (LV) used in Spain and the single nontransferable vote (SNTV) previously used in Japan. All three systems have citizens vote for individual candidates, rendering representation by individuals rather than by parties, and they all use multiple member districts and a plurality electoral formula, but they differ in their ballot structure. In a district electing five representatives, SNTV would grant each voter only one vote, whereas LV would grant voters between two and four votes: in each case, voters use a categorical ballot to vote for fewer candidates than there are seats in the district, and they can cast only one vote per candidate. Conversely, CV uses a cumulative ballot that grants voters five votes. Voters can then distribute their five votes among the candidates by granting one vote for five candidates, cumulating all five votes on one candidate, or cumulating a few votes on a few candidates. This crucial difference in ballot structure increases the propensity for wasted votes under CV, thereby decreasing its proportionality.

Typically, these systems use a plurality electoral formula, not a proportional electoral quota. This leads to some curious properties. Imagine a three-member district with 100 votes cast. If candidate A gets 50 votes, B 23, C 10, D 9, and E 8, candidates A, B, and C are elected, despite the fact that A gained five times as many votes as C. Indeed, it would be possible for A, B, and C to be elected if A received 98 votes and B and C only received one vote each, or if A, B, and C each received 33 votes each. This reveals that these systems lack any real threshold of inclusion, the minimum number of votes necessary to gain election under the best circumstances.[115] On the other hand, all three systems have clear thresholds of exclusion, the minimum number of votes necessary to guarantee election under the worst of circumstances. For CV and SNTV, the threshold of exclusion can be calculated as $100\%/(DM + 1) + 1$: this is the same as the Droop quota used in the STV. For LV, which varies in the number of votes citizens can cast independently of the DM, the threshold of exclusion is expressed as $(\text{\# of votes}/\text{\# of votes} + DM) \times 100$.[116]

The proportionality of these systems tends to increase as the number of votes granted to citizens declines and the DM increases.[117] Keeping DM constant, the SNTV tends to be more proportional than LV and CV respectively. The multiple votes in LV and CV provide more opportunities for wasted votes and thus increase their disporportionality over SNTV. In these systems, wasted votes tend to harm large parties or groups, which must carefully calculate how many candidates to run in a given district. If they run too many, they may dilute their voting support; if they run too few, they may fail to take full advantage of the voting support that they have. Conversely, small parties that appeal to a very narrow group of voters can simply run one candidate per district.[118] Because CV tends to place the greatest burdens upon larger groups to avoid disproportional vote dilution, it may be particularly valuable in bolstering minority representation. However, this comparative advantage will be most effective where minorities are geographically dispersed, as in the case of Black Americans in Alabama.[119] Where minorities are geographically concentrated, as in the case of Blacks in Illinois, CV need not improve minority representation over SMDP systems with minority–majority districts.[120] Indeed, in multimember districts where Blacks are the majority, CV's disproportionality might actually dilute its voting strength.

In terms of aggregative equality, the disproportionality of CV has ambiguous results. Lani Guinier asserts that CV will greatly reduce minority vote dilution when compared to SMDP.[121] However, this claim overlooks the different situations faced by majority versus minority groups. CV diminishes vote dilution only among geographically dispersed minorities; it does no better than SMDP when applied to geographically concentrated minorities, and it may increase vote dilution in Black-majority districts. In addition, Guinier falsely claims that CV will minimize wasted votes; yet this clearly need not be the case, given the lack of vote transfer mechanisms.[122] It is not hard to imagine lumping lots of wasted votes on a candidate who has already secured election. Nevertheless, small minorities are likely to waste fewer votes, particularly if their demographic population is near the Droop quota for the district. It is precisely the differential capacity for wasted votes that recommends CV as a means of enhancing minority representation among geographically dispersed minorities: majority-group voters are much more likely to waste their votes than are cohesive minority-group voters.

With respect to aggregative autonomy, CV confronts many of the same dilemmas as STV. CV and STV have the same relatively low threshold of exclusion; both systems can enable minority voters to coalesce as a subjective constituency after campaign deliberation, especially as DM increases. CV's cumulative ballot, like STV's ordinal ballot, enables voters to rank and identify with multiple subjective constituencies. Thus, a socialist, Chinese-American, pro-life citizen could support representation of his ethnic perspective, life world-view, and economic opinion by casting one vote each to a Chinese candidate, a pro-life candidate, and a socialist candidate. Alternatively, he could rank his ethnic perspective higher than his pro-life world-view by casting two ballots for the Chinese candidate, one for the socialist, and none for the pro-lifer.

On the other hand, CV suffers some of the same disadvantages as STV. Like STV, CV requires a relatively small DM, as a large number of seats and candidates places heavy burdens on voters. This lower DM opens CV to STV's problems of racial gerrymandering, a decline in parliamentary parties, and an increased threshold of exclusion, three factors that lower aggregative autonomy over constituency and representation. But in sharp contrast to STV, CV faces a distinct constraint on aggregative autonomy over representation when more than one minority-group candidate contests an election. Whereas STV's ordinal ballot and transfer mechanism allows two or more minority candidates to compete without fear of splitting the minority vote, CV remains prone to this danger.[123] In fact, this very outcome occurred in the town of Centre, Alabama, where its second CV election saw two Black candidates split the Black vote and lose.[124]

In terms of deliberative equality, the effect of CV is unclear. One analysis of CV voting in nineteenth-century British local elections depicts electoral campaigning among a broad array of ideological and religious perspectives, the latter reflecting an especially divisive social cleavage in this setting.[125] Another analysis of CV voting in Alabama suggests significant racial diversity among candidates there.[126] Still, wasting votes, especially among members of majority groups, can depress the number of elective candidates through Duverger's psychological effect.

Deliberative reciprocity across groups is similarly difficult to evaluate. On the one hand, the multiple ballots allow voters to support candidates who make appeals across group lines without requiring them to reject group-specific candidates entirely. Thus, in a three-seat district, Black voters can support a Black candidate with two votes while supporting an inclusive White candidate with one. In this way, CV's vote-splitting option, like the vote transfer capacity in STV and AV, avoids the voter dilemma found in party list PR. On the other hand, the opportunity to cumulate votes can also benefit racially exclusive candidates. If a Black voter wishes to cumulate three votes on a Black extremist candidate, CV lacks the transfer mechanism of STV that would moderate such exclusivist support. Exclusive or inclusive candidates can fare equally well under CV; the thin support that an inclusive candidate can expect from across group boundaries can be matched by the intense support that exclusive candidates can gain from cumulated votes from their own group.

Because the CV has been adopted in very few jurisdictions, there is little empirical evidence on how its incentive structure shapes deliberative reciprocity.[127] The study of CV in London suggests that it does not enhance it, as few candidates made appeals across religious group divisions. Instead, it was more common for the lone Catholic candidate in each of London's CV districts to gain multiple votes, presumably from the minority Catholic voters, while the multiple Protestant candidates mainly received split votes from the Protestant majority.[128] These majority and minority plumping strategies, then, might lead to a continuation of polarized voting within CV systems, limiting their potential to motivate deliberation across group boundaries. However, we cannot take this possibility as a necessity. The danger of intensified, exclusivist voting was raised as a possible criticism of CV, but evidence from its use in Chilton County, Alabama, revealed a moderate Black candidate defeating a more extreme Black candidate.[129] Still, the Chilton County study is the only detailed analysis of the possibility of racial polarization, so this danger persists as a possibility.

The indeterminate character of CV incentives replicates itself in terms of aggregative reciprocity. Although candidates do have the opportunity to create electoral alliances across group boundaries, there is no specific incentive to do so. Exclusive candidates who campaign alone might do better than inclusive candidates who seek cross-group alliances. Again, pace Guinier, there are no specific incentives favoring electoral coalitions in CV, as opposed to the clear ones under AV or STV. Nor does CV include any specific incentives to encourage aggregative reciprocity at the legislative level. Inclusive or exclusive tactics remain open possibilities under CV: everything depends upon the preferences of the voters, and CV provides no specific incentives to transform them in a manner that will accommodate the interests, opinions, perspectives, or world-views of members of other groups.

CONTEXT, APPLICATION, AND ADOPTION

As the preceding sections demonstrate, the fairness conditions of plural deliberation can help us develop a normative assessment of electoral systems for a plural polity. The assessment is based not only on each system's aggregative properties with respect to enhancing the representation of internally diverse, minority collective identities; it also assesses the capacity of each electoral system to enhance plural deliberation across the potentially shifting boundaries of various minority, majority, and plurality groups. Although this assessment focuses on the suitability of an electoral system with respect to the realization of deliberative democracy in a plural polity, it nevertheless remains excessively abstract. All plural polities are not the same. Thus, prior to suggesting which electoral systems are best suited to an America populated by diverse and constructed collective identities, it is important to examine various contextual factors that will shape the application of an electoral reform to a specific political context. These factors and others will also affect the prospects for adopting any given electoral system. In my judgment, the application of new electoral systems, even those designed to counter the political dynamic of group conflict, requires addressing five contextual factors: stability, size and complexity, political culture, political parties, and popular acceptance.

Stability refers to the concern that adopting a new electoral system will itself undermine peaceful coexistence among diverse groups. As I mentioned in chapter 3, the political dynamic of conflict applies to the adoption of new political institutions. Indeed, constitutional choices about formal, decision-making institutions are among the most conflict inducing of all political phenomena.[130] This is because the political actors authorized to enact institutional reforms are often the very people most affected by them. Moreover, constitutionally entrenched decision-making institutions establish the rules of the game for political competition, thereby structuring payoffs for political groups long into the future.[131] In plural polities marked by additional dynamics of conflict, the political actors creating new institutions may be motivated less by an interest in stable and fair institutions than by an interest in gaining an advantageous position over competing groups.[132] Thus, proponents of new formal, decision-making institutions, even those designed to mitigate group conflict, must consider whether institutional alterations will initiate new conflicts.

We must also address questions of *size and complexity.* The size of the jurisdiction slated to adopt a new electoral institution should match the complexity of the system to be adopted. All things being equal, jurisdictions that have large populations and cover considerable territory should adopt electoral institutions that are relatively simple to use. In general, SMDP, party list PR, and AV tend to be more applicable to large national institutions, whereas STV and CV, with their more complex ballot structures and counting processes, are usually considered best applied to smaller jurisdictions.

The *political culture* of the polity or jurisdiction that is to adopt a new electoral institution should also be considered. In particular, we should note whether the existing electoral system is strongly rooted in the political culture. If this is the case, we might think about reforming the existing electoral system or replacing it with a relatively similar one. We must consider the most widely shared characteristics of the political culture, but we should also recognize that collective identities within that polity may have their own political subcultures with different assessments of the existing electoral system.

A polity's political culture will influence two extremely important issues: the political parties that exist under the present system and that are likely to develop under a new system, and the willingness of the populace to accept the new electoral system. With respect to *political parties,* we should first determine whether the political culture favors representation by party or by individuals. We should also consider whether the political parties are strong and ideologically coherent or weak and ideologically fragmented. *Popular acceptance* of electoral reform will reflect a number of considerations, perhaps most important the allegiance to the existing political system and how much electoral variation the citizenry has previously experienced.

Consideration of these five contextual factors should lead us to make distinct suggestions for electoral reform at the national versus the state and local levels of government. National level problems have dominated discussions of pluralism and electoral reform in the Supreme Court,[133] contemporary political and legal theory,[134] and even Congress.[135] Unfortunately, electoral reform at this level will remain most difficult, given the contextual factors outlined above. Concerns about stability are most important in national elections because there are no higher authorities to adjudicate conflicts over altering these institutions. While ostensibly the United States Supreme Court could adjudicate such conflicts, as illustrated in its intervention into the 2000 presidential election, its hesitancy to interfere with coequal national institutions is well established. Moreover, the problem of size and complexity most powerfully applies to national-level jurisdictions. House districts are extremely large in terms of population and territory. Thus, we must consider only those electoral systems that are relatively simple to use and administer, which of course will rule out STV and CV.

On top of this, we must note that American political culture is most strongly attached to the SMDP system at the national level. Whereas various state and local jurisdictions have experimented with different electoral systems, the SMDP system has dominated House and Senate elections; this may undermine popular acceptance of new electoral systems at this level. Finally, the role and character of American political parties will hinder the adoption of the electoral system most suitable for national elections, party list PR. Americans are more familiar with individual level representation, to the extent that voters who have been incorporated into a new district would rather vote for their new incumbent than maintain their party allegiance.[136] And although party affiliation does help voters to determine general characteristics of individual candidates, American political parties remain fairly weak and have little ideological coherence. Of course, we should not reify the existing two-party system or the existing two parties: minor parties can and should play an important role in national elections. However, American political parties remain far from the disciplined, ideological parties present in list PR systems or even in SMDP parliamentary systems. And though new electoral systems, like party list PR, can shape political parties, other factors, like the executive-legislative structure, are also crucial.

Given that size and complexity rule out STV and CV at the national level, and that the role and character of American parties hinder the adoption of list PR, we seem stuck with SMDP at the national level. But as I pointed out earlier, SMDP can be improved by increasing the number of districts in the House of Representatives. The American lower chamber has far fewer seats and districts than the lower chambers of smaller countries, for example, Great Britain. Increasing the number of districts can improve the proportionality of SMDP, especially when districts are drawn to minimize minority vote dilution. Indeed, it can also facilitate the simultaneous creation of minority–majority and democratic-leaning districts, enhancing the descriptive and substantive representation of minority voters. Plural deliberation's fairness conditions and problems of identity construction do not favor SMDP minority–majority districts; however, contextual problems of application may favor reforming rather than replacing it.

If we believe that risks in terms of complexity and public acceptance are not too high, we could go beyond increasing the number of House districts and introduce AV elections. There are good reasons for thinking that AV would not be too complex; in most instances only a few candidates would run in each single-member district. Popular acceptance would be aided by the fact that it would retain the single member districts so closely associated with the House of Representatives and would not require the development of strongly disciplined, ideologically coherent political parties. The greatest benefit, of course, would be AV's incentives toward deliberative reciprocity across group boundaries. Such incentives will require heterogeneous districts, where members of a single group cannot win election on their own. Thus, AV will have its greatest effect on minority influence districts, where racial minorities can form coalitions with liberal Whites, and on interracial, minority–majority districts, where typically Blacks and Latinos together constitute the majority.

Whereas electoral reform faces greater constraints at the national level, there is more room for change at the state and local levels. Stability, for example, becomes less of an issue; Congress and the federal judiciary can more easily adjudicate conflicts over electoral reforms at a lower level of government. In addition, more complex electoral systems like STV and CV can more easily be used and administered in smaller, subnational jurisdictions. Indeed, empirical studies suggest that American citizens have relatively little difficulty using these two systems at the state, county, and local levels.[137]

With respect to the political culture, we should note that there has been much greater variation in electoral design at the state and local level, from the poorly suited MMDP systems, to the CV formerly used in the Illinois House and more recently adopted in several southern counties, to the STV formerly used in several Ohio cities and presently still used in Cambridge, Massachusetts. The strong connection to SMDP at the national level is simply not replicated in most state and local jurisdictions. We should also note that several state and local jurisdictions admit greater variety in the role and character of political parties. Nonpartisan elections are common in many jurisdictions, New York State has several important elective parties, and several states commonly elect independent or minor party candidates. The range of variation in electoral systems and political parties suggests that popular acceptance of electoral reform at the state and local level may be forthcoming.

One great obstacle to adopting new electoral systems at the state level, however, is the fact that several state constitutions, including those of Connecticut, Kansas, and Michigan, require SMDP elections for their state legislatures.[138] Attempts to alter electoral rules for these states will encounter significant difficulties. However, even here there may be more room for electoral innovation within municipal elections. And given that racial and ethnic diversity is often greatest in large, urban municipalities, these may be the jurisdictions most in need of an alternative electoral system to enhance plural deliberation across group boundaries.

That being said, what contours should electoral reform follow at this level? First and foremost, the MMDP at-large systems should be replaced. As I pointed out earlier, these systems have little redeeming value for a plural polity, given their extreme tendency to dilute minority voting strength and their utter lack of incentives toward deliberative reciprocity. The most likely candidates to replace MMDP are CV and STV. Although CV has gained the most attention of late, largely due to the influence of Lani Guinier, this system does not score well according to plural deliberation's fairness conditions. Cumulative voting equally encourages and discourages deliberative reciprocity, while also allowing for wasted votes for popular candidates. Where racial minorities are in the majority, as is the case in many local jurisdictions, CV could actually dilute minority voting strength.

On the other hand, STV's ordinal ballot can provide incentives toward deliberative reciprocity while also enhancing aggregative reciprocity and aggregative autonomy. And although aggregative equality suffers because of nonmonotonicity, it is also enhanced by the minimization of wasted votes through the transfer of lower-preference votes. Note, however, that the need for lower-preference votes, and thus the incentives for deliberative reciprocity, will diminish if candidates can win election through first-preference votes alone. Although Horowitz cites this problem as a reason for favoring multimember AV over STV, AV must be assessed in light of its own failure to require lower-preference votes if there is a coherent majority bloc. For these reasons, STV probably remains a better alternative for state and local jurisdictions.

Thus, I tentatively suggest that electoral reform at the state and local level seek to eliminate MMDP and SMDP electoral systems and replace them with STV. Electoral reform at the national level should focus on increasing the number of House districts and, perhaps, adopting AV elections. Of course, this leaves open the question of whether there is any chance that these reforms could be enacted. Two methods of adoption seem most promising. First, there is the judicial strategy. Since *Thornburg v. Gingles,* Voting Rights Act jurisprudence has threatened MMDP electoral systems by comparing their ability to elect minority representatives with SMDP systems. However, MMDP systems are usually replaced with SMDP or CV. This tendency has largely resulted from SMDP's familiarity and the legal advocacy of Lani Guinier. Both tendencies can be countered by greater acknowledgment in the legal community of STV's relative value when compared to CV. Here, the advocacy of legal scholars like Donald Horowitz will come to the forefront. A second method of adoption is also possible. Many state and local jurisdictions allow for electoral reform through referendum. STV won approximately 45% of such referendums in Cincinnati and San Francisco.[139] For STV to be adopted through such methods, public sphere actors must more effectively promote this system. Certain politically oriented associations representing women and Latinos have voiced support for PR systems in general.[140] It will be up to politically engaged scholars to promote the specific value of STV to these and other public sphere actors.

Electoral reform at the national level may be more difficult, given the concerns for stability and the inability to alter the system through referendum. However, the judicial strategy remains viable. In particular, Voting Rights Act jurisprudence includes a doctrine of nonretrogression: the number of minority–majority seats must not decline from its present status. It is becoming more and more difficult to draw such districts, and so increasing the number of districts may well become necessary in order to comply with the Voting Rights Act. *Thornburg v. Gingles* allowed counterfactual comparisons of minority representation under SMDP versus MMDP, in order to challenge the latter's use in local and state elections. Perhaps voting rights lawyers could suggest using counterfactual comparisons of minority representation under party list PR versus SMDP. This could apply more pressure to increase the number of House districts, which would enhance the proportionality of the national SMDP system.

Still, this leaves open the question of adopting AV voting processes. Here, Congressional action will be necessary. Congress has already entertained debate over much more radical alterations to House elections, and so this more moderate alteration might enjoy a relatively realistic chance for adoption. Again, scholarly advocacy will remain crucial. But in this case, we should also recognize the role of quasi-formal, deliberative institutions, which have provided venues for legal scholars to deliberate with Congressional representatives over the costs and benefits of alternative electoral systems. Most famous have been the 1999 hearings held by the House Judiciary Committee's Subcommittee on the Constitution, which discussed the possibility of allowing states to introduce new electoral systems for House seats.[141] Deliberation within quasi-formal, deliberative settings, along with activity within the informal, deliberative institutions of civil society and the public sphere, will remain crucial to the adoption of new electoral systems. This, of course, reveals a point I raised earlier: deliberative democracy in a plural polity requires multiple deliberative settings. Just as campaigning candidates can introduce new issues into public sphere deliberation, so too can deliberation within the public sphere and advisory panels affect how citizens and their representatives alter formal, decision-making institutions. Deliberative democracy in a plural polity is a complex matter, and realizing it requires work by many actors in many settings. By more precisely outlining the contours of deliberative institutions and processes, deliberative democratic theory can inform such action and the citizens who remain free to adopt or ignore its counsel.

APPENDIX: PARTY LIST PR ELECTORAL FORMULAS

Party list PR electoral formulas differ primarily in their method of awarding seats for fractional proportions of votes. For instance, it is rarely the case that the number of seats can be divided into perfect proportions according to the number of votes won. More likely is the following scenario. In a district with 5 seats and 100 votes cast, Party A wins 36 votes, Party B wins 30 votes, Party C wins 14 votes, Party D wins 12, and Party E wins 8. Given the likelihood of this circumstance, PR systems usually assign a vote quota needed to gain election. Under the "least remainders" formula, the number of votes cast is divided by the number of seats, generating an initial quota. In this case, with 5 seats, each party gains one seat for every 20 votes received, and thus Party A will win 1 seat and Party B will win 1 seat. The next three seats will be awarded to the largest remainders left after the 20 votes taken to elect Parties A and B are removed. Thus, the remainders are 16 (A), 10 (B), 14 (C), 12 (D), and 8 (E). As a result, a second seat will be awarded

Table 5.3 Seat Distribution under a d'Hondt Formula Part List PR System

Party	V/1	V/2	V/3	Seats
A	36	18	12	2
B	30	15	10	2
C	14	7	4⅔	1
D	12	6	4	0
E	8	4	2⅔	0

to A, and C and D will also win one seat each. The final seat allocation will be A (2), B (1), C (1), D (1), E (0).

Alternatively, seats can be awarded not by an initial quota and remainders but through divisors. For instance, the d'Hondt method divides the votes received by each party using successive integers (1, 2, 3 . . .). In each division, the largest vote quotient is granted a seat. Thus, in our example the vote divisions will be as represented in Table 5.3. If we award the seats to the top 5 vote quotients, those will be 36 (A), 30 (B), 18 (A), 15 (B), and 14 (C). The rest of the vote quotients will gain no seats. Thus, whereas Party D gained a seat according to largest remainders, in a d'Hondt system Party D gains no seats and Party B gains a second seat. Another divisor method, the Sainte-Lague method, uses odd-numbered divisors (1, 3, 5 . . .). In general, the largest remainders method tends to be the most proportional and tends to benefit smaller parties. The d'Hondt formula most benefits large parties, and the Sainte-Lague method falls in between.[142]

Conclusion

At the outset of this book, I contended that questions of justice and stability should be more carefully integrated into the examination of democratic polities that have a plurality of intergenerational groups. I criticized empirical social scientists for failing to scrutinize the normative presuppositions behind the institutions and policies they recommend to enhance stability in a plural polity. I then criticized normative political philosophers for failing to examine how problems of identity construction, dynamics of group conflict, and institutional incentives can complicate the recommendations they proffer for realizing justice among groups. I have attempted to integrate questions of justice and stability through a deliberative, institutional approach to pluralism, one that can guide normative responses to injustices within a plural polity while remaining sensitive to problems of identity construction, dynamics of group conflict, and institutional incentives.

The normative core of this approach is a model of fair, plural deliberation, which can be used to assess and reform democratic processes and institutions. This model demands that the scope of deliberation remain unrestricted with respect to the contributions proffered within democratic deliberation. It also incorporates substantive and procedural elements, as fair deliberation in a plural polity requires not only the satisfaction of certain procedural rules but also the substantive achievement of understanding across group boundaries. Deliberative understanding aims to generate an exchange of justifications and criticisms across group boundaries, which in turn should prompt participants to reflect upon the preferences they act upon in making democratic, collective decisions. Such deliberatively reflective preferences should contribute to collective decision-making through processes like deliberative voting and elections. Finally, processes of deliberation and decision-making must be assessed through the aggregative and deliberative fairness conditions of political equality, political autonomy, and political reciprocity.

This normative model of deliberation can better respond to the three oversights committed by most normative theories regarding identity construction, dynamics of group conflict, and institutional incentives. It responds to the problem of identity construction in two ways. By focusing on the democratic processes through which a plural polity reaches collective decisions, it allows members of diverse but constructed collective identities to respond to the problems faced by specific groups and subgroups in a flexible, contextually sensitive manner. Instead of directly tying certain types of group-specific measures to certain types of groups, this approach seeks to foster deliberative processes that include members of all relevant collective identities. Through such processes, they can develop and justify more precise group-specific or group-neutral measures, which can more flexibly apply to collective identities marked by internal diversity, shifting boundaries, and multiple modes of identity construction. However, deliberation may require group-based representation in order to include all relevant perspectives. Consequently, this approach also remains sensitive to identity construction by distinguishing among three different types of institutions and their suitability for group-based representation. Informal and quasi-formal deliberative institutions are more amenable to group-specific representation because these bodies are not constitutionally established and do not reach collective decisions that legally bind the entire polity. Constitutionally established, formal, decision-making institutions are less amenable to group-specific representation. Instead, these institutions should incorporate electoral systems that enable but do not require group-based representation.

This deliberative, institutional approach to pluralism also responds to the strategic dynamics of group conflict, foremost by recognizing that plural deliberation must rely not only on deliberative motivations but also on strategic incentives. Deliberative motivations, grounded in moral psychology, cultural self-understandings, publicity constraints, and the deliberative generation of trust, remain necessary for plural deliberation. However, they are clearly not sufficient. For this reason, I examine how strategic incentives can bolster plural deliberation. This leads me to identify which actors are best positioned strategically to engage in plural deliberation, to recommend specific policies in order to mitigate dynamics of group conflict, to accommodate problems of identity construction, and to outline possible reforms to our deliberative and decision-making institutions.

Finally, this approach takes into account institutional incentives within the public sphere and electoral systems. It recognizes that the public sphere remains an indispensable site for plural deliberation across group boundaries, particularly because it facilitates the flexible representation of emerging and submerging collective identities. However, my analysis also reveals the public sphere to be vulnerable to strategic dynamics of group conflict. As a result, we must pursue reforms to realize plural deliberation and mitigate dynamics of group conflict in the public sphere, including measures to promote intergroup associations, diversify media ownership, improve journalistic ethics, and monitor racial biases in the media. Institutional incentives play an important role in my examination of electoral systems. Because electoral systems may effectively force some candidates to seek the votes of members of different groups, they provide incentives for candidates to extend deliberative reciprocity across group boundaries.

Although the deliberative, institutional approach to pluralism cannot resolve all problems of identity construction, dynamics of group conflict, and institutional incentives, it places these issues at the forefront of normative theory. In this way, it can enable us to develop judgments of justice and fairness that more precisely take into account the complex political relations within and among diverse and constructed collective identities. Having provided fairly precise discussions of the public sphere and electoral systems, I now wish to extend my argument by making brief suggestions regarding how the criteria of plural deliberation can be applied to other formal, decision-making institutions connected to the democratic state.

Consider legislatures. These formal, decision-making institutions are the key sites of policy formation in representative democracies, and thus they would appear to be crucial for deliberative, democratic theory. And when we recall that the English term *parliament* derives from the French term *parlement,* which in turn derives from *parler* (to speak), we recognize an etymological link between legislatures and the idea of deliberation. Let me emphasize that I have no objection to applying deliberative criteria to the assessment of legislatures, as some scholars have done.[1] In this way, I differ from theorists who remain skeptical about deliberation within the formal, decision-making institutions of the democratic state.[2] Attention to legislative deliberation will be crucial to realizing the deliberative aims sought by electoral reform. The election of minority representatives, one of several goals pursued by alternative electoral systems, can lose its significance if these representatives lack power within the legislature. Although the election of minority representatives is a necessary prerequisite for plural deliberation at the legislative level, it is not sufficient. For this reason, let me briefly suggest how one might assess legislatures according to the model of plural deliberation, the problem of identity construction, and the dynamics of group conflict.

First, recall that the criterion of deliberative autonomy was not helpful in distinguishing among electoral systems because it was consistently violated in the vertical deliberation between representatives and citizens. But when we turn to the horizontal deliberation among representatives in a legislature, this condition becomes more applicable because in principle, all members should have relatively equal access to parliamentary procedural rules. Deliberative equality would also require equal allotments of speaking time among different perspectives, regardless of their numerical representation within the assembly. In order to realize deliberative equality more substantively, reforms could attend to the egalitarian distribution of legislative research staff and resources so that representatives of minority groups do not suffer in relation to representatives of majority groups. Still, such an egalitarian distribution of resources does not address whether representatives of different groups enjoy the capacity to exploit such resources equally. Although I cannot dismiss this danger, it may be lessened in the case of representatives who remain members of the political elite, even if they come from disadvantaged minority groups.[3]

Deliberative equality and autonomy might be enhanced through special caucuses for disadvantaged, minority representatives, for reasons similar to those favoring minority counterpublics within the public sphere. But even if minority caucuses enhance deliberative autonomy among representatives, the formal, decision-making character of legislatures may hinder the flexibility to respond to internal diversity. Whereas new counterpublics can easily emerge to represent internal minorities and shifting boundaries within the public sphere, such flexibility cannot be guaranteed in a formal, decision-making institution. If minority caucuses can proliferate in response to the proliferation of internal minority perspectives, then they can enhance deliberative autonomy and equality. But if the formal character of legislatures hinders such proliferation, we run the risk that a minority caucus could undermine deliberative equality for internal minorities. In the end, the validity of minority caucuses may rest upon a contextual judgment assessing not only the formal, decision-making character of legislatures but also the extent to which a collective identity admits of internal diversity, shifting boundaries, and multiple modes of construction. Given the analysis of different groups in chapter 1, a minority caucus for Blacks might make more sense than one for Asians.

I remain uncertain about which parliamentary rules could enhance deliberative reciprocity among representatives. Some theorists advocate group vetoes or cumulative voting within legislatures to enhance the power of minority representatives, but I have strong reservations about both methods. I suspect that enshrining a legislative group-veto requires fixing a constructed collective identity within a constitutionally established, formal, decision-making institution. Problems of internal diversity, shifting boundaries, and multiple modes of identity construction make this measure seem sharply at odds with the deliberative, institutional approach that I have advocated here. In addition, in chapter 5 I argued that cumulative voting does not provide strong incentives favoring deliberative reciprocity in the election of representatives. I am not sure that it will enhance deliberative reciprocity among representatives if it is applied to legislative voting. I have argued that the preferential, ordinal ballots in the alternative vote and the single-transferable vote can enhance deliberative reciprocity in elections. However, I have not discovered studies of preferential voting at the legislative level and thus cannot speak of its effects on deliberative reciprocity there.

However, there are empirically based arguments suggesting that alternative voting can enhance deliberative reciprocity among diverse groups when it is applied to the election of executive offices.[4] The alternative vote can also enhance deliberative equality by encouraging elective candidates for executive office, like the Green party's Ralph Nader. This system might be preferable to the plurality formula, which would allow a candidate to win executive office by catering only to a cohesive plurality. We can apply the alternative vote directly to the election of executives only in presidential systems, where the executive is elected separately from the legislature. This raises the thorny question of whether presidential or parliamentary systems are more conducive to plural deliberation. On the one hand, Arend Lijphart favors parliamentary systems with party list PR elections because they enable the formation of cabinets that include representatives of different ethnic or racial political parties. On the other hand, Donald Horowitz favors a presidential system with alternative voting, so that the single executive can serve as a unifying figure beholden to voters from different groups.[5]

I will not pretend to resolve this debate here, but I will suggest how plural deliberation can assess either proposal. The Lijphart approach generally favors proportional representation of ethnic groups within the executive cabinet, which would realize only aggregative, not deliberative, equality among groups. The locus of plural deliberation would shift to the legislature; its reliance on party list PR means that voters would experience strong pressure to vote for their own, group-based parties rather than for cross-group parties. The realization of plural deliberation would thus require cabinet procedures that enhance deliberative equality, deliberative autonomy, and deliberative reciprocity among group representatives.

Horowitz's approach, on the other hand, locates plural deliberation at the campaign level. His advocacy of alternative voting and electoral requirements obligating candidates to attain diverse, regional support, may enhance deliberative reciprocity across racial, ethnic, or regional lines. The alternative vote's incentives favoring elective candidates can also enhance deliberative equality. However, the majority formula of alternative voting may limit descriptive representation within the executive, something clearly envisioned by the Lijphart plan. The key to assessing the two systems, then, depends on the weight one attaches to descriptive representation versus the generation of deliberative reciprocity across group boundaries.

Finally, we might inquire whether judicial institutions can be assessed according to the criteria of plural deliberation. On the one hand, judicial institutions seem clearly related to deliberation, given the need for juries to reach consensus on a decision through extended discussion. On the other hand, they are not meant to represent the interests of citizens. This disinterested character leads John Rawls to envision the United States Supreme Court as a deliberative institution;[6] however, plural deliberation's inclusion of individual and group interests within the deliberative process does not require this. Still, the criteria of deliberative equality, deliberative autonomy, and deliberative reciprocity could be used to assess judicial institutions and processes. Thus, jury deliberation might be a fruitful area of research, as some theorists have already noted.[7]

For example, the equal inclusion of a diverse set of jurors, regardless of the demographic size of their respective groups, would reflect the criterion of deliberative equality. Realizing this criterion might be of great importance, given persistent race-related disparities in the criminal punishment of similar crimes.[8] However, Lynn Sanders suggests that White, middle-class males deploy cultural power on juries through their assertive speaking style,[9] a problem that would diminish deliberative autonomy in a diverse jury. Combating this danger might require enhancing deliberative reciprocity among jurors, but I cannot provide a clear means of doing so. Alternative voting systems are not easily applicable to juries, given their small size and common use of consensus as a decision rule. James Fishkin, in his proposals for deliberative opinion polls, has participants spend an extended period of time together in order to enhance deliberative reciprocity.[10] However, he does not provide clear evidence that this manages to reduce the deployment of cultural power among diverse participants. Still, this type of inquiry is precisely what is necessary to determine whether plural deliberation can be realized in jury deliberation.

One institutional innovation clearly pertinent to plural deliberation is local self-governance. I have discussed the suitability of different electoral systems in relation to municipal elections, but I have not examined how more participatory institutions at the local level should be analyzed according to the criteria of plural deliberation. As an entry to this issue, I will engage two important studies of local, participatory self-government: the five-city comparative study conducted by Jeffrey Berry, Kent Portney, and Ken Thomson, and Archon Fung's analysis of participatory structures governing Chicago schools and policing.[11] Fung clearly locates his inquiry within the ambit of deliberative democratic theory; Berry and his collaborators are primarily concerned with testing the viability of participatory democratic theory. Nevertheless, I believe that both studies introduce important issues for plural deliberation.

These participatory structures involve citywide neighborhood institutions that devolve governing power to citizens. Thus, they are formal, decision-making institutions. They are formal through their creation by and connections to municipal governments. In the case of Chicago, the city government created these institutions and also monitors them in order to assess the effectiveness of their substantive decisions and the fairness of their decision-making procedures.[12] These institutions have the power to make decisions that bind the residents within their neighborhoods. In Chicago, the local school councils (LSCs) can hire, fire, and monitor school principals and create school budgets; neighborhood "police beat" meetings influence the operations of officers in their areas.[13] In the five cities studied by Berry and colleagues, neighborhood institutions could affect city funding, the allocation of resources to neighborhoods, and local development. More detailed analysis reveals that business developers were more effective at placing items on the city government agenda, whereas neighborhood councils were more effective at shaping ultimate policy outcomes, primarily through their potential to obstruct unwanted development.[14]

In highlighting how the Chicago institutions differ from informal or quasi-formal deliberative institutions, Archon Fung and Erik Olin Wright emphasize that they are "not merely advisory" but have real and binding decision-making powers.[15] Even though these institutions are formal and decision-making, both studies emphasize their participatory character. Chicago's police beat meetings are open to all, and although the LSC positions are elected offices, most are uncontested, rendering them closer to a volunteer activity.[16] Neighborhood institutions in the five-city study are open to all residents, although actual participation varies considerably, as it does in Chicago as well.

In assessing these urban, participatory schemes according to plural deliberation, one must immediately recognize that understanding and criticism across group boundaries are not their central concerns. Although all of the urban centers included in these studies contain diverse racial and ethnic groups, residential segregation often divides these groups geographically. Thus, the focus on neighborhood participation immediately limits plural deliberation across group boundaries. Moreover, Berry and colleagues find troubling evidence that neighborhood participation may foster parochialism, such that neighborhood participants fight for their own interests rather than entertaining the interests of other neighborhoods or the city at large. Even worse, they find that race, wealth, and organization are most often cited as determining whether a neighborhood obtains disproportionate benefits from the city government.[17] Consequently, we are confronted with the danger that urban participatory opportunities, when combined with racial or ethnic segregation, could actually undermine plural deliberation. This should remind us that heterogeneous neighborhoods, like heterogeneous electoral districts, are necessary (but insufficient) conditions for plural deliberation. Where neighborhoods are not heterogeneous, plural deliberation will require interneighborhood deliberative processes, something neglected in both sets of studies.[18]

Beyond this, plural deliberation can guide assessments of how these local participatory arrangements function. Consider first the question of linking local deliberation to collective decision-making. Berry's group does not clarify how its urban participatory institutions reach collective decisions; Fung and Wright, in their deliberative approach, vaguely suggest either a loose consensus, akin to the workable agreements discussed in chapter 2, or deliberative voting. In articulating the latter method, they distinguish deliberative voting, which requires citizens to vote for the most reasonable proposal, from aggregative voting, whereby citizens vote according to their own personal interests.[19] This suggestion, unfortunately, neglects the crucial issue. Whether citizens base their votes on personal interests or on opinions of reasonableness, voting is an aggregative mechanism that requires distinct aggregative criteria, as I argue in chapter 2. However, Fung and Wright fail to articulate aggregative criteria for collective decision-making, something that plural deliberation provides. Moreover, I suspect that they draw too sharp a distinction between aggregation and deliberation. Although the two are analytically distinct, the discussion of electoral systems in chapter 5 strongly suggests that aggregative voting mechanisms can structure deliberation. The framework of plural deliberation should provide greater guidance on voting methods, especially regarding the election of members of local school councils.

Apart from the lack of aggregative criteria, these studies insufficiently apply deliberative criteria. Most prominent in both studies is a concern with substantive resources and capacities for deliberative equality (the equally effective representation of different viewpoints, regardless of numerical support) and deliberative autonomy (the possession of critical, reflective preferences). In terms of deliberative equality, Berry and colleagues show how city governments provide the resources needed for effective participation at the local level and how participation can enhance participants' political knowledge and general sense of political efficacy.[20] Fung and Wright are centrally concerned with participants' "capacities of argument." Fung's casework documents how the Chicago city government provided LSC members with training for practical matters, like preparing budgets, and more abstract skills, like collective problem solving.[21] Regarding substantive deliberative autonomy, both studies pay careful attention to how local participants can improve their ability to develop critical and reflective preferences on the issues they confront. Indeed, the examination of substantive capacities and resources remains perhaps the strongest contribution of these studies. Fung also documents how third party intervention can mitigate procedural violations of deliberative autonomy, whereby wealthier or more educated participants dominate others.[22]

Less satisfying, however, is the utter lack of attention to the procedural aspects of deliberative equality (the equal representation of diverse viewpoints, regardless of numerical strength) and deliberative reciprocity. This clearly reveals an inattention to problems of deliberative understanding and criticism across group boundaries, the concern that these criteria most clearly reflect. This, then, restates my earlier point that local participatory structures; if they are to contribute to deliberative democracy in a plural polity, they must include cross-neighborhood deliberative processes that can realize conditions of deliberative equality and reciprocity. Without such processes, the fact of residential segregation might render neighborhood participation an obstacle, rather than a support, to plural deliberation.

In these ways, plural deliberation can inform our assessments of other formal, decision-making institutions, such as legislatures, executives, judiciaries, and local self-government structures. Clearly, any possible reforms of these institutions must take into account important contextual problems, like those discussed at the end of chapter 5. Still, plural deliberation can guide more detailed, context-sensitive research into these types of institutions. Such institutional guidance, along with attention to problems of identity construction and dynamics of group conflict, reveals more general advantages to my deliberative, institutional approach when compared to other normative theories of racial, ethnic, and cultural pluralism. Let me conclude by briefly examining a few alternative theories.

Most prominent is the liberal, group rights approach popularized by Will Kymlicka. I have discussed this approach with respect to the problem of identity construction in chapter 1, but I wish now to focus on the dynamics of group conflict and other pragmatic concerns. Before doing so, let me first acknowledge some areas of agreement between plural deliberation and Kymlicka's theory. For the most part, I agree with Kymlicka's conclusion that self-government rights are more applicable to national minorities that share a common language, common institutions, and a contiguous territory. Because most immigrant ethnic groups are territorially dispersed and tend to seek only those political measures that will aid their integration into the new, host society, self-government rights are less viable for them. However, my agreement with Kymlicka's conclusion stems not from his theory of distributive justice among groups, with its sharp distinction between the modes of identity construction associated with each type of group. And I do not agree that national cultures, as opposed to religious or other cultural frameworks, are necessarily most important for exercising individual autonomy. Rather, pragmatic concerns ground my concurrence with Kymlicka. In the modern world of territorial nation-states, it is simply more feasible to grant self-government to national minorities that share a language, a territory, and institutions.

However, I suspect that contiguous territory and shared institutions may be more important than a common language to the granting of self-government rights. Several states share a common language but nevertheless govern themselves separately. At the level of sovereign nation-states, the United States and English-speaking Canada or Germany and Austria provide perhaps the most prominent examples of populations that share a common language but inhabit separate states, the result of accidents of history. Whether they remain separate or become unified may depend upon two countervailing features: the persistence of distinct political institutions, cultures, and constitutional attachments versus the integrating pressures of market economies. At the level of jurisdictions without full sovereignty, the fact that several Indian states share a common language while remaining distinct reinforces the lack of fit between territorial jurisdiction and language. Common administrative and social institutions may also eclipse language as the key to a politicized national identity. Benedict Anderson argues that the limited reach of state bureaucracies and the popular press generated multiple nationalisms rather than a single nationalism among the many Spanish-speaking colonies of South America. Conversely, a strong colonial state bureaucracy under the Dutch fostered a relatively unified nationalism in Indonesia, despite the plethora of languages present in that territory.[23] The territorial boundaries of self-governing jurisdictions depend upon much more than a common language, and we should not try to attach too much moral significance to what are often morally arbitrary factors. The congruence of language, territory, and institutions may aid in the feasibility of self-government, but this should be seen as a pragmatic issue that should be factored into context-sensitive deliberation.

Kymlicka's tendency to conflate moral and pragmatic questions can become even more troubling when we consider the thorny question of disputed territorial and linguistic boundaries. These issues often raise the questions of political motivation to which Kymlicka is so blind. Elie Kedourie notes that nineteenth-century German nationalists asserted their right to annex the Netherlands by claiming that Dutch was merely a dialect of German. Russian nationalists used similar claims to justify a pan-Slavic union dominated by Russia.[24] These nationalists may have been motivated purely by their linguistic beliefs, but it is hard to overlook how their claims can be sustained by incentives associated with the instrumental-agency mode of identity construction and the political and resource dynamics of group conflict.

A more recent example also complicates Kymlicka's claims. When the idea of dividing India and Pakistan was introduced during the first half of the twentieth century, leaders of the militant Sikh party, Akali Dal, emulated the Muslim League's successful articulation of a Muslim national identity and mobilized for a Sikh religious nationality. When this failed, Sikhs migrated to the Punjab region of India, creating a territorial majority there. This led Akali Dal leaders to adopt a new strategy. Secular India rejected religion but accepted language as a basis for territorial, political jurisdiction, and so the Akali Dal fought to have Punjabi, until now merely a regional dialect, recognized as a distinct language. Concomitantly, they promoted the Gurumukhi script, hitherto used only for Sikh religious purposes, as the Punjabi language's script. Ultimately, Akali Dal leaders succeeded in creating a Sikh-majority Punjabi state in 1966 by mobilizing middle-class Sikhs, not religious leaders, through constructed appeals to linguistic rights and questionable claims of job discrimination.[25]

This case clearly reveals how a national identity can be constructed through instrumental agency, which in turn can be motivated by incentives associated with resource and political dynamics. It reveals that strategic manipulations by political elites can construct a national identity out of a religious identity, a troubling occurrence given Kymlicka's sharp distinction between the claims of national and religious groups.[26] Moreover, as the rise of violent Sikh separatism suggests, such strategic dynamics can also lead to heightened group conflict. Kymlicka is aware of how secessionist demands can incite violent group conflict, and he does not simply argue that secessions are directly justified through his theory of self-government rights.[27] But his failure to attend to the question of motivations, instrumental modes of identity construction, and the dynamics of group conflict reveals important lacunae in his model. I in no way claim that plural deliberation can resolve all the thorny problems involved with group conflict in general and secessionism in particular; however, this deliberative, institutional approach avoids reifying collective identities and outlines some of the motivational problems associated with the dynamics of group conflict and institutional incentives. In this way, it opens the door to new lines of inquiry generally excluded from most normative theories, including Kymlicka's.

Attention to the dynamics of group conflict, instrumental modes of identity construction, and institutional incentives also distinguishes my approach from that of Iris Marion Young. In many ways, my approach resembles Young's, through its focus on democratic deliberation and its rejection of sharp distinctions between different types of groups. However, Young overlooks the role of instrumental agency in the construction of collective identities and inadequately attends to dynamics of group conflict. In the one instance where she directly addresses group conflict, she concentrates only on the positional dynamic, overlooking how other strategic dynamics can undermine deliberative reciprocity across group boundaries.[28] In her later work, Young circumvents problems of group conflict and simply assumes that political actors in a plural polity will adopt Habermasian communicative action rather than various forms of strategic action. This assumption relieves her of the need to assess institutional incentives within the public sphere and electoral systems. The failure to address electoral incentives is particularly unfortunate, as she has come to view alternative electoral systems as the best means for enhancing group-based representation. My deliberative, institutional theory thus complements Young's approach by providing a more detailed assessment of how electoral systems can not only enhance minority representation but can also encourage deliberation across group boundaries.

I have argued that my approach can complement Young's theory; however, its clearest complementary relationship lies with detailed, contextual assessments of justice among groups, like that of Joseph Carens.[29] And as I suggested in the Introduction and in chapter 1, such contextual analysis can be seen as a necessary corollary to my deliberative, institutional approach because it can provide assessments of the substantive outcomes of the democratic processes evaluated by plural deliberation. Such contextual assessments can also function as contributions to deliberative, democratic processes of collective decision-making in a plural polity. In this way, the contextual theorist acts as a politically engaged intellectual or social critic, whose specialized knowledge can contribute to democratic deliberation. In providing specialized contributions, however, the social critic's expertise cannot grant him any greater social or political power. Deliberative autonomy requires the social critic to play on the same field as all other citizens. In this way, he enters the public sphere not as the vanguard of social change but as a fellow citizen, whose contributions may be affirmed or rejected in the process of deliberative decision-making.

The role of the social critic has occupied more attention in theories of deliberative democracy than in most other contemporary normative theories. This attention clearly stems from the influence of Jürgen Habermas, whose approach grows out of the intellectual tradition of critical theory. The Hegelian and Marxist roots of critical theory forced it to grapple with the role of the social critic; neo-Marxists like Lenin justified their assumption of political power through their status as interpreters and implementers of Marxist doctrine. Thus, critical theorists have sought to reconcile the political engagement of the social critic with the requirements of democratic, political autonomy. The result is subtle, theoretical reflection on the role of political and social theory within a deliberative, democratic polity.[30]

In my deliberative, institutional approach to democracy in a plural polity, the social critic has at least two distinctive contributions to make. First, there is the careful assessment of substantive outcomes, exemplified by Carens's contextualist approach to pluralism. But social criticism must go beyond this, to assess not only substantive outcomes but also the democratic processes and institutions through which a plural polity reaches such outcomes. Politically engaged theorists must contribute to our understanding of how to improve our democratic institutions and processes. They must criticize processes, institutions, and even specific political actors that fail to fulfill the requirements of plural deliberation. When possible, they should suggest ways to reform our institutions and processes and identify which political actors to support. I hope I have provided this second type of contribution, by outlining criteria for assessing democratic processes and institutions and by suggesting possible institutional and policy reforms. But my contributions remain subject to the affirmation or rejection of participants within the processes of democratic deliberation and decision-making. More than most theories, deliberative democratic theory recognizes its subservience to the people it serves. A theory of deliberative democracy in a plural polity merely emphasizes the diversity of the people, who remain sovereign.

Notes

INTRODUCTION

1. Alvin Rabushka and Kenneth Shepsle, *Politics in Plural Societies: A Theory of Democratic Instability* (Columbus, OH: Merrill, 1971).

2. Crawford Young, *The Politics of Cultural Pluralism* (Madison, WI: The University of Wisconsin Press, 1976); Arend Lijphart, *Democracy in Plural Societies* (New Haven, CT: Yale University Press, 1979).

3. Lijphart, *Democracy in Plural Societies;* Donald Horowitz, *A Democratic South Africa?* (Berkeley, CA: University of California Press, 1991).

4. Jack Snyder, *From Voting to Violence* (New York: Norton, 2000).

5. Ann Phillips, *The Politics of Presence* (New York: Oxford University Press, 1995); Melissa Williams, *Voice, Trust, and Memory* (Princeton, NJ: Princeton University Press, 1998); Iris Marion Young, *Justice and the Politics of Difference* (Princeton, NJ: Princeton University Press, 1990); idem, *Inclusion and Democracy* (New York: Oxford University Press, 2000).

6. Will Kymlicka, *Multicultural Citizenship* (New York: Oxford University Press, 1995); Jeff Spinner, *The Boundaries of Citizenship* (Baltimore, MD: Johns Hopkins University Press, 1993); Michael Rosenfeld, *Affirmative Action and Justice* (New Haven, CT: Yale University Press, 1991).

7. Nancy Fraser, "Rethinking the Public Sphere," in *Habermas and the Public Sphere,* ed. Craig Calhoun (Cambridge, MA: MIT Press, 1992), 108–142.

8. Consider Kymlicka's summary dismissal of identity construction in *Multicultural Citizenship,* 185. Jeff Spinner, *The Boundaries of Citizenship,* chapter 2, is one of the few normative philosophers to address the problem of identity construction, but his response is insufficient. I examine Kymlicka and Spinner on identity construction in chapter 1.

9. Kymlicka provides a clear example of this problem. On the one hand, concerns for stability ground his contention that self-government rights can mitigate violence if they are limited to national minorities that have a common language, history, and territory. On the other hand, he expects that disputes over self-government and other minority rights can be

managed "peacefully and fairly, assuming that there is some level of good will" (*Multicultural Citizenship,* 193). Of course, Kymlicka realizes that good will is not always forthcoming, but he never examines the specific motivations, social conditions, or institutional incentives that might foster good will rather than conflict among groups.

10. Phillips, *The Politics of Presence,* 151.

11. In my opinion, the best contextually sensitive approach to specific policies concerning diverse groups in a plural polity is Joseph Carens's *Culture, Citizenship, and Community* (New York: Oxford University Press, 2001). My main concern with this book is its relative lack of attention to the processes through which a democratic polity could fairly authorize the specific policies he advocates. Amy Gutmann and Dennis Thompson, *Democracy and Disagreement* (Cambridge, MA: Harvard University Press, 1996), link specific policy outcomes to a model of the deliberative, democratic process. However, the policies they examine do not specifically address problems of pluralism, except for their discussion of affirmative action. Moreover, they do not examine or assess institutional mechanisms for achieving deliberative democracy, a problem that clearly undermines their theory of deliberative representation. Consequently, my project focuses on these questions of a model of fair deliberation in order to evaluate democratic institutions and processes.

12. Other theorists seem to base their theories of justice between groups on similar modes of identity construction. For instance, Emily Gill adopts Tamir's use of interpretive agency in arguing that cultural membership should be regarded as an expression of autonomous choice. *Becoming Free: Autonomy and Diversity in the Liberal Polity* (Lawrence, KS: University Press of Kansas, 2001), 78. Similarly, Melissa Williams comes close to Spinner's reliance on instrumental, structural identity when she defends group representation for those marginalized groups that suffer inequality, are associated with negative meanings, and whose members are involuntarily and immutably incorporated into these groups. Williams, *Voice, Trust, and Memory,* 15–16.

13. Jean Cohen and Andrew Arato, *Civil Society and Political Theory* (Cambridge, MA: MIT Press, 1992), 435–442.

14. For a critique of Kymlicka's assumption that other plural polities will share Canada's rather genteel form of politics, see David Laitin, "Liberal Theory and the Nation," *Political Theory* 26 (April 1998): 231. For an argument that Canada's motivation for intergroup reconciliation stems from its self-comparison to the United States, see Hugh Donald Forbes, "Canada: From Bilingualism to Multiculturalism," in *Nationalism, Ethnic Conflict, and Democracy,* ed. Larry Diamond and Marc F. Plattner (Baltimore, MD: Johns Hopkins University Press, 1994), 80–101. Forbes even suggests that the Canadian tradition of Anglophone–Francophone accommodation developed in the nineteenth century due to the two communities' shared perception of a common American enemy. A perceived common enemy is thought to be a general motivation for intergroup accommodation in consociational politics. See Lijphart, *Democracy in Plural Societies,* 66–67. In this sense, the Canadian case may be generalizable only to other small countries that feel in some way threatened by a much larger neighbor, such as Belgium or the Netherlands. It would clearly not apply to large, powerful countries, like India, Great Britain, or Russia, or to polities marked by groups that fear mutually exclusive external threats, like Northern Ireland, Bosnia, or Sri Lanka.

15. This foundational concern is especially apparent in the works of Jürgen Habermas. See *Theory of Communicative Action,* vol. 1, trans. Thomas McCarthy (Boston: Beacon, 1984); *Theory of Communicative Action,* vol. 2, trans. Thomas McCarthy (Boston: Beacon,

1987); *Moral Consciousness and Communicative Action,* trans. Christian Lenhardt and Shierry Weber Nicolsen (Cambridge, MA: MIT Press, 1990); *Between Facts and Norms: Contributions to a Discourse Theory of Law and Democracy,* trans. William Rehg (Cambridge, MA: MIT Press, 1996).

16. See Habermas, *Moral Consciousness and Communicative Action.*

17. See Michael Rabinder James, "Critical Intercultural Dialogue," *Polity* 31 (Summer, 1999): 587–607.

1. THE NORMATIVE CONSEQUENCES OF IDENTITY CONSTRUCTION

1. Yen Le Espiritu, *Asian American Panethnicity* (Philadelphia: Temple University Press, 1992), 124–125.

2. Discussions of internal diversity have typically focused on cultural beliefs or practices. However, diverse social conditions and shifting boundaries affect Iris Marion Young's theory of social oppression as experienced by broad identity categories. See Iris Marion Young, *Inclusion and Democracy* (New York: Oxford University Press, 1990), 63–65. I will discuss Young later in this chapter.

3. Paula McClain and Joseph Stewart, *Can We All Get Along? Racial and Ethnic Minorities in American Politics* (Boulder, CO: Westview Press, 1999), 4.

4. Donald Horowitz, *Ethnic Groups in Conflict* (Berkeley, CA: University of California Press, 1985), 65.

5. Charles Taylor, "The Politics of Recognition," in *Multiculturalism and the Politics of Recognition,* ed. Amy Gutmann (Princeton, NJ: Princeton University Press, 1993), 25–73.

6. The most important sources in developing this framework have been Stephen Cornell and Douglas Hartmann, *Ethnicity and Race: Making Identities in a Changing World* (Thousand Oaks, CA: Pine Forge Press, 1998); Espiritu, *Asian American Panethnicity;* Joane Nagel, *American Indian Ethnic Renewal* (New York: Oxford University Press, 1996); Michael Omi and Howard Winant, *Racial Formation in the United States* (New York: Routledge, 1994); and Crawford Young, *The Politics of Cultural Pluralism* (Madison, WI: University of Wisconsin Press, 1977).

7. Nathan Glazer and Daniel Patrick Moynihan, *Beyond the Melting Pot* (Cambridge, MA: MIT Press, 1970), 17.

8. Mary Waters, *Ethnic Options* (Berkeley: University of California Press, 1990).

9. Will Kymlicka, *Multicultural Citizenship* (New York: Oxford University Press, 1995), 76.

10. Ibid., 96, emphasis in original.

11. Ibid., 109.

12. For an example of this debate, see the symposium on Kymlicka's *Multicultural Citizenship* in *Constellations* 4, Number 1 (1997): 35–87.

13. James Johnson, "Why Respect Culture?," *American Journal of Political Science* 44 (July 2000): 416.

14. Brian Barry, *Culture and Equality* (Cambridge, MA: Harvard University Press, 2001), 309.

15. Indeed, the empirical literature on nationalism seems to emphasize the instrumental conditions that engender national identities, even where multiple languages and cultures

exist. Consider Benedict Anderson's discussion of the rise of a common Indonesian national identity versus fragmented Southeast Asian national movements in *Imagined Communities* (London: Verso, 1983), 47–65, 120–124.

16. Yael Tamir, *Liberal Nationalism* (Princeton, NJ: Princeton University Press, 1993), 21.

17. Ibid., 71–72.

18. Ibid., 84–85.

19. Ibid., 100.

20. Ibid., 73.

21. Ibid., 69–70.

22. Ibid., 66.

23. Horowitz, *Ethnic Groups in Conflict.*

24. Russell Hardin, *One for All: On the Logic of Group Conflict* (Princeton, NJ: Princeton University Press, 1995), 46.

25. Ibid., 6–10, 186–189, 195.

26. Ibid., 46–49.

27. Ibid., 72.

28. Hardin's explanatory account of group conflict is flawed by his tendency to select his cases based on the variable he wishes to explain, in this case violent conflict. Thus, he tends to overlook cases where there are strong levels of group identification and perhaps also group-specific norms but little group conflict. As a result, group-specific norms need not have the disastrous consequences implicit in his account. See James Fearon and David Laitin, "Explaining Interethnic Cooperation," *American Political Science Review* 90 (December 1996): 715–735; and David Laitin, "Liberal Theory and the Nation," *Political Theory* 26 (April 1998): 221–236. Nevertheless, Hardin is right to perceive the conflict-inducing incentive structure found in the combination of instrumental agency and particularistic norms, even if he overstates the prevalence of this danger. I augment Hardin's account with other sources of group conflict in chapter 3.

29. Hardin, *One for All,* 180, 216, 226–227.

30. Jeff Spinner, *The Boundaries of Citizenship* (Baltimore, MD: Johns Hopkins University Press, 1994), 19.

31. Ibid., 24.

32. Ibid., 19. Moreover, as Anthony Appiah notes, racial identities often include multiple cultures. Thus, to speak of a single African-American culture is fundamentally misleading and can even place unjust cultural constraints upon the members of that group. Racial identities have less to do with the interpretive significance of cultural meaning than with problems of political and economic power. Anthony Appiah, "Race, Culture, Identity: Misunderstood Connections," in Anthony Appiah and Amy Gutmann, *Color Conscious* (Princeton, NJ: Princeton University Press, 1996), 88–89.

33. Spinner, *The Boundaries of Citizenship,* 23.

34. Ibid., 123–134.

35. Ibid., 136.

36. Ibid., 192, 202.

37. Cornell and Hartmann, *Ethnicity and Race;* Anthony Marx, *Making Race and Nation* (New York: Cambridge University Press, 1998).

38. William Van Deburg, *New Day in Babylon: The Black Power Movement and American Culture, 1965–1975* (Chicago: University of Chicago Press, 1992), 113–129.

39. Stephen Cornell, *The Return of the Native* (New York: Oxford University Press, 1988), 73–76, 155.

40. Ibid., 132; Nagel, *American Indian Ethnic Renewal,* 235. Indeed, as of 1988 there were more Native Americans in Los Angeles County than in any tribal reservation other than the Navajo nation. Cornell, *The Return of the Native,* 149.

41. Cornell, *The Return of the Native,* 104; Nagel *American Indian Ethnic Renewal,* 235.

42. Nagel, *American Indian Ethnic Renewal,* 242–245.

43. Ibid., 115, 239.

44. Ibid., 5, 86–94.

45. Ibid., 193, 236.

46. Cornell, *The Return of the Native,* 114–115; Nagel, *American Indian Ethnic Renewal,* 115–121.

47. Cornell, *The Return of the Native,* 133–135; Nagel, *American Indian Ethnic Renewal,* 148.

48. Nagel, *American Indian Ethnic Renewal,* 30.

49. Jennifer L. Brown, "Tribal Members Were Like Brothers and Sisters until Dispute over Race and Money Split Them," *The Associated Press,* 21 September 2002.

50. A total of 56 million dollars was awarded to the Seminole nation, but a quarter of that amount was granted to the Seminole members who remained in Florida. See Brian Ford, "Court Ruling Blocks Black Seminoles," *The Tulsa World,* 28 April 2002.

51. William Glaberson, "Who is a Seminole, and Who Gets to Decide?" *New York Times,* 29 January 2001.

52. Tribes retain the right to name their own members; however, changes in membership can potentially conflict with federal treaties. Consequently, the federal Bureau of Indian Affairs has refused to disburse the forty-two million to the Seminole Nation of Oklahoma because the terms of its original treaty included the Black Seminoles as full members. Brown, "Tribal Members Were Like Brothers and Sisters." However, because the Seminole Nation is a sovereign entity, a federal district court has ruled that the Black Seminoles cannot sue the nation within the federal judiciary to recover their share of any federal payment. Ford, "Court Ruling Blocks Black Seminoles."

53. Will Kymlicka, "Ethnic Associations and Democratic Citizenship," in *Freedom of Association,* ed. Amy Gutmann (Princeton, NJ: Princeton University Press, 1998), 209. Strangely enough, Kymlicka also draws arbitrary distinctions among different Hispanic immigrant groups and their status, associating Central Americans with legal immigration, Mexicans with illegal immigration, and Cubans with refugee status. This categorization clearly misses the overlapping statuses among various Hispanic groups. It also ignores more important divisions within this group, including the quasi-racial identity dynamics of American-born Hispanics.

54. Enrique Trueba, *Latinos Unidos: From Cultural Diversity to the Politics of Solidarity* (Totowa, NJ: Rowman and Littlefield, 1999), 35.

55. Michael Jones-Correo, *Between Two Nations: The Political Predicament of Latinos in New York City* (Ithaca, NY: Cornell University Press, 1998), 115.

56. Edward Chang and Jeanette Diaz-Veizades, *Ethnic Peace in the American City: Building Community in Los Angeles and Beyond* (New York: New York University Press, 1999), 109–119.

57. Trueba, *Latinos Unidos,* 154.

58. We should note, however, that although the American census does not presently have a separate Hispanic race category, it did include "Mexican" as a separate racial group in 1930. Melissa Nobles, *Shades of Citizenship* (Stanford, CA: Stanford University Press, 2000), 188.

59. Clara Rodriguez, *Changing Race: Latinos, the Census, and the History of Ethnicity in the United States* (New York: New York University Press, 2000), 159–176. As we shall see in chapter 4, Hispanic associations successfully resisted this change, demonstrating the role of quasi-formal deliberative settings in generating forms of collective identity categorization that are more amenable to the affected parties.

60. Indeed, the relative insignificance of legal categorization comes into view by the fact that the first official use of the term *Hispanic* came only when President Richard Nixon declared a National Hispanic Heritage Week in 1969, at least a century after informal perceptions of a unified Hispanic identity had already developed. Suzanne Oboler, *Ethnic Labels, Latino Lives* (Minneapolis: University of Minnesota Press, 1995), 81.

61. Ibid., 24–26, 35.

62. Ibid., 139–144, 171.

63. Ibid., 130.

64. Rodriguez, *Changing Race,* 56.

65. Ibid., 50–51.

66. Oboler, *Ethnic Labels, Latino Lives,* 132–133.

67. Ibid., 61–68.

68. Rodriguez, *Changing Race,* 6–14.

69. Ibid., 139–147.

70. Oboler, *Ethnic Labels, Latino Lives,* 139–140; Rodriguez, *Changing Race,* 53.

71. Mia Tuan, *Forever Foreigners or Honorary Whites? The Asian Ethnic Experience Today* (New Brunswick, NJ: Rutgers University Press, 1998).

72. Espiritu, *Asian American Panethnicity,* 107.

73. Ian Haney Lopez, *White by Law: The Legal Construction of Race* (New York: New York University Press, 1996), 80–89.

74. Nobles, *Shades of Citizenship,* 188–189.

75. Espiritu, *Asian American Panethnicity,* 91–94, 124–125.

76. Ibid., 124–126.

77. Ibid., 91–99.

78. Ibid., 107.

79. Ibid., 141–143.

80. Ibid., 157–159.

81. Ibid., 148–149.

82. Tuan, *Forever Foreigners or Honorary Whites?,* 24–37.

83. Ibid., 35.

84. Ibid., 130.

85. Ibid., 100.

86. Cornell and Hartmann, *Ethnicity and Race,* 114–119.

87. Noel Ignatiev, *How the Irish Became White* (New York: Routledge, 1994); Karen Brodkin *How the Jews Became White Folks* (New Brunswick, NJ: Rutgers University Press, 1998).

88. Timothy Egan, "When to Campaign with Color," *New York Times,* 20 June 2000.

89. In what follows, I use "West Indian" to signify African-descended, English-speaking immigrants from the Caribbean, "African American" to identify descendants of Africans born in the United States, and "Black" to connote a common racial identity shared by West Indians and African Americans. See Philip Kasinitz, *Caribbean New York* (Ithaca, NY: Cornell University Press, 1992), 4–7; and Mary Waters, *Black Identities* (Cambridge, MA: Harvard University Press, 1999), 65.

90. F. James Davis, *Who is Black?* (University Park, PA: Penn State University Press, 1991), 35, 126; Kasinitz, *Caribbean New York,* 47–48.

91. South Africa, Latin America, and the Caribbean use distinct categories to identify mixed-race persons, whereas in the United States, even nonWhite persons are usually not subject to hypo-descent rules. For instance, a person with a distant Korean ancestor will not be categorized as Asian, but a person with an equally distant African ancestor will be categorized as Black. Davis, *Who is Black?,* 13–16.

92. Nobles, *Shades of Citizenship,* 137–141.

93. Waters, *Black Identities,* 94–95.

94. Kasinitz, *Caribbean New York,* 98–99.

95. Ibid., 225–237.

96. Davis, *Who is Black?,* 40–41, 62; Cornell and Hartmann, *Ethnicity and Race,* 104–105.

97. Cornell and Hartmann, *Ethnicity and Race,* 106.

98. Cheryl Harris, "Whiteness as Property," in *Critical Race Theory,* ed. Kimberle Crenshaw, Neil Gotanda, Garry Peller, and Kendall Thomas (New York: The New Press, 1995), 276–277.

99. Doug McAdam, *Political Process and the Development of Black Insurgency, 1930–1970* (Chicago: University of Chicago Press, 1982); Marx, *Making Race and Nation.*

100. Davis, *Who is Black?,* 11–13.

101. Ibid., 18, 29, 180; Cornell and Hartmann, *Ethnicity and Race,* 33.

102. Nobles, *Shades of Citizenship,* 137.

103. Kasinitz, *Caribbean New York,* 219.

104. Ibid., 10, 225–227.

105. Ibid., 10.

106. Nobles, *Shades of Citizenship,* 141.

107. Kasinitz, *Caribbean New York,* 26–31, 54–59, 96–110; Waters, *Black Identities,* 112–113.

108. Waters, *Black Identities,* 64, 66, 130.

109. Kasinitz, *Caribbean New York,* 32; Waters, *Black Identities,* 4–5, 65, 76–79, 105–116, 124.

110. Waters, *Black Identities,* 28–31, 53–55.

111. Kasinitz, *Caribbean New York,* 96–110; Waters, *Black Identities,* 116–168, 120–123, 153–172.

112. Waters, *Black Identities,* 169–171.

113. Ibid., 169.

114. Kasinitz, *Caribbean New York,* 246–250.

115. Waters, *Black Identities,* 288–302.

116. Most immigrants come from economically impoverished or politically repressive countries, so their degree of volition is open to argument. For compelling critiques of Kym-

licka's response to this problem, see Laitin, "Liberal Theory and the Nation," 231; and Bikhu Parekh, "Dilemmas of a Multicultural Theory of Citizenship," *Constellations* 4 (1997): 54–62.

117. Ronald Schmidt, *Language Policy and Identity Politics in the United States* (Philadelphia, PA: Temple University Press, 2000), 188. Kymlicka has recently devoted more attention to race, but his analysis remains hamstrung by his adherence to the fundamental distinction between voluntary immigrant identities and involuntary national identities. Thus, he makes an excessively strong distinction between the situations of West Indian immigrants and African Americans, given the involuntary migration of the latter. Kymlicka, *Politics in the Vernacular* (New York: Oxford University Press, 2001), chapter 9. This follows from his insistence that African Americans constitute an atypical case, an almost unique violation of the putatively more common distinction between voluntary ethnic immigrants and involuntary national minorities. *Multicultural Citizenship,* 24. Yet many of the group-based problems faced by African Americans result from contemporary anti-Black discrimination, not from the legacy of slavery. West Indian immigrants are often involuntarily incorporated into this despised Black identity, and so their group-based harms might render the instrumental-structural, racial dimension of their identity more salient than the agent-based dimension related to their status as ethnic immigrants. Kymlicka's discussions of Asian, Arab, and Hispanic minority identities exhibit similar problems, leading him to emphasize the socioeconomic success of some Asian ethnics while underestimating the socioeconomic disadvantages of others and the extent to which Asians of various ethnicities are involuntarily incorporated into racialized identities through formal laws, informal perceptions, and threats of violence. *Politics in the Vernacular,* 188–192. When we consider racialized Black, Hispanic, Arab, and Asian identities in light of the multiple modes of construction involved in tribal, subtribal, and supratribal Native American identities, Kymlicka's sharp distinction between agent-centered versus structural identities is severely challenged.

118. Thus far, I have focused only on American cases. That instrumental agency is common in nationalist movements outside of North America is commonly recognized in the literature on ethnic conflict. See, for instance, Horowitz, *Ethnic Groups in Conflict,* chapter 2; Laitin, "Liberal Theory and the Nation," 233–234; Crawford Young, *The Politics of Cultural Pluralism,* chapter 4. Kymlicka's failure to attend to this fact is notable in his summary dismissal of constructivist accounts of national identity construction. *Multicultural Citizenship,* 185. This likely stems from his assumption of "a (rather rosy) view of the political process that may fit Canada but few other societies." Laitin, "Liberal Theory and the Nation," 231. According to this viewpoint, the real exception to intergroup politics is not the atypical case of African Americans but the atypical case of Canadian politics.

119. Iris Marion Young, *Justice and the Politics of Difference* (Princeton, NJ: Princeton University Press, 1990), 33–38, 43.

120. Iris Marion Young, "Difference as a Resource for Democratic Communication," in *Deliberative Democracy: Essays on Reason and Politics,* ed. James Bohman and William Rehg (Cambridge, MA: MIT Press, 1997), 392; Iris Marion Young, "Deferring Group Representation," in *Ethnicity and Group Rights,* ed. Ian Shapiro and Will Kymlicka (New York: New York University Press, 1997), 365; Iris Marion Young, *Inclusion and Democracy,* 99–102.

121. Iris Marion Young, "A Multicultural Continuum: A Critique of Will Kymlicka's Ethnic-nation Dichotomy, *Constellations* 4 (1997): 54–62.

122. Iris Marion Young, *Justice and the Politics of Difference,* 186.

123. Ibid., 48–65. Indeed, Young for the most part views internal diversity solely in cross-cutting terms. Thus, she realizes that an intergenerational collective identity, like Hispanic, will be divided in terms of gender, sexuality, and political interests. She much less often examines intergenerational groups within intergenerational groups, exemplified, of course, by the multiple ethnicities within the broader, racialized identities of Asian or Hispanic.

124. Ibid., 48.

125. A similar but more thoroughgoing critique of Iris Marion Young's theory of social perspective can be found in Seyla Benhabib, *The Claims of Culture* (Princeton, NJ: Princeton University Press, 2002), 137, 205 n. 9. I address this criticism and, more generally, how social perspectives relate to democratic deliberation in chapter 2.

126. In fairness, Kymlicka does admit that group claims, even when distinguished according to his ethnic-national dichotomy, will unavoidably confront indeterminacies that require negotiation and deliberation through fair procedures. *Multicultural Citizenship,* 131. However, he addresses the issue of fair deliberation and negotiation only through a discussion of group representation, not through a careful analysis of fair procedures themselves.

127. Joseph Carens, *Culture, Citizenship, and Community* (New York: Oxford University Press, 2000).

128. I should add that I am not entirely comfortable with how Carens normatively grounds his investigations. He adopts Michael Walzer's approach, which seeks to identify the shared normative commitments within a political community, but Carens rightly transforms this in a more universalistic fashion. Unlike Walzer, Carens emphasizes that Western, liberal democracies contain some normative commitments that apply only to the specific polity in question (e.g., Canada), some that apply to all Western liberal democracies (e.g., Canada, the United States, and Western Europe), and some that apply to all polities around the world. Ibid., 33–35. While I find considerable merit to this framework, I fear that it propagates two problematic assumptions. First, it underestimates the diversity of political values within a given liberal democracy. As Rogers Smith rightfully notes, American political history includes not only a liberal-egalitarian political culture but also illiberal, hierarchical, racist, and theological traditions. See Rogers M. Smith, "Beyond Tocqueville, Myrdal, and Hartz: The Multiple Traditions in America," *American Political Science Review* 87 (September 1993), 549–566. Second, it assumes excessively sharp demarcations between different political cultures. However, Seyla Benhabib rightly argues that cultures do not admit of firm boundaries but are fluid and open horizons, to use Hans-Georg Gadamer's formulation. Thus, it will remain difficult to identify what is "our" culture or, for that matter, who "we" are, and political theorists will do best to define communities as communities of conversation rather than communities of shared values. However, Benhabib rightly points out that communities of conversation must necessarily share some values in order to make conversation possible. *The Claims of Culture,* 33–42. Attention to Benhabib's concerns leads to some interesting questions for Carens. For instance, Carens is more willing to criticize the restrictive citizenship laws of Germany than those of Japan as the "cultural differences between Japan and North America are much greater than the cultural differences between Germany and North America." *Culture, Citizenship, and Community,* 32. However, one wonders whether a North American of Japanese descent, one who maintains ongoing ties to Japan, might feel the opposite sentiment and more enthusiastically criticize Japan rather than Germany. This example reveals how communities of conversation and criticism do not neatly coincide with legal or political boundaries.

129. Carens, *Culture, Citizenship, and Community,* 51.

130. Ibid., 1. Carens himself understands his investigations as a contribution not to democratic deliberation but "to an ongoing conversation among contemporary political theorists."

131. Jack Knight and James Johnson, "Aggregation and Deliberation: On the Possibility of Democratic Legitimacy," *Political Theory* 22 (May 1994): 287–289.

132. Robert Dahl, *A Preface to Democratic Theory* (Chicago: University of Chicago Press, 1956), 137.

133. Horowitz, *Ethnic Groups in Conflict,* 564–566.

2. PLURAL DELIBERATION AND COMPLEX LEGITIMACY

1. Thus, plural deliberation rejects John Rawls's limitation of the exercise of public reason to constitutional essentials. See John Rawls, *Political Liberalism* (New York: Columbia University Press, 1993), 214.

2. This type of constrained dialogue via ex ante stipulation is usually attributed to political thinkers in the liberal school of thought, but it is unclear which specific thinker or thinkers advocate this position. Although I do not wish to enter into this controversy here, my sense is that this position is most applicable to Bruce Ackerman, "Why Dialogue?," *Journal of Philosophy* 86 (January 1989): 5–22. It is least applicable to Charles Larmore, "Political Liberalism," *Political Theory* 18 (August 1990): 339–360; and J. Donald Moon, *Constructing Community* (Princeton, NJ: Princeton University Press, 1993). More ambiguous are the positions of John Rawls, *Political Liberalism;* and Amy Gutmann and Dennis Thompson, *Democracy and Disagreement* (Cambridge, MA: Harvard University Press, 1996). I provide a more detailed assessment of the relationship between political liberalism and deliberation amidst a plurality of perspectives and world-views in Michael Rabinder James, "Critical Intercultural Dialogue," *Polity* 31 (Summer 1999): 587–607; and "Tribal Sovereignty and the Intercultural Public Sphere," *Philosophy and Social Criticism* 25 (September 1999): 57–86.

3. Iris Marion Young, *Inclusion and Democracy* (New York: Oxford University Press, 2000), 110.

4. Because this would presuppose a prior consensus on the political life as the good life, for the most part, citizens in a pluralistic, deliberative democracy should not be expected to perceive political activity as an end in itself, but rather as a means to securing interests that lie beyond politics. However, this implies that part of the good life that actors seek must make room for political activity. Conceptions of the good life that entirely preclude political participation are incompatible with plural deliberation.

5. The distinction that I draw between preferences and interests mirrors the distinction between policy preferences (what I call preferences) and fundamental preferences (what I call interests) in Jon Elster, "Deliberation and Constitution Making," in *Deliberative Democracy,* ed. Jon Elster (Cambridge: Cambridge University Press), 100. It does not square with Jane Mansbridge's definition of interests as "enlightened preferences," which I would call the reflective preferences generated by deliberation. See Jane Mansbridge, *Beyond Adversary Democracy* (Chicago: University of Chicago Press, 1980), 24–26. Such reflective preferences may be based on individual or group interests or on opinions about the common interest.

6. See Iris Marion Young, *Inclusion and Democracy.* Some democratic theorists use the term *judgments* to characterize what I call opinions. Voting as the aggregation of judgments (opinions) is often portrayed as an "epistemic" conception of democracy. See Thomas

Christiano, *The Rule of the Many* (Boulder, CO: Westview Press, 1996), 29–32. I prefer the term *opinion* for two reasons. First, it coheres with the idea of public opinion found within the literature on the public sphere, as discussed in chapter 4. Second, it allows me to reserve the term *judgment* for the activity of assessing the legitimacy of democratic processes according to the elements and conditions of plural deliberation.

7. See Iris Marion Young, *Inclusion and Democracy.*

8. James Johnson defines a world-view as "a symbolically constituted, comprehensive, and more or less coherent conception of social and natural order—of the way the world is, the sorts of entities it contains, and the ways that relevant actors expect those entities to behave." See James Johnson, "Arguing for Deliberation," in *Deliberative Democracy,* ed. Jon Elster (New York: Cambridge University Press, 1998), 179.

9. John Dryzek's term *discourse* is worth comparing. "A discourse is a shared means of making sense of the world embedded in language. Any discourse will always be grounded in assumptions, judgments, contentions, dispositions, and capabilities. These shared terms of reference enable those who subscribe to a particular discourse to perceive and compile bits of sensory information into coherent stories or accounts that can be communicated in intersubjectively meaningful ways. Thus, a discourse will generally revolve around a central storyline, containing opinions about both facts and values." Dryzek, *Deliberative Democracy and Beyond* (Oxford: Oxford University Press, 2000), 18. Although Dryzek draws an analogy between discourses and Alasdair MacIntyre's conception of traditions in order to suggest that this shows the different frameworks within different cultural world-views, he generally uses discourse in a narrower manner, more closely tied to specific political issues like environmental justice or crime. Ibid., 74–80; and "Legitimacy and Economy in Deliberative Democracy," *Political Theory* 29 (October 2001): 658. Accordingly, individuals within a modern industrial society would share a world-view but not a common discourse.

10. Adam Przeworski, "Deliberation and Ideological Domination," in *Deliberative Democracy,* ed. Jon Elster (New York: Cambridge University Press, 1998), 143.

11. James Bohman, *Public Deliberation* (Cambridge, MA: MIT Press, 1996), 5.

12. Johnson, "Arguing for Deliberation," 174.

13. William Wei, *The Asian American Movement* (Philadelphia: Temple University Press, 1993), 250.

14. Elster, "Deliberation and Constitution Making," 102.

15. Seyla Benhabib, *The Claims of Culture* (Princeton, NJ: Princeton University Press, 2002), 137, 205 n. 9.

16. Iris Marion Young, "Deferring Group Representation," in *Ethnicity and Group Rights,* ed. Ian Shapiro and Will Kymlicka (New York: New York University Press, 1997), 370–371.

17. I owe this example to Amy McCready.

18. I will examine how perspectives are tested in this way in chapters 4 and 5.

19. See Joshua Cohen, "Procedure and Substance in Deliberative Democracy," in *Deliberative Democracy: Essays on Reason and Politics,* ed. James Bohman and William Rehg (Cambridge, MA: MIT Press, 1996); and "Democracy and Liberty," in *Deliberative Democracy,* ed. Jon Elster (Cambridge: Cambridge University Press, 1998).

20. Seyla Benhabib, "Toward a Deliberative Model of Democratic Legitimacy," in *Democracy and Difference: Contesting the Boundaries of the Political,* ed. Seyla Benhabib (Princeton, NJ: Princeton University Press, 1996), 75–76.

21. Cohen, "Democracy and Liberty," 188–189.

22. See James, "Critical Intercultural Dialogue."

23. Johnson, "Arguing for Deliberation," 177.

24. Ibid.; and Dryzek, *Deliberative Democracy and Beyond.*

25. Hans-Georg Gadamer, *Truth and Method,* rev. 2nd ed., trans. Donald Marshall and Joel Weinsheimer (New York: Crossroad Publishing Company, 1990), 302–306.

26. I translate as "transposition" the idea of *Versetzen.* See Gadamer, *Truth and Method,* 304.

27. Iris Marion Young, "Asymmetrical Reciprocity," *Constellations* 3 (1997): 343–344.

28. Georgia Warnke, *Gadamer: Hermeneutics, Tradition, and Reason* (Stanford, CA: Stanford University Press, 1987), 100–106.

29. See Karl-Otto Apel, *Towards a Transformation of Philosophy,* trans. G. Adey and D. Frisby (London: Routledge, 1980).

30. Stephen Cornell, *The Return of the Native* (New York: Oxford University Press, 1988), 114–115.

31. See Melissa Williams, *Voice, Trust, and Memory* (Princeton, NJ: Princeton University Press, 1998), 163.

32. Lee Sigelman and Susan Welch, *Black Americans' View of Racial Equality* (New York: Cambridge University Press, 1991), 64–65.

33. Gadamer, *Truth and Method,* 293–294.

34. I associate this deductive method most closely with the political liberalism of Charles Larmore, "Political Liberalism"; and J. Donald Moon, *Constructing Community.*

35. Young, "Asymmetrical Reciprocity," 355–357.

36. This type of outcome is demonstrated in Plato's *Theatetus* (210c). Here, despite the failure to reach any final conclusion regarding the meaning of knowledge (*episteme*), Socrates nevertheless hopes to achieve a practical goal. By pointing out the limits of Theatetus's knowledge, Socrates believes that the brilliant youth may become gentler with his own comrades. For an insightful account of how the aporetic character of certain Socratic dialogues can contribute to toleration of different perspectives, see Gerald M. Mara, "Socrates and Liberal Toleration," *Political Theory* 16 (August 1988): 468–495.

37. This point resonates with Jürgen Habermas's assertion that a discursive normative framework demands a "postconventional morality," where one's norms and beliefs are held as hypothetical and open to revision. Habermas uses this notion to show how discourse is incompatible with fundamentalist cultures that close off their religious or metaphysical world-views from critical scrutiny. Jürgen Habermas, *Moral Consciousness and Communicative Action,* trans. Christian Lenhardt and Shierry Weber Nicolsen (Cambridge, MA: MIT Press, 1990), 87; Jürgen Habermas, *Between Facts and Norms: Contributions to a Discourse Theory of Law and Democracy,* trans. William Rehg (Cambridge, MA: MIT Press, 1996), 371; Stephen K. White, *The Recent Work of Jürgen Habermas* (Cambridge: Cambridge University Press, 1988), 57–58. As is well known, Habermas tries to arrive at this point through a defense of the normative content and communicative rationality of the modern ways of thinking. An analysis of Habermas's position is impossible here; my main concern is that it frees modern cultures from recognizing their own contingency and the possibility that they may have something to learn from cultures which, at least in some ways, might not be considered modern.

38. My approach thus differs from that of Bohman, *Public Deliberation,* 89, who focuses

less on criticism across world-views in favor of "moral compromises," or alternative frameworks shared by neither world-view that can serve as impartial methods for resolving conflicts.

39. Robert Goodin, "Democratic Deliberation Within," *Philosophy and Public Affairs* 29 (2000): 92–99.

40. Ibid., 101–102.

41. Dryzek, "Legitimacy and Economy in Deliberative Democracy," 663.

42. Jean Cohen and Andrew Arato, *Civil Society and Political Theory* (Cambridge, MA: MIT Press, 1992), 508; Doug McAdam, "Movement Strategy and Dramaturgic Framing in Democratic States: The Case of the American Civil Rights Movement," in *Deliberation, Democracy, and the Media,* ed. Simone Chambers and Anne Costain (Lanham, MD: Rowman and Littlefield, 2001).

43. Simone Chambers, *Reasonable Democracy: Jürgen Habermas and the Politics of Discourse* (Ithaca, NY: Cornell University Press, 1996), 169–170.

44. Simone Chambers, "Discourse and Democratic Practices," in *The Cambridge Companion to Habermas,* ed. Stephen K. White (Cambridge: Cambridge University Press, 1995), 249.

45. Habermas, *Between Facts and Norms,* 339, italics in original.

46. Benhabib, *The Claims of Culture,* 144–145; Chambers, "Discourse and Democratic Practices," 248–250.

47. Habermas, *Moral Consciousness and Communicative Action,* 72.

48. Dryzek, *Deliberative Democracy and Beyond,* 47–50.

49. Ibid., 50.

50. Christiano, *The Rule of the Many,* 88.

51. Habermas, *Between Facts and Norms;* Benhabib, "Toward a Deliberative Model of Democratic Legitimacy"; Chambers, "Discourse and Democratic Practices"; Chambers, *Reasonable Democracy.*

52. Chambers, "Discourse and Democratic Practices," 250.

53. Tali Mendelberg, *The Race Card* (Princeton, NJ: Princeton University Press, 2001), 74–75, 81–84.

54. See Bohman, *Public Deliberation,* 172–181.

55. Dryzek admits that measuring the relative weight of discourses will be difficult because it requires not only the aggregation of public opinion on policy positions typical of survey research, but also some measurement of the intensity or strength of attachment of people to a particular discourse. Dryzek, "Legitimacy and Economy in Deliberative Democracy," 660–661.

56. Ibid., 661.

57. Marc Lynch, *State Interests and Public Spheres* (New York: Columbia University Press, 1999), 68.

58. Bernard Manin, *The Principles of Representative Government* (New York: Cambridge University Press, 1997), 359–360.

59. Jack Knight and James Johnson, "Aggregation and Deliberation: On the Possibility of Political Legitimacy," *Political Theory* 22 (1994): 279–281.

60. Gerry Mackie, *Democracy Defended* (New York: Cambridge University Press, 2003), chapter 4.

61. Johnny Goldfinger, "Deliberation, Preference Formation, and Voting: Empirical Real-

ities" (Paper presented at the annual meeting of the American Political Science Association, Washington, DC, August 2000), 7.

62. Dryzek, *Deliberative Democracy and Beyond,* 42–47. Dryzek's formulation counters criticisms that certain models of deliberation violate the axiom of unrestricted domain through ex ante preclusion strategies that limit deliberation within the bounds of reasonable pluralism. If reasonable pluralism is the ex post outcome of deliberation, then domain restriction is not antidemocratic. See also Knight and Johnson, "Aggregation and Deliberation," 283–287; and Johnson, "Arguing for Deliberation," 165–168.

63. Dryzek, *Deliberative Democracy and Beyond,* 38–42; Knight and Johnson, "Aggregation and Deliberation," 282.

64. Goldfinger, "Deliberation, Preference Formation, and Voting," 6–13.

65. Manin, *Principles of Representative Government,* 223.

66. Gutmann and Thompson, *Democracy and Disagreement,* 55, 82–85.

67. Charles Beitz, *Political Equality* (Princeton, NJ: Princeton University Press, 1989), 53; Emily Hauptmann, *Putting Choice Before Democracy* (Albany, NY: SUNY Press, 1996), 20.

68. Mackie, *Democracy Defended,* chapter 3.

69. Dryzek, *Deliberative Democracy and Beyond,* 54.

70. Dryzek, "Legitimacy and Economy in Deliberative Democracy," 653–654.

71. Ibid., 665.

72. Donald Horowitz, *A Democratic South Africa?* (Berkeley, CA: University of California Press, 1991). In chapter 5, I will provide an analysis of deliberative dynamics and incentives in electoral systems.

73. Dryzek, "Legitimacy and Economy in Deliberative Democracy," 665–666; Goodin, "Democratic Deliberation Within," 108.

74. Dryzek, *Deliberative Democracy and Beyond* and "Legitimacy and Economy in Deliberative Democracy."

75. Bohman, *Public Deliberation,* 188.

76. Habermas, "Three Normative Models of Democracy."

77. Bohman, *Public Deliberation;* Cohen, "Procedure and Substance in Deliberative Democracy"; Cohen, "Democracy and Freedom"; James Fishkin, *Democracy and Deliberation* (New Haven, CT: Yale University Press, 1991); Jack Knight and James Johnson, "What Sort of Equality does Deliberative Democracy Require?" in *Deliberative Democracy: Essays on Reason and Politics,* ed. James Bohman and William Rehg (Cambridge, MA: MIT Press, 1997); Young, *Inclusion and Democracy.*

78. Cohen, "Procedure and Substance in Deliberative Democracy," 106–107, seems to conflate the two in defining the equal opportunity for "effective influence" on collective decisions in terms of "equal rights of participation, including rights of voting, association, and political expression, with a strong presumption against restrictions on the content or viewpoint of expression; rights to hold office; a strong presumption in favor of equally weighted votes; and a more general requirement of equal opportunity for effective influence. This last requirement condemns inequalities in opportunities for office-holding and political influence that result from the design of arrangements of collective decision-making." This conflation is deepened in two footnotes that elaborate on violations of political equality by referring to problems of vote dilution through gerrymandering, an issue that according to my formulation would fall under aggregative equality.

79. Christiano, *The Rule of the Many,* 91.

80. Ibid., 92. Mark Warren equates jointness of supply and nonexcludability. As such, this characteristic can apply to material entities, like highways, that generally function only as public goods, from which individuals cannot exclude others. See Mark Warren, *Democracy and Association* (Princeton, NJ: Princeton University Press, 2001), 125.

81. Lani Guinier, *The Tyranny of the Majority: Fundamental Fairness in Representative Democracy* (New York: The Free Press, 1994), 71–73.

82. However, it does entail a substantive aspect, given that major philosophers such as Plato, Aristotle, and Mill reject equal voting power. Robert Dahl, *Democracy and Its Critics* (New Haven, CT: Yale University Press, 1989), 174. See Beitz, *Political Equality,* 32–40, for a critique of Mill's defense of plural voting.

83. Notably, Charles Beitz argues that equal votes ⇔ equal value is not a requirement of political equality. While recognizing the inequality implied by wasted votes, Beitz claims that it is normatively insignificant because it does not impinge upon any inviolable citizen interests like recognition, equitable treatment, or deliberative responsibility. Instead, he argues, specific circumstances may require race-conscious districting to protect minorities likely to suffer from majority tyranny, which would impinge upon the inviolable interest in equitable treatment. Based on a minimal theory designed not to identify optimal institutions but only to rule out which institutions are indefensible, Beitz's argument is unsatisfying. Moreover, it requires an ex ante identification of which groups deserve remedial representation, a stance that fits poorly with the constructed character of collective identities discussed in chapter 1 and the requirement of deliberative autonomy defended in the next section. See Beitz, *Political Equality,* 100, 132–140, 155–158.

84. Christiano, *The Rule of the Many,* 110–113; Bohman, *Public Deliberation,* 110.

85. Knight and Johnson, "What Sort of Equality does Deliberative Democracy Require?" 290–292.

86. Bohman, *Public Deliberation,* 110; Knight and Johnson, "What Sort of Equality does Deliberative Democracy Require?" 293–294.

87. Participatory theorists, following the lead of Rousseau and Marx, initiated the contemporary articulation of this ideal. For a detailed defense of this approach, see Carol Gould, *Rethinking Democracy* (New York: Cambridge University Press, 1988). Deliberative theorists adopting the condition of political autonomy include Cohen, "Procedure and Substance in Deliberative Democracy," 222–223 and, especially, Warren, *Democracy and Association,* 62–70. The classic definition of democracy as the choice of competitive elites is, of course, Joseph Schumpeter, *Capitalism, Socialism, and Democracy* (New York: Harper & Row, 1942).

88. Warren, *Democracy and Association,* 62.

89. Ibid., 62–70.

90. Christiano, *The Rule of the Many,* 37–38.

91. See Susan Bickford, "Reconfiguring Pluralism: Identity and Institutions in the Inequalitarian Polity," *American Journal of Political Science* 43 (January 1999): 86–108; Jane Mansbridge, "Should Women Represent Women and Blacks Represent Blacks? A Contingent Yes," *The Journal of Politics* 61 (August 1999): 628–657; Melissa Williams, *Voice, Trust, and Memory;* Iris Marion Young, *Justice and the Politics of Difference* (Princeton, NJ: Princeton University Press, 1990).

92. Carol Swain, *Black Faces, Black Interests* (Cambridge, MA: Harvard University Press, 1995), 170–188.

93. See Guinier, *The Tyranny of the Majority;* Horowitz, *A Democratic South Africa?;*

Arend Lijphart, *Democracy in Plural Societies* (New Haven, CT: Yale University Press, 1977); and especially Williams, *Voice, Trust, and Memory,* 49–53.

94. Beitz, *Political Equality,* 132–133.

95. The term *critical skills* comes from Warren, *Democracy and Association,* 75–77.

96. Jon Elster, *Sour Grapes* (New York: Cambridge University Press, 1983).

97. Cass Sunstein, *The Partial Constitution* (Cambridge, MA: Harvard University Press, 1993), 176–177.

98. For a more detailed analysis of this type of problem, see James, "Critical Intercultural Dialogue" and "Tribal Sovereignty and the Intercultural Public Sphere."

99. Benjamin Page and Robert Shapiro, *The Rational Public* (Chicago: University of Chicago Press, 1992), 372.

100. Bohman, *Public Deliberation,* 115–116.

101. Young, "Communication and the Other," in *Democracy and Difference: Contesting the Boundaries of the Political,* ed. Seyla Benhabib (Princeton, NJ: Princeton University Press, 1996), 133–134.

102. Ibid., 128–133; Lynn Sanders, "Against Deliberation," *Political Theory* 25 (June 1997): 347–376.

103. Young, *Inclusion and Democracy,* 70–77.

104. Ibid., 63–70.

105. Ibid., 57–62.

106. Gould, *Rethinking Democracy,* 71.

107. Ibid., 77.

108. Gutmann and Thompson, *Democracy and Disagreement,* 55.

109. For a discussion of this point, see James Johnson, "Habermas on Strategic and Communicative Action," *Political Theory* 19 (May 1991): 181–201. The specific recognition of others not as objects or parameters but as rational actors recommends depicting this relationship as strategic, not as instrumental. Thus, I avoid using Gould's terminology of "instrumental reciprocity," even though the actors within aggregative reciprocity engage others only in order to further their own interests. See Gould, *Rethinking Democracy,* 76–77.

110. Christiano, *The Rule of the Many,* 89, succinctly summarizes the spirit of aggregative reciprocity: "When there are many alternative to choose from and many issues to decide, bargaining and coalition building become very important components of collective decision-making. . . . I . . . vote with them on issues that are important to them, and they agree to vote with me on issues that are important to me."

111. This formulation is somewhat distinct from Gould's conception of "social reciprocity," which demands "a respect and concern by each agent for the aims and interests of the other as having independent value." *Rethinking Democracy,* 77. Clearly, deliberative reciprocity requires a provisional respect for the interests of others prior to the deliberative exchange of justifications, but should deliberation reveal those interests to be unjustifiable, then further respect would be unwarranted.

112. Dryzek, *Deliberative Democracy and Beyond,* 163–166.

113. See Bruce Lawrence, *Defenders of God* (San Francisco: Harper & Row, 1989).

114. Lijphart, *Democracy in Plural Societies,* 66–68, 137.

115. Jane Mansbridge, "Altruistic Trust," in *Democracy and Trust,* ed. Mark Warren (New York: Cambridge University Press, 1999).

116. Robert Dahl, *A Preface to Democratic Theory* (Chicago: University of Chicago Press, 1956), 138.

117. Gutmann and Thompson, for instance, see deliberative reciprocity as their framework's central principle, which shapes the other principles of publicity and accountability. Reciprocity's centrality stems from its median position between strategic, aggregative reciprocity, wherein actors merely pursue their preferences, and the altruistic effacement of preferences through what they call "impartiality." *Democracy and Disagreement,* 52–53. Gutmann and Thompson's specific formulation problematically ties it to the ex ante constraint of deliberation within the bounds of reasonable pluralism criticized earlier. For them, the spirit of reciprocity is evident when actors use only reasons that others can accept as publicly reasonable, thus precluding appeals to world-views that remain controversial to others. However, their basic portrait of the reciprocal willingness to give and receive justifications remains compelling.

118. Bohman, *Public Deliberation,* 328, 338.

119. Ibid., 116–117.

120. The exemplary agonistic challenge is William Connolly's open letter to St. Augustine and his "harangue" against excessive hopes for unity and equality within a Rousseauian democracy. See William Connolly, *Identity/Difference* (Ithaca, NY: Cornell University Press, 1991), 123–157, 194–197. Iris Marion Young uses the term *activist* to depict the nondeliberative contestation of existing political and economic structures. See Iris Marion Young, "Activist Challenges to Deliberative Democracy," *Political Theory* 29 (October 2001): 670–690.

121. Connolly's agonism implicitly and imprecisely relies on such egalitarian justifications. For instance, he believes that contemporary conditions do not justify the harangue he levies against Rousseauian democracy, a position "already excluded from democratic politics." *Identity/Difference,* 197. On the other hand, contemporary conditions do justify agonistic challenges to "hegemonic discourses" like Augustinian theism and secularism. Ibid., 155. In contrast to Connolly's implicit and imprecise justifications, plural deliberation explicitly provides more precise criteria for assessing when, where, and against whom agonism is justifiably employed.

122. Sanders's opposition to deliberation "for now" is an example of a response incompatible with plural deliberation. See Sanders, "Against Deliberation," 369.

123. In this way, plural deliberation responds to the criticism of Emily Hauptmann that leftist deliberative democrats are insufficiently precise in their formulations of legitimacy to justify criticisms of existing politics or to point to possible institutional reforms. "Can Less be More? Leftist Deliberative Democrats' Critique of Participatory Democracy" *Polity* 33 (Spring 2001): 397–421.

3. DELIBERATIVE MOTIVATIONS AND THE DYNAMICS OF GROUP CONFLICT

1. James Fearon and David Laitin, "Explaining Interethnic Cooperation," *American Political Science Review* 90 (December 1996): 715–735.

2. I get this term from Jane Mansbridge, "Altruistic Trust," in *Democracy and Trust,* ed. Mark Warren (New York: Cambridge University Press, 1999).

3. Jürgen Habermas, *Theory of Communicative Action,* vol. 1, trans. Thomas McCarthy (Boston: Beacon, 1984), 86.

4. Habermas, *Theory of Communicative Action,* vol. 2, trans. Thomas McCarthy (Boston: Beacon, 1987), 86; Habermas, *Justification and Application,* trans. Ciaran P. Cronin

(Cambridge, MA: MIT Press, 1993), 6. Note that strategic action is a subset of teleological action. Teleological action reflects the basic pursuit of predetermined preferences. It may include either parametric action, where actors pursue preferences in the context of fixed constraints or parameters, or strategic action, where actors pursue preferences in the context of other rational agents who may react to the first actors' actions. For a clear discussion of this distinction, see James Johnson, "Habermas on Strategic and Communicative Action," *Political Theory* 19 (May 1991): 181–201.

5. Iris Marion Young, *Inclusion and Democracy* (New York: Oxford University Press, 2000), 47–51.

6. The most detailed account of the resource logic is found in Russell Hardin, *One for All: The Logic of Group Conflict* (Princeton, NJ: Princeton University Press, 1995), 6–10, 46, 186–189, 195. Hardin acknowledges that many of our potential identifications are given to us externally, through objective factors like sex or skin color. However, the presence of multiple potential objective and subjective identities provides individuals great autonomy over which identification is salient in a given situation. Crawford Young, *The Politics of Cultural Pluralism* (Madison, WI: University of Wisconsin Press, 1976) provides substantial empirical evidence of the fluidity of racial, ethnic, and cultural identities within conflict-prone plural societies. For other accounts of ethnic conflict based on the resource logic, see Robert Bates, "Ethnic Competition and Modernization in Contemporary Africa," *Comparative Political Studies* 6 (January 1974): 457–484; David Lake and Donald Rothchild, "Containing Fear: The Origins and Management of Ethnic Conflict," *International Security* 21 (Fall 1996): 41–57; Susan Olzak, *The Dynamics of Ethnic Competition and Conflict* (Stanford, CA: Stanford University Press, 1992).

7. Hardin, *One For All,* 49–55.

8. Ibid., 56–59.

9. Ibid., 29, 142–147. Of course, other causes were also necessary. Zero-sum inter-group competition over scarce state-controlled resources can remain peaceful whenever the state retains its capacity to punish violent action. But when the state is somehow weakened—as was the case during the Yugoslavian power struggle following the death of Tito—coordination within groups and conflict among groups may go unpunished by a common coercive power. Ibid., 156–163. I discuss how the decline of the state can enable group resource competition to become group conflict under the rubric of the security dynamic.

10. Donald Horowitz, *Ethnic Groups in Conflict* (Berkeley, CA: University of California Press, 1985), 217. See also Crawford Young, *The Politics of Cultural Pluralism.*

11. Alvin Rabushka and Kenneth Shepsle, *Politics in Plural Societies* (Columbus, OH: Merrill, 1971); Horowitz, *Ethnic Groups in Conflict;* idem, *A Democratic South Africa?* (Berkeley, CA: The University of California Press, 1991).

12. Horowitz, *A Democratic South Africa?*

13. On Spain, see David Laitin, "National Revivals and Violence," *Archives Europennes de Sociologie* 36 (Spring 1995): 3–43. On Northern Ireland, see Caroline Kennedy-Pipe, *The Origins of the Present Troubles in Northern Ireland* (London and New York: Longman, 1997).

14. Horowitz, *Ethnic Groups in Conflict.*

15. Ibid., 157–158, 165.

16. Jack Snyder and Karen Ballentine, "Nationalism and the Marketplace of Ideas," *International Security* 21 (Fall 1996): 5–40. See also Hardin, *One for All,* 88–91; and Lake and Rothchild, "Containing Fear," 102.

17. Robert Entman and Andrew Rojecki, *The Black Image in the White Mind* (Chicago: University of Chicago Press, 2000), 46–54, 70–75. See also Howard J. Ehrlich, "Reporting Ethnoviolence: Newspaper Treatment of Race and Ethnic Conflict," in *Race and Ethnic Conflict,* ed. Fred L. Pincus and Howard J. Ehrlich (Boulder, CO: Westview Press, 1999); and Claire Jean Kim, *Bitter Fruit: The Politics of Black-Korean Conflict in New York City* (New Haven, CT: Yale University Press, 2000), 192.

18. Paul Brass, *Theft of an Idol: Text and Context in the Representation of Collective Violence* (Princeton, NJ: Princeton University Press, 1997), 156.

19. Hardin, *One for All,* 156–163; See also Lake and Rothchild, "Containing Fear."

20. See Patrick Buckland, *A History of Northern Ireland* (Dublin: Gill and Macmillan, 1981), 120–121; and Kennedy-Pipe, *The Origins of the Troubles,* 44–45.

21. Brass, *Theft of an Idol,* 274.

22. Iris Marion Young, "Together in Difference: Transforming the Logic of Group Conflict," in *Principled Positions: Postmodernism and the Rediscovery of Value,* ed. Judith Squires (London: Lawrence and Wishart, 1993).

23. Hardin, *One for All,* 142–147.

24. Carol Conaway, "Crown Heights: Politics and Press Coverage of the Race War that Wasn't," *Polity* 32 (Fall 1999), 101–102; Paula McClain and Joseph Stewart, *Can We All Get Along? Racial and Ethnic Minorities in American Politics* (Boulder, CO: Westview Press, 1999), 149–154.

25. Edward Chang and Jeanette Diaz-Veizades, *Ethnic Peace in the American City: Building Community in Los Angeles and Beyond* (New York: New York University Press, 1999), 109–110.

26. Sumi Cho, "Korean Americans vs. African Americans: Conflict and Construction," in *Reading Rodney King: Reading Urban Uprising,* ed. Robert Gooding-Williams (New York: Routledge, 1993), 210.

27. Olzak, *The Dynamics of Ethnic Competition and Conflict.*

28. Paula McClain and Joseph Stewart, *Can We All Get Along?,* 145, 149.

29. Paula McClain and Albert Karnig, "Black and Hispanic Socioeconomic and Political Competition," *American Political Science Review* 84 (June 1990): 539, 542.

30. Jose E. Cruz, "Interminority Relations in Urban Settings: Lessons from the Black-Puerto Rican Experience," in *Black and Multiracial Politics in America,* ed. Yvette M. Alex-Assensoh and Lawrence J. Hanks (New York: New York University Press, 2000), 93–95.

31. Chang and Diaz-Veizades, *Ethnic Peace in the American City,* 122; McClain and Stewart, *Can We All Get Along?,* 147.

32. Conaway, "Crown Heights," 101.

33. McClain and Stewart, *Can We All Get Along?,* 148, 162–163.

34. Ibid., 129.

35. J. Harvie Wilkinson, *From Brown to Bakke* (New York: Oxford University Press, 1979), 88–89.

36. Kenneth Karst, *Law's Promise, Law's Expression: Visions of Power in the Politics of Race, Gender, and Religion* (New Haven, CT: Yale University Press, 1993).

37. Paula McClain and Albert Karnig, "Black and Hispanic Socioeconomic and Political Competition," *American Political Science Review* 84 (June 1990): 539, 542.

38. Cruz, "Interminority Relations in Urban Settings," 97.

39. Melissa Williams, *Voice, Trust, and Memory* (Princeton, NJ: Princeton University Press, 1998), 81.

40. Conaway, "Crown Heights," 101–102.

41. McClain and Stewart, *Can We All Get Along?*, 156.

42. Raphael Sonnenshein and Susan Pinkus, "The Dynamics of Latino Political Incorporation: The 2001 Los Angeles Mayoral Election as Seen in *Los Angeles Times* Exit Polls," *PS: Political Science and Politics* 35 (March 2002): 67–74.

43. Chang and Diaz-Veizades, *Ethnic Peace in the American City,* 17.

44. Cohen and Arato, *Civil Society and Political Theory,* 435–442.

45. Simone Chambers, *Reasonable Democracy: Jürgen Habermas and the Politics of Discourse* (Ithaca, NY: Cornell University Press, 1996), 245.

46. Fearon and Laitin, "Explaining Interethnic Cooperation," 715.

47. Note that moral universality, understood as norms justifiable to all, need not mean normative uniformity, understood as norms that treat all individuals the same. Thus, group specific rights or policies, such as affirmative action, self-government rights, and mirror representation, can be universally justified even though they may not treat all individuals uniformly. For a discussion of this point, see Michael Rabinder James, "Tribal Sovereignty and the Intercultural Public Sphere," *Philosophy and Social Criticism* 25 (September 1999), 66. Note that Hardin defines universalistic norms in terms of uniformity. He defends them because they provide fewer incentives for group-based mobilization and conflict. *One for All,* 77–79, 107–142. Communicative theory would treat Hardin's position as one possible argument within an inclusive dialogue, yet one that can be rejected without violating normative universality.

48. William Rehg, "Discourse and the Moral Point of View: Deriving a Dialogical Principle of Universality," *Inquiry* 34 (1991): 27–48, 77.

49. Entman and Rojecki, *The Black Image in the White Mind,* 17–22, 55.

50. Ibid., 22.

51. Cohen and Arato, *Civil Society and Political Theory,* 387–388; Habermas, *Moral Consciousness and Communicative Action,* 207. Note that Cohen and Arato conclude that this motivation precludes reflective communicative action with nonmodern groups. A modern culture can only tolerate such groups but cannot generate communicatively grounded solidarity with them.

52. Rogers M. Smith, "Beyond Tocqueville, Myrdal, and Hartz: The Multiple Traditions in America," *American Political Science Review* 87 (September 1993): 549–566.

53. Philip Klinkner with Rogers M. Smith, *The Unsteady March: The Rise and Decline of Racial Equality in America* (Chicago: University of Chicago Press, 1999), 3–4.

54. Jürgen Habermas, *Between Facts and Norms: Contributions to a Discourse Theory of Law and Democracy,* trans. William Rehg (Cambridge, MA: MIT Press. 1996), 340; James Bohman, *Public Deliberation* (Cambridge, MA: MIT Press, 1996), 26, 39, 200–224.

55. Jon Elster, "Deliberation and Constitution Making," in *Deliberative Democracy,* ed. Jon Elster (Cambridge: Cambridge University Press, 1998).

56. Tali Mendelberg, *The Race Card* (Princeton, NJ: Princeton University Press, 2001), 67.

57. I adopt this term from Kim, *Bitter Fruit.*

58. Mark Warren, "Democratic Theory and Trust," in *Democracy and Trust,* ed. Mark Warren (New York: Cambridge University Press, 1999).

59. Nancy Fraser, "Rethinking the Public Sphere," in *Habermas and the Public Sphere,* ed. Craig Calhoun (Cambridge, MA: MIT Press, 1992), 121–128. The concern with seg-

mented ethnic media markets is found in Snyder and Ballentine, "Nationalism and the Marketplace of Ideas," 67–81. See also Bohman, *Public Deliberation,* 81.

60. Mark Warren, "Democratic Theory and Trust," 340–342.

61. Ibid., 340.

62. Ibid., 342.

63. Hasia Diner, *In the Almost Promised Land: American Jews and Blacks, 1915–1935* (Baltimore, MD: Johns Hopkins University Press, 1977), 52, 139, 151, 182, 207.

64. Ibid., 62, 71–77, 92, 104, 141.

65. Ibid., 74, 177–178.

66. Ibid., 72, 89, 114–115, 237–238.

67. Ibid., 15, 72–73.

68. Ibid., 14, 98, 153, 228.

69. Leonard Dinnerstein, *Anti-Semitism in America* (New York: Oxford University Press, 1994), 184.

70. Dan Carter, *Scottsboro: A Tragedy of the American South* (New York: Oxford University Press, 1969), 258–259.

71. Dinnerstein, *Anti-Semitism in America,* 185.

72. Deborah Dash Moore, "Separate Paths: Blacks and Jews in the American South," in *Struggles in the Promised Land: Toward a History of Black-Jewish Relations in the United States,* ed. Jack Salzman and Cornel West (New York: Oxford University Press, 1997), 281; Stephen Whitfield, *Voices of Jacob, Hands of Esau: Jews in American Life and Thought* (Hamden, CT: Archon Books, 1984), 219–223.

73. Seth Forman, *Blacks in the Jewish Mind: A Crisis of Liberalism* (New York: New York University Press, 1998), 38, 47–49.

74. Michael Rogin, *Black Face, White Noise* (Berkeley, CA: University of California Press, 1996).

75. James Glaser, "Toward an Explanation of the Racial Liberalism of American Jews," *Political Research Quarterly* 50 (June 1997): 437–458.

76. Karen Brodkin, *How Jews Became White Folks, and What That Says About Race in America* (New Brunswick, NJ: Rutgers University Press, 1994), 36.

77. Thomas Christiano, *The Rule of the Many: Fundamental Issues in Democratic Theory* (Boulder, CO: Westview Press, 1996), 110–113.

78. Cohen and Arato, *Civil Society and Political Theory,* 506.

79. John Paul Lederach, *Sustainable Reconciliation in Divided Societies* (Washington, DC: United States Institute of Peace Press, 1997), 38–43.

80. Brian Smith, "Memory and India's Identity Crisis," *The World and I* (May 1994).

81. Eileen O'Brien, "Privileged Polemics: White Antiracist Activists." In *Race and Ethnic Conflict: Contending Views on Prejudice, Discrimination, and Ethnoviolence,* ed. Fred L. Pincus and Howard J. Ehrlich (Boulder, CO: Westview Press, 1999).

82. David Laitin, "The Sharia Debate and the Origins of Nigeria's Second Republic," *Journal of Modern African Studies* 20 (1982): 411–430.

83. Chang and Diaz-Veizades, *Ethnic Peace in the American City,* 107.

84. Warren, "Democratic Theory and Trust," 340.

85. Simone Chambers and Jeffrey Kopstein, "Bad Civil Society," *Political Theory* 29 (December 2001): 837–865.

86. Christopher Winship and Jenny Berrien, "Boston Cops and Black Churches," *The*

Public Interest 136 (Summer 1999): 52–69; Orlando Patterson and Christopher Winship, "Boston's Police Solution," *New York Times,* 3 March 1999, sec. A, p. 17.

87. Cohen and Arato, *Civil Society and Political Theory.*

88. Snyder and Ballentine, "Nationalism and the Marketplace of Ideas."

89. John Dryzek, "Legitimacy and Economy in Deliberative Democracy," *Political Theory* 29 (October 2001): 665.

90. Donald Horowitz, *A Democratic South Africa?*

91. Andrew Reynolds and Timothy Sisk, "Elections and Electoral Systems: Implications for Conflict Management," in *Elections and Conflict Management in Africa,* ed. Timothy Sisk and Andrew Reynolds (Washington, DC: The United States Institute of Peace Press, 1998), 17, 19.

4. PLURAL DELIBERATION AND THE PUBLIC SPHERE

1. Jürgen Habermas, *Between Facts and Norms: Contributions to a Discourse Theory of Law and Democracy,* trans. William Rehg (Cambridge, MA: MIT Press, 1996), 360.

2. Jean Cohen and Andrew Arato, *Civil Society and Political Theory* (Cambridge, MA: MIT Press, 1992), 411.

3. John Dryzek "Legitimacy and Economy in Deliberative Democracy," *Political Theory* 29 (October 2001): 662–663.

4. John Dryzek, *Deliberative Democracy and Beyond: Liberals, Critics, Contestations* (Oxford: Oxford University Press, 2000), 103.

5. Seyla Benhabib, *The Claims of Culture* (Princeton, NJ: Princeton University Press, 2002), 106. Emphasis in the original. Cf. 131–132.

6. Dryzek, *Deliberative Democracy and Beyond,* 100.

7. Habermas seems to realize this point, at least with respect to larger publics. *Between Facts and Norms,* 374.

8. Dryzek, "Legitimacy and Economy in Deliberative Democracy," 665.

9. Mark E. Warren, *Democracy and Association* (Princeton, NJ: Princeton University Press, 2001), 94.

10. Ibid., 70–93.

11. Ibid., 96–97.

12. Ibid., 109. Following Talcott Parsons, Warren uses the term *media* to depict what I call the means of social integration. I substitute *means* because in this chapter I use the word "media" in its more common usage to depict the methods of communicating information, such as newspapers, radio, and television.

13. Ibid., 117.

14. Ibid., 123–133. I have altered some of Warren's terminology in order to highlight the characteristics that are shared among different constitutive goods. Thus, whereas Warren speaks of "public material goods," I use "inclusive material goods" to highlight how these goods and "inclusive social goods" are nonexcludable public goods that can only be enjoyed by an indeterminate number of people, not by an individual or definable group. Similarly, I use "exclusive personal identity" and "exclusive collective identity" to highlight how these identities are excludable and can be enjoyed by an individual or a small group of people.

15. Ibid., 142. Warren believes that most associations achieve this goal, but I fear that

the quality of information can vary greatly among associations. I will delay further discussion on this issue until I examine deliberative reciprocity because, according to the information dynamic of conflict, the greatest danger with group-specific information concerns the perception of out-groups.

16. Ibid., 145–147.

17. Ibid., 143.

18. Ibid., 75–76.

19. Ibid., 160.

20. Ibid., 152–154.

21. Ibid., 152.

22. Ibid., 210.

23. Dryzek, "Legitimacy and Economy in Deliberative Democracy," 660–661.

24. Warren, *Democracy and Association,* 202–203.

25. Ibid., 176.

26. Ibid., 183.

27. Doug McAdam, *Political Process and the Development of Black Insurgency, 1930–1970* (Chicago: University of Chicago Press, 1982), 25.

28. Ibid., 44–48.

29. Sydney Tarrow, *Power in Movement: Social Movements, Collective Action, and Politics* (Cambridge: Cambridge University Press, 1994), 126.

30. Cohen and Arato, *Civil Society and Political Theory,* 502; McAdam, *Political Process and the Development of Black Insurgency,* 77–82.

31. Ron Eyerman and Andrew Jamison, *Social Movements: A Cognitive Approach* (University Park, PA: Penn State University Press, 1991), chapter 4. Cf. Cohen and Arato, *Civil Society and Political Theory,* 587, and Habermas, *Between Facts and Norms,* 383.

32. Eyerman and Jamison, *Social Movements: A Cognitive Approach,* 60, 64.

33. Doug McAdam, "Movement Strategy and Dramaturgic Framing in Democratic States: The Case of the American Civil Rights Movement" in *Deliberation, Democracy, and the Media,* ed. Simone Chambers and Anne Costain (Lanham, MD: Rowman and Littlefield, 2000), 120–124.

34. Eyerman and Jamison, *Social Movements: A Cognitive Approach,* 102.

35. Habermas identifies only two groups addressed by social movements: the general public and political officials. His inattention to strategically engaged adversaries highlights his tendency to downplay the strategic character of social movements. *Between Facts and Norms,* 383.

36. McAdam, "Movement Strategy and Dramaturgic Framing," 126.

37. Ibid., 127–128.

38. McAdam, *Political Process and the Development of Black Insurgency,* 177–178.

39. Ibid., 84; Philip Klinkner with Rogers M. Smith, *The Unsteady March: The Rise and Decline of Racial Equality in America* (Chicago: University of Chicago Press, 1999), 154–160.

40. See, for example, James Bohman, *Public Deliberation: Pluralism, Complexity, and Democracy* (Cambridge, MA: MIT Press, 1996); and Dryzek "Legitimacy and Economy in Deliberative Democracy." However, Cohen and Arato, *Civil Society and Political Theory,* 520–522, do acknowledge the role of strategic action within social movements.

41. Bohman, *Public Deliberation;* Dryzek, *Deliberative Democracy and Beyond.*

42. William Van Deburg, *New Day in Babylon: The Black Power Movement and American Culture, 1965–1975* (Chicago: University of Chicago Press, 1992), 76, 104, 165–167, 217.

43. Ibid., 13, 74.

44. Ibid., 76, 96, 113–114.

45. McAdam, *Political Process and the Development of Black Insurgency,* 197–200, 221.

46. Van Deburg, *New Day in Babylon,* 140, 206, 217, 223, 251.

47. Ibid., 113–114, 127–128, 137, 147.

48. Ibid., 122, 162–164.

49. Joane Nagel, *American Indian Ethnic Renewal* (New York: Oxford University Press, 1996), 130; Suzanne Oboler, *Ethnic Labels, Latino Lives* (Minneapolis: University of Minnesota Press, 1995), 65; Yen Le Espiritu, *Asian American Panethnicity* (Philadelphia: Temple University Press, 1992), 12, 25; William Wei, *The Asian American Movement* (Philadelphia: Temple University Press, 1993), 25–26, 41–42.

50. Wei, *The Asian American Movement,* 135, 208, 228.

51. Nagel, *American Indian Ethnic Renewal,* 225–226.

52. Pyong Gap Min, *Caught in the Middle: Korean Communities in New York and Los Angeles* (Berkeley, CA: University of California Press, 1996), 101.

53. Claire Jean Kim, *Bitter Fruit: The Politics of Black-Korean Conflict in New York City* (New Haven, CT: Yale University Press, 2000), 116–124.

54. Ibid., 121, 126–133, 164, 173–180.

55. Ibid., 138–144, 180–187.

56. James Fishkin, *The Voice of the People: Public Opinion and American Democracy* (New Haven, CT: Yale University Press, 1994); John Keane, *The Media and Democracy* (Cambridge: Polity Press, 1991); Habermas, *Between Facts and Norms,* 367.

57. James Bohman, "The Division of Labor in Democratic Discourse: Media, Experts, and Deliberative Democracy," in *Deliberation, Democracy, and the Media,* ed. Simone Chambers and Anne Costain (Lanham, MD: Rowman and Littlefield, 2000).

58. McAdam "Movement Strategy and Dramaturgic Framing in Democratic States," 125–127. For a detailed account of the role of cold war foreign policy in the success of the civil rights movement, see Klinkner and Smith, *The Unsteady March,* chapters 7–8.

59. Habermas, *Between Facts and Norms,* 374–375.

60. Benjamin Page, *Who Deliberates? Mass Media in Modern Democracy* (Chicago: University of Chicago Press, 1996), 1–11.

61. Ibid.

62. William Gamson, *Talking Politics* (Cambridge: Cambridge University Press, 1994).

63. Robert Entman and Andrew Rojecki, *The Black Image in the White Mind* (Chicago: University of Chicago Press, 2000), 68–69.

64. Ibid., 86–88.

65. Ibid., 135–139.

66. Bohman, "The Division of Labor in Democratic Discourse."

67. Tali Mendelberg, *The Race Card: Campaign Strategy, Implicit Messages, and the Norm of Equality* (Princeton, NJ: Princeton University Press, 2001), 152.

68. Entman and Rojecki, *The Black Image in the White Mind,* 132–133.

69. Donald Kinder and Lynn Sanders, *Divided by Color: Racial Politics and Democratic Ideals* (Chicago: University of Chicago Press, 1996), 238.

70. Mendelberg, *The Race Card.*

71. Susan Herbst, *Politics at the Margins: Historical Studies of Public Expression Outside the Mainstream* (Cambridge: Cambridge University Press, 1994), 77–78.

72. Elizabeth Maguire, "University Presses and the Black Reader," in *The Black Public Sphere: A Public Culture Book,* ed. The Black Public Sphere Collective (Chicago: University of Chicago Press, 1995).

73. Espiritu, *Asian American Panethnicity,* 155.

74. Michael Dawson, "A Black Counterpublic?: Economic Earthquakes, Racial Agenda(s), and Black Politics," in *The Black Public Sphere: A Public Culture Book,* ed. The Black Public Sphere Collective (Chicago: University of Chicago Press, 1995), 199–201, 221.

75. Philip Kasinitz, *Caribbean New York* (Ithaca, NY: Cornell University Press, 1992), 233, 249.

76. Wei, *The Asian American Movement,* 102, 106, 114–117, 128.

77. Herbst, *Politics at the Margins,* 77.

78. Wei, *The Asian American Movement,* 109.

79. Carol Conaway, "Crown Heights: Politics and Press Coverage of the Race War that Wasn't," *Polity* 32 (Fall 1999): 96.

80. Edward Chang and Jeanette Diaz-Veizades, *Ethnic Peace in the American City: Building Community in Los Angeles and Beyond* (New York: New York University Press, 1999), 44, 63, 73.

81. Sumi Cho, "Korean Americans vs. African Americans: Conflict and Construction," in *Reading Rodney King: Reading Urban Uprising,* ed. Robert Gooding-Williams (New York: Routledge, 1993), 200.

82. Kim, *Bitter Fruit,* 117, 164–165.

83. Conaway, "Crown Heights," 97, 115–118.

84. Kim, *Bitter Fruit,* chapter 6; Chang and Diaz-Veizades, *Ethnic Peace in the American City,* 61, 69–74, 79; Min, *Caught in the Middle,* 107.

85. Cohen and Arato, *Civil Society and Political Theory,* 411.

86. Warren, *Democracy and Association,* 54.

87. Habermas, *Between Facts and Norms,* 365.

88. Bohman, *Public Deliberation,* 189.

89. Melissa Nobles, *Shades of Citizenship* (Stanford, CA: Stanford University Press, 2000), 79–81.

90. Ibid., 82.

91. Clara Rodriguez, *Changing Race: Latinos, the Census, and the History of Ethnicity in the United States* (New York: New York University Press, 2000), 153.

92. Ibid., 130, 170.

93. Ibid., 155, 159–176.

94. Nobles, *Shades of Citizenship,* 82.

95. Rodriguez, *Changing Race,* 170–172.

96. Nobles, *Shades of Citizenship,* 83.

97. Yael Tamir, "Revisiting the Civic Sphere," in *Freedom of Association,* ed. Amy Gutmann (Princeton, NJ: Princeton University Press, 1998); Nancy Rosenblum, *Membership and Morals: The Personal Uses of Pluralism in America* (Princeton, NJ: Princeton University Press, 1998).

98. Warren, *Democracy and Association,* 217, emphasis in original.

99. Dryzek, *Deliberative Democracy and Beyond,* 114.

100. Warren, *Democracy and Association,* 218–221.

101. Chang and Diaz-Veizades, *Ethnic Peace in the American City,* 34, 65, 112.

102. Ibid., 115.

103. Ibid., 115–118.

104. Entman and Rojecki, *The Black Image in the White Mind,* 220.

105. Jack Snyder, *From Voting to Violence: Democratization and Nationalist Conflict* (New York: Norton, 2000), 336.

106. Entman and Rojecki, *The Black Image in the White Mind,* 214, 217.

107. Ibid., 217–218.

5. PLURAL DELIBERATION, REPRESENTATION, AND ELECTORAL DESIGN

1. Michael Dummett, *The Principles of Electoral Reform* (Oxford: Oxford University Press, 1997), 6.

2. Burt Monroe, "Fully Proportional Representation," *American Political Science Review* 89 (December 1995): 925–940.

3. Charles Beitz, *Political Equality* (Princeton, NJ: Princeton University Press, 1989), 107–117.

4. Ibid., 132–140.

5. Thomas Christiano, *The Rule of the Many* (Boulder, CO: Westview Press, 1996), 224–238.

6. Beitz primarily assesses deliberation according to the inclusion of diverse positions and the thoughtful, comparative assessment of policies. *Political Equality,* 114–115. Christiano depicts deliberation primarily as instrumental in improving citizens' understanding of their own interests. *The Rule of the Many,* 84–87. This portrait, in my opinion, reduces deliberation to little more than the pooling of information associated with aggregative democratic procedures, and I will characterize Christiano's approach as such below. In general, neither Beitz nor Christiano portrays deliberation as communication aimed at understanding, criticism, and justification across world-views, perspectives, opinions, and interests.

7. Both Beitz and Christiano do devote some attention to the representation of minority groups, but neither treatment is comprehensive. Beitz, for instance, argues that attention to historical and social context justifies the creation of majority-Black districts, in order to mitigate majority tyranny. *Political Equality,* chapter 7. However, I believe his contextual analysis is not contextual enough, because it does not examine the myriad problems related to collective identity construction and does not investigage how electoral systems mitigate dynamics of conflict. Christiano parenthetically alludes to problems of identity construction when he argues that PR allows for voluntary proportionality among groups rather than juridically forming SMDP districts with a specific racial majority. *The Rule of the Many,* 221. However, he, too, neglects the relationship between electoral systems and the political dynamic of conflict.

8. Susan Bickford, "Reconfiguring Pluralism: Identity and Institutions in the Inegalitarian Polity," *American Journal of Political Science* 43 (January 1999): 86–108; Jane Mansbridge, "Should Women Represent Women and Blacks Represent Blacks? A Contingent

Yes," *The Journal of Politics* 61 (August 1999): 628–657; Melissa Williams, *Voice, Trust, and Memory* (Princeton, NJ: Princeton University Press, 1998).

9. Donald Horowitz, *A Democratic South Africa?* (Berkeley, CA: University of California Press, 1991), 165.

10. Andrew Reynolds and Timothy Sisk, "Elections and Electoral Systems: Implications for Conflict Management," in *Elections and Conflict Management in Africa,* ed. Timothy Sisk and Andrew Reynolds (Washington, DC: The United States Institute of Peace Press, 1998), 17, 19.

11. My analysis of electoral systems focuses only on the procedural aspects of plural deliberation's fairness conditions and not on more substantive aspects of either the fairness conditions or the requirement of understanding prior to criticism. I limit my analysis in this way because the more substantive characteristics are meant to judge specific candidates or campaign contributions. Electoral systems, as institutions, cannot themselves embody such substantive characteristics, although incentives for deliberative reciprocity can affect the likely success of candidates who unfairly criticize perspectives or world-views that they do not accurately understand.

12. Lani Guinier, *The Tyranny of the Majority: Fundamental Fairness in Representative Democracy* (New York: The Free Press, 1994), 71–73.

13. Michael Dummett exclaims that the "concept of the wasted vote is thoroughly confused and wholly unhelpful in thinking about electoral systems." *The Principles of Electoral Reform,* 118. He grounds this assertion on an ambiguity in the meaning of wasted votes. On the one hand, a wasted vote is one that, if cast differently under the same electoral system, would have led to a different candidate's being elected. This definition would apply to Nader voters in Florida who, if they had strategically voted for Gore, would have defeated Bush. Instead, by voting for Nader, they supposedly wasted their votes. However, this definition is terribly unstable because strategic voting can greatly alter which candidate actually wins under any electoral system. If, for example, Nader voters were more evenly split between Gore and Bush, we cannot say who really wasted their votes. Presumably, it would be the Nader>Gore>Bush (the sign > indicates a transitive ordering of preferences) voters because their sincere vote for Nader led Gore to lose. However, their votes can be thought of as wasted only if the Nader>Bush>Gore voters were to continue to vote sincerely for Nader. If this latter group were to vote strategically for Bush, then Bush would have won anyway, and the Nader>Gore>Bush voters could not be said to have wasted their votes. On the other hand, wasted votes can refer simply to votes that do not contribute to a winning candidate. Dummett finds this definition vacuous because all elections lead to some losers. Ibid., 117. However, this definition becomes less so when we consider that some electoral systems lead to far more losers than others, to the point that in some SMDP elections with an ethnically fractured electorate the winner could receive perhaps only 15 percent of the vote, leaving 85 percent of the voters with wasted votes.

14. Arend Lijphart, *Electoral Systems and Party Systems* (New York: Oxford University Press, 1994), 70.

15. Keith Bybee, *Mistaken Identity: The Supreme Court and the Politics of Minority Representation* (Princeton, NJ: Princeton University Press, 1998) expresses this intuition in his argument that voting rights jurisprudence errs by assuming, prior to political activity, that voters already know their relevant political identities.

16. Arend Lijphart, *Democracy in Plural Societies* (New Haven, CT: Yale University Press, 1977); Horowitz, *A Democratic South Africa?*

17. Richard Katz, *Democracy and Elections* (New York: Oxford University Press, 1997).

18. Mark Button and Kevin Mattson, "Deliberative Democracy in Practice: Challenges and Prospects for Civil Deliberation," *Polity* 31 (Summer 1999): 622–626.

19. William T. Bianco, *Trust: Representatives and Constituents* (Ann Arbor, MI: University of Michigan Press, 1994); Gerry Mackie, "All Men are Liars: Is Democracy Meaningless?," in *Deliberative Democracy,* ed. Jon Elster (Cambridge: Cambridge University Press, 1997).

20. Jürgen Habermas, *Moral Consciousness and Communicative Action,* trans. Christian Lenhardt and Shierry Weber Nicolsen (Cambridge, MA: MIT Press, 1990).

21. On citizens' judgment of representatives' actions, see Bianco, *Trust.* On citizens' comparative judgment of candidates, see Benjamin Page and Robert Y. Shapiro, *The Rational Public* (Chicago: University of Chicago Press, 1992).

22. Amy Gutmann and Dennis Thompson, *Democracy and Disagreement* (Cambridge, MA: Harvard University Press, 1996), 128–144.

23. Iris Marion Young, *Inclusion and Democracy* (New York: Oxford University Press, 2000), 128–133.

24. Bianco, *Trust,* 49–55, 154.

25. Christiano, *The Rule of the Many,* 213–219.

26. Bianco, *Trust,* 18.

27. Bernard Manin, *Principles of Representative Government* (New York: Cambridge University Press, 1997), 218–223; Anne Phillips, *The Politics of Presence* (New York: Oxford University Press, 1995), 155–160.

28. Philllips, *The Politics of Presence,* 155–160.

29. Katz, *Democracy and Elections,* 154.

30. Bianco, *Trust,* 55–62.

31. Williams, *Voice, Trust, and Memory,* chapter 5.

32. David Lublin, *The Paradox of Representation: Racial Gerrymandering and Minority Interests in Congress* (Princeton, NJ: Princeton University Press, 1997), 71, 96–97.

33. Ibid., 57, 66–71.

34. Young, *Inclusion and Democracy,* 147.

35. Ibid., 128–133.

36. Beitz, *Political Equality,* 150.

37. Lijphart, *Electoral Systems and Party Systems,* 28.

38. Ibid., 25.

39. Richard Engstrom, "The Political Thicket, Electoral Reform, and Minority Voting Rights," in Mark Rush and Richard Engstrom, *Fair and Effective Representation? Debating Electoral Reform and Minority Rights* (Lanham, MD: Rowman and Littlefield, 2001), 41.

40. Katz, *Democracy and Elections,* 262.

41. Jane Mansbridge, "Motivating Deliberation in Congress," in *Constitutionalism in America, Volume II: E Pluribus Unum,* ed. Sarah Baumgartner Thurow (New York: University Press of America, 1998), 79.

42. Beitz, *Political Equality,* 135, 156.

43. Williams, *Voice, Trust, and Memory,* 110–115.

44. Lijphart, *Electoral Systems and Party Systems,* 82.

45. Katz, *Democracy and Elections,* 145; Mark Rush, "The Hidden Costs of Electoral Reform," in Rush and Engstrom, *Fair and Effective Representation?,* 78–79.

46. Reynolds and Sisk, "Elections and Electoral Systems."

47. Lublin, *The Paradox of Representation,* 57–61.

48. See Rush, "The Hidden Costs of Electoral Reform"; and Lisa Disch, *The Tyranny of the Two-Party System* (New York: Columbia University Press, 2002).

49. Lublin, *The Paradox of Representation,* 119.

50. Lijphart, *Electoral Systems and Party Systems,* 82.

51. Lublin, *The Paradox of Representation,* 47, 87.

52. Morris Fiorina and Paul Peterson, *The New American Democracy* (Needham Heights, MA: Allyn & Bacon, 1999), 347. Cf. Bianco, *Trust,* 62.

53. Christiano, *The Rule of the Many.*

54. Disch, *The Tyranny of the Two-Party System.*

55. Philip Williams, "The United States: Members of Congress and their Districts," in *Representatives of the People? Parliaments and Constituents in Western Democracies,* ed. Vernon Bogdanor (Brookfield, VT: Gower Publishing Company, 1985), 66.

56. Katz, *Democracy and Elections,* 129–134.

57. Douglas Amy, *Behind the Ballot Box* (Westport, CT: Praeger, 2000), 56–57.

58. Ibid., 56–59; idem, *Real Choices, New Voices: The Case for Proportional Representation in the United States* (New York: Columbia University Press, 1993), 118–119; Bybee, *Mistaken Identity,* 15, 19.

59. Bybee, *Mistaken Identity,* 118–125.

60. Guinier, *The Tyranny of the Majority,* 91.

61. Amy, *Behind the Ballot Box,* 60.

62. Ibid., 55–56.

63. Williams, *Voice, Trust, and Memory,* 208–212.

64. Arend Lijphart, "Proportionality by Non-PR Methods: Ethnic Representation in Belgium, Cyprus, Lebanon, New Zealand, West Germany, and Zimbabwe," in *Electoral Laws and their Political Consequences,* ed. Arend Lijphart and Bernard Grofmann (New York: Agathon Press, 1986); Marc Galanter, *Competing Equalities: Law and the Backward Classes in India* (New Delhi: Oxford University Press, 1991), 45.

65. Katz, *Democracy and Elections,* 189.

66. Williams, *Voice, Trust, and Memory,* 209.

67. Lijphart "Proportionality by Non-PR Methods."

68. See appendix for an explanation of the different electoral formulas.

69. Katz, *A Theory of Parties and Electoral Systems* (Baltimore: Johns Hopkins University Press, 1980), 84–94.

70. Lijphart, *Electoral Systems and Party Systems,* 26–27.

71. Ibid., 26.

72. Katz, *Democracy and Elections,* 128–138.

73. Arend Lijphart argues that LR tends to be the most proportional formula, followed by the Droop, the St. Lague, and the D'Hondt, respectively. See Lijphart "Degrees of Proportionality of Proportional Representation Formulas," in *Electoral Laws and their Political Consequences,* ed. Arend Lijphart and Bernard Grofmann (New York: Agathon Press, 1986), 178; and Lijphart, *Electoral Systems and Party Systems,* 64. Richard Katz challenges this claim in a study using a larger data set. Katz, *Democracy and Elections,* 129.

74. Lijphart, *Electoral Systems and Party Systems,* 75, 82, 90, 92, 141.

75. Katz, *Democracy and Elections,* 151–160; Christiano, *The Rule of the Many.*

76. Christiano, *The Rule of the Many,* 221; Lijphart, *Electoral Systems and Party Systems,* 140–141.

77. Williams, *Voice, Trust, and Memory,* 219–220.

78. Donald Horowitz, *Ethnic Groups in Conflict* (Berkeley, CA: University of California Press, 1985), 643–646.

79. James Bohman, *Public Deliberation* (Cambridge, MA: MIT Press, 1996), 137.

80. The relationship between the environmental movement and Green parties suggests that this formulation is not far fetched.

81. Christiano, *The Rule of the Many,* 231.

82. Lijphart, *Electoral Systems and Party Systems,* 142, attributes this to the weakness of Duverger's psychological effect. Duverger's law holds that electoral systems have both a mechanical effect, which reflects the number of parliamentary parties that can successfully win seats, and a psychological effect, which affects the willingness of politicians to create new parties. The data suggest, however, that the former prong of Duverger's law is much stronger than the latter.

83. Horowitz, *A Democratic South Africa?,* 172.

84. Arend Lijphart, "The Alternative Vote: A Realistic Alternative for South Africa? *Politikon* 18 (June 1991): 93.

85. Lijphart, *Electoral Systems and Party Systems,* 150.

86. Clive Bean, "The Personal Vote in Australian Federal Elections," *Political Studies* 33 (1990): 253–268.

87. Jack Wright, "Australian Experience with Majority-Preferential and Quota-Preferential Systems," in *Electoral Laws and Their Political Consequences,* ed. Arend Lijphart and Bernard Grofmann (New York: Agathon Press, 1986), 128.

88. Lijphart, *Electoral Systems and Party Systems,* 97.

89. Ben Reilly, "Preferential Voting and Political Engineering: A Comparative Study," *Journal of Commonwealth and Comparative Politics* 35 (March 1997): 27.

90. Lijphart, "The Alternative Vote," 95.

91. Wright, "Australian Experience," 131–132.

92. Amy, *Behind the Ballot Box,* 104–105.

93. This is a slight alteration of the example found in David M. Farrell, *Comparing Electoral Systems* (New York: Prentice Hall, 1997), 134–136. For another example, see Dummett, *Principles of Electoral Reform,* 99–103.

94. Dummett, *Principles of Electoral Reform,* 103.

95. Gerry Mackie, *Democracy Defended* (New York: Cambridge University Press, 2003), chapter 3.

96. Horowitz, *A Democratic South Africa?,* 165.

97. Ibid., 189.

98. Reilly, "Preferential Voting," 10–11.

99. Ibid., 12–14.

100. Lijphart, *Electoral Systems and Party Systems,* 24.

101. Lijphart, "Degrees of Proportionality."

102. Amy, *Real Choices, New Voices,* 52.

103. Katz, *Democracy and Elections,* 180–184.

104. Katz, *A Theory of Parties and Electoral Systems;* Lijphart, *Electoral Systems and Party Systems,* 150.

105. Dummett, *Principles of Electoral Reform,* 184–185.

106. Ralph Straetz, *PR Politics in Cincinnati* (New York: New York University Press, 1958), 121–124.

107. Engstrom, "The Political Thicket, Electoral Reform, and Minority Voting Rights," 43.

108. David M. Farrell, Malcolm Mackerras, and Ian McAllister, "Designing Electoral Institutions: STV Systems and their Consequences," *Political Studies* 44 (1996): 32.

109. Amy, *Real Choices, New Voices,* 133–134.

110. Farrell, Mackerras, and McAllister, "Designing Electoral Institutions," 34.

111. Horowitz, *A Democratic South Africa?,* 171–174; Cornelius O'Leary, "Northern Ireland, 1921–1929: A Failed Consociational Experiment," in *Electoral Politics,* ed. Dennis Kavanagh (Oxford: Clarendon Press, 1986), 256–260.

112. O'Leary, "Northern Ireland, 1921–1929," 251–256.

113. Amy, *Real Choices, New Voices,* 133.

114. Straetz, *PR Politics in Cincinnati,* 154.

115. Lijphart, *Electoral Systems and Party Systems,* 40.

116. Engstrom, "The Political Thicket, Electoral Reform, and Minority Voting Rights," 40–43. In order to avoid the haphazard electoral dynamics caused by a lack of real threshold of inclusion, Lani Guinier introduces a Droop quota as a minimal threshold for her CV proposals, as it tends to reflect the threshold of exclusion. Guinier, *The Tyranny of the Majority,* 96–97. This solution is deeply problematic, however, because without the ordinal ballot and transfer mechanism of the STV, we do not know how to fill any seats for which no candidate has secured the Droop quota.

117. Lijphart, *Electoral Systems and Party Systems,* 40.

118. Ibid., 42; Shaun Bowler, Todd Donovan, and David Farrell, "Party Strategy and Voter Organization under Cumulative Voting in Victorian England," *Political Studies* 47 (1999): 910.

119. Edward Still, "Cumulative Voting and Limited Voting in Alabama," in *United States Electoral Systems: Their Impact on Women and Minorities,* ed. Wilma Rule and Joseph F. Zimmerman (New York: Greenwood Press, 1992).

120. David H. Everson, "The Effect of the Cutback on the Representation of Women and Minorities in the Illinois General Assembly," in *United States Electoral Systems: Their Impact on Women and Minorities.*

121. Guinier, *The Tyranny of the Majority,* 71–73.

122. Ibid., 99; Bowler, Donovan, and Ferrell, "Party Strategy and Voter Organization under the Cumulative Vote," 912.

123. Engstrom, "The Political Thicket, Electoral Reform, and Minority Voting Rights," 43.

124. Amy, *Behind the Ballot Box,* 121.

125. Bowler, Donovan, and Ferrell, "Party Strategy and Voter Organization under the Cumulative Vote," 910–911.

126. Still, "Cumulative Voting and Limited Voting in Alabama."

127. Amy, *Behind the Ballot Box,* 109.

128. Bowler, Donovan, and Ferrell, "Party Strategy and Voter Organization under the Cumulative Vote," 910–911.

129. Richard Engstrom, "The Political Thicket, Electoral Reform, and Minority Voting Rights," 54–56.

130. Jack Knight and James Johnson, "Aggregation and Deliberation: On the Possibility of Political Legitimacy," *Political Theory* 22 (1994): 287–289.

131. Robert Dahl, *A Preface to Democratic Theory* (Chicago: University of Chicago Press, 1956), 137.

132. Horowitz, *Ethnic Groups in Conflict*, 564–566.

133. Shaw v. Reno, 509 U.S. 630 (1993); Miller v. Johnson 512 U.S. 622 (1995); Bush v. Vera 517 U.S. 952 (1996).

134. Phillips, *The Politics of Presence;* Williams, *Voice, Trust, and Memory.*

135. Consider the debate in the House Judiciary Committee on introducing new electoral systems for House elections. See Rush, "The Hidden Costs of Electoral Reform."

136. Mark Rush, *Does Redistricting Make a Difference? Partisan Representation and Electoral Behavior* (Baltimore, MD: Johns Hopkins University Press, 1993).

137. Engstrom, "The Political Thicket," 47–49; Straetz, *PR Politics in Cincinnati.*

138. Amy, *Behind the Ballot Box*, 115.

139. Engstrom, "The Political Thicket," 65 n. 35.

140. Williams, *Voice, Trust, and Memory,* 236; Edward Chang and Jeanette Diaz-Veizades, *Ethnic Peace in the American City: Building Community in Los Angeles and Beyond* (New York: New York University Press, 1999).

141. See Rush, "The Hidden Costs of Electoral Reform," 69.

142. See Lijphart "Degrees of Proportionality of Proportional Representation Formulas," 178.

CONCLUSION

1. See Joseph Bessette, *The Mild Voice of Reason: Deliberative Democracy and American National Government* (Chicago: University of Chicago Press, 1994); and Jane Mansbridge, "Motivating Deliberation in Congress," in *Constitutionalism in America, Volume II: E Pluribus Unum,* ed. Sarah Baumgartner Thurow (New York: University Press of America, 1998).

2. For example, John Dryzek, *Deliberative Democracy and Beyond* (New York: Oxford University Press, 2000).

3. Consider the fact that Black American representatives have been able to exploit the significant resources associated with seniority and committee chairs in the House of Representatives. Latino representatives do not have such resources, but this stems primarily from their relative lack of seniority. See David Lublin, *The Paradox of Representation* (Princeton, NJ: Princeton University Press, 1997), 63–66.

4. Donald Horowitz, *A Democratic South Africa?* (Berkeley, CA: University of California Press, 1991), 205–214; Douglas Amy, *Behind the Ballot Box* (Westport, CT: Praeger, 2000), chapter 6.

5. Arend Lijphart, *Democracy in Plural Societies* (New Haven, CT: Yale University Press, 1977); Horowitz, *A Democratic South Africa?*

6. John Rawls, *Political Liberalism* (New York: Columbia University Press, 1993), 231–240.

7. Lynn Sanders, "Against Deliberation," *Political Theory* 25 (June 1997): 347–376.

8. David Cole notes that whereas Black and White defendants might face equal odds of receiving the death penalty, capital punishment is much more likely when the victim is White. David Cole, *No Equal Justice: Race and Class in the American Criminal Justice System* (New York: The New Press, 1999), 132.

9. Sanders, "Against Deliberation."

10. James Fishkin, *The Voice of the People* (New Haven, CT: Yale University Press, 1995), 143, 173.

11. Jeffrey M. Berry, Kent E. Portney, and Ken Thomson, *The Rebirth of Urban Democracy* (Washington, DC: The Brookings Institute, 1993); Archon Fung, "Accountable Autonomy: Toward Empowered Deliberation in Chicago Schools and Policing," *Politics and Society* 29 (March 2001): 73–103; Archon Fung and Erik Olin Wright, "Deepening Democracy: Innovations in Empowered Participatory Governance," *Politics and Society* 29 (March 2001): 5–41.

12. Fung, "Accountable Autonomy," 83–87.

13. Ibid., 76–80.

14. Berry, Portney, and Thomson, *The Rebirth of Urban Democracy,* 46, 63–69, 107, 141–149.

15. Fung and Wright, "Deepening Democracy," 21.

16. Fung, "Accountable Autonomy," 87–89.

17. Berry, Portney, and Thomson, *The Rebirth of Urban Democracy,* 180–188.

18. Fung discusses one police beat that included wealthy and poor sections, but he does not document the racial or ethnic divisions that may accompany this class difference. "Accountable Autonomy," 96.

19. Fung and Wright, "Deepening Democracy," 19–20, 27.

20. Berry, Portney, and Thomson, *The Rebirth of Urban Democracy,* 57–63, 270–275.

21. Fung and Wright, "Deepening Democracy," 32; Fung, "Accountable Autonomy," 80–83.

22. Fung, "Accountable Autonomy," 96.

23. Benedict Anderson, *Imagined Communities* (London: Verso, 1983), 47–65, 120–124.

24. Elie Kedourie, *Nationalism* (London: Blackwell, 1960), 118.

25. Crawford Young, *The Politics of Cultural Pluralism* (Madison, WI: University of Wisconsin Press), 110–114.

26. Will Kymlicka, *Multicultural Citizenship* (New York: Oxford University Press, 1995), 92–93. E. J. Hobsbawm argues that national identity is often fostered by overlapping religious and territorial identities. See *Nations and Nationalism since 1780* (New York: Cambridge University Press, 1990), 67–68.

27. Kymlicka, *Multicultural Citizenship,* 186.

28. Iris Marion Young, "Together in Difference: Transforming the Logic of Group Conflict," in *Principled Positions: Postmodernism and the Rediscovery of Value,* ed. Judith Squires (London: Lawrence and Wishart, 1993).

29. Joseph Carens, *Culture, Citizenship, and Community* (New York: Oxford University Press, 2000).

30. For a sophisticated examination of this problem, see James Bohman, *Public Deliberation* (Cambridge, MA: MIT Press, 1996), 203–208, 213–229.

Index